GEORGE INNESS
Writings and Reflections on Art and Philosophy

———◆◆◆———

The greatness of Art is not in the display of knowledge,
or in material accuracy, but in the distinctness with which
it conveys the impressions of a personal vital force,
that acts spontaneously, without fear or hesitation.

—George Inness

GEORGE INNESS

Writings and Reflections on Art and Philosophy

EDITED BY

ADRIENNE BAXTER BELL

GEORGE BRAZILLER, PUBLISHERS / NEW YORK

Published in 2006 by George Braziller, Inc., New York
Copyright © 2006 by George Braziller, Inc.
Foreword and Acknowledgments, "George Inness: Artist, Writer, Philosopher,"
prefatory texts, and backmatter copyright © 2006 by Adrienne Baxter Bell
See References for information on copyright holders of all other texts
See captions for copyright holders of images

For information, please address the publisher:
George Braziller, Inc.
171 Madison Avenue
New York, New York 10016

Library of Congress Cataloging-in-Publication Data:
George Inness : writings and reflections on art and philosophy /
edited by Adrienne Baxter Bell.—1st ed.
p. cm.
Includes all known writings by George Inness.
Includes bibliographical references (pp. 285–88).
ISBN-13: 978-0-8076-1567-6 (hardcover)
ISBN-10: 0-8076-1567-6 (hardcover)
1. Inness, George, 1825–1894—Written works. 2. Inness, George, 1825–1894—Criticism and
interpretation. I. Bell, Adrienne Baxter. II. Inness, George, 1825–1894. Works. 2006. III. Title.
ND237.I5A35 2006
759.13—dc22

Half-title page quotation: George Inness in E., "Mr. Inness on Art-Matters," *The Art Journal* 5
(1879): 377

Frontispiece: Mathew Brady, *George Inness*, photograph, 1862, reproduced in George Inness, Jr.,
Life, Art, and Letters of George Inness (New York: The Century Co., 1917), p. 59.

Designed by Rita Lascaro

Printed in Singapore
First edition

CONTENTS

Foreword and Acknowledgments

THE LANDSCAPES OF GEORGE INNESS (1825–1894), especially paintings from his final fifteen years, together constitute one of America's greatest treasures. The aura of suggestiveness and the nimble handling of paint in these works so effectively invite our scrutiny and stimulate our curiosity that they regularly remind us of the complexity and excitement of engaging with art. On balance, they fulfill Inness's preeminent goal: not to instruct and not to edify his viewers but to awaken an emotion in them.

A percipient student of nature, Inness possessed the full range of expressive abilities. He could create refined or assertive highlights on trees; he could judiciously striate farmland or suggest it through pools of crystallized color. He could choke a stormy sky with ashen clouds or adorn it on a clear day with a delicate necklace of white puffs. He could labor in one painting over the representation of a cow's pink ears and, in another, take pleasure in flecking color from a fully loaded brush. His portrayal of individual features and his facility with paint unified the tenor and purpose of each landscape representation.

Indeed, Inness was a virtuosic painter. Working with a mass of nacreous yellowocher or piquant vermillion, his vascular brush conjured anything from a cluster of flowers to the liminal sun. At other times, a deep breath and a dozen slashes of dull gray produced the illusion of a wheelbarrow or the side of a weather-beaten barn. When needed, he would use his brush handle or fingernail to score seemingly random lines into the still-wet paint. On one occasion, this technique produced thin, deep shadows beneath a hillside blanketed with snow; on another, it made wind swirl through friable autumn leaves. Extending the legendary tradition of painting with fingers, Inness stamped an orange/white/black mass onto one canvas. In so doing, and quite improbably, he accomplished four things at once: he produced the illusion of a small farm animal in the grass; he generated visual interest in an otherwise quiet compositional space; he kindled the modern idea of painting as an arena for the play of pure colors; and he left an incontrovertible signature on the surface of his canvas—in all, a tour de force of the artist's working hand.

Inness also understood the power of compositional order. Selecting discreet brushwork from his arsenal of pictorial tools, he would nimbly assemble the components of a terrain—the hills, shadows, trees, body of water, sky—to evoke nature's underlying rationale, always ensuring that order served the greater pictorial intentions of each painting, whatever they might be. Although this feature appears in the works of many artists and serves their own purposes, it may have alluded, in Inness's case, to his belief that order and structure characterize the spiritual realm and that those same qualities produce counterparts, or correspondences, in nature.

Humanistic concerns seem always to have been at the forefront of Inness's consciousness. He signaled his commitment to this idea by creating opportunities for extended engagement with his work, by using demonstrative brushwork that left ample traces of his directorial presence, and by including human figures—often eidolonic ones—in nearly all of his landscapes. Frequently created with only the thinnest veils of color, these figures stimulate our powers of perception; in a sense, we generate them along with Inness. And although we may debate the number and nature of Inness's sources of inspiration, his humanistic daubs remind us that his underlying preoccupation was always the plight of the individual.

Essentially, Inness was a self-taught artist. In the 1820s, his hometown of Newburgh, New York, provided almost no access to an artistic education. Fortunately, he and his family soon moved to New York City, where he discovered engraved reproductions of old master paintings—notably landscapes by the seventeenth-century Frenchman Claude Lorrain. Then, as he put it, "the light began to dawn." Inness understood that he could translate his close study of nature into organized, pleasing landscape paintings. His exposure to the works of his Hudson River School predecessors, especially Thomas Cole and Asher B. Durand, corroborated his nascent grasp of the artist's role in transforming vision into pictorial representation. His early paintings—from the late 1840s to mid-1850s—prove that, as with many artists, he needed to digest the past before setting out on his own.

The Barbizon paintings to which Inness was exposed in Paris in 1852 and again in 1853-54 presented an exciting alternative to extant pictorial models. From the circle of artists that included Jean-Baptiste-Camille Corot and Théodore Rousseau, he gained his freedom to paint more liberally and to bypass, when he saw fit, the convention of representing familiar or even identifiable locations. Furthermore, Barbizon aesthetics accorded with his impassioned temperament; in his first major interview, he spoke admiringly of the "inspirational power" of Corot's paintings and of the "pure ideas" expressed by Rousseau. From these artists, he refined his intention to express what he would later describe to the art critic Ripley Hitchcock as "the subjective mystery of nature with which wherever I went I was filled." Ultimately, Inness would transport Barbizon's sensuousness through the pragmatic tendencies of nineteenth-century American art into Tonalism, the major native art movement of the 1880s and 1890s; it would reemerge in the painterly, atmospheric photographs of Edward Steichen, Alfred Stieglitz, and turn-of-the-century American Pictorialists.

Dissatisfied with the study of any single artistic movement, Inness extended his search for understanding to the works of Eugène Delacroix, Jean-Louis-Ernest Meissonier, and Jean-Leon Gérôme; he came to know the paintings of John Constable and J. M. W. Turner; he derived inspiration from the landscapes of Meindert Hobbema and Rembrandt; he disparaged the aesthetics of the Pre-Raphaelites and Impressionists. In interviews of the late 1870s and 1880s, he revealed a limber familiarity with Egyptian, Greek, Early Christian, Renaissance, and Native American (termed "American Indian") art. Although his knowledge may have been shallow in these fields, its wide embrace evinces the reach of his imagination and intimates a precocious cognizance of his place within the history of art.

A well-known and highly respected figure in mid- to late-nineteenth-century America, Inness may have been one of the most inquisitive artists of his generation, absorbing as much literary culture as he did art history. He searched relentlessly for knowledge; he read avidly, wrote for hours every night, and discoursed extemporaneously, often to perplexed but devoted friends and family members. Favorite topics included science, optics, evolutionary history, mathematics, numerology, psychology, philosophy, spirituality, and theology. He grappled with questions, mainly metaphysical ones, on the omnipresence of spirit, the value of sensuality in art and life, the meaning of "truth," and the nature of the relationship between man and God, or, as he described the latter, "the Infinite Spirit." The inscrutability of these questions kept him fully engaged in their analysis; indeed, throughout his life, it was this inscrutability that he struggled to express in pictorial form.

Inness's paintings are the primary expression of his ideas. *George Inness: Writings and Reflections on Art and Philosophy* makes the primary *literary* expressions of these ideas available. It includes the four interviews that he gave to major newspapers and art journals; his essays and articles on art, philosophy, and religion; his debates on aesthetics with leading critics and editors; his political speeches; and his spirited, albeit ingenuous poetry. Several texts are published here for the first time. Alternately confrontational and amusing, informative and misguided, periodically vague but always provocative, these texts represent a vital, diastolic counterpart to Inness's ambitious and influential landscape paintings.

Inness's contestation of American pictorial norms and his assimilation of then-radical French ones; his commitment to the spiritual nature of art and life; his outspoken disdain for art establishments (from museums to critics to private collectors); his determination to elevate the role of the artist in society; and, especially, his pictorial inventiveness attracted countless admirers and critics. They responded to his work from the time it entered its first major exhibition in 1847 by visiting his studio, watching him paint, and by writing profiles on him for newspapers and magazines. During his life and soon after his death, they transcribed and published their recollections of his discourses and working habits. Their texts grant us unprecedented access to the artist at work in his studio, often as he simultaneously (and rather theatrically) lectured and painted. Unable to include every worthy recollection, I have focused on those that contain Inness's statements, even if transmitted through a secondary voice. (As American art history has not yet fully benefited from the tradition, ubiquitous in the study of European art, of publishing reflections by and about artists, it is hoped that this volume will not only bring fresh insights into Inness's life and work but also inspire a new effort to publish the primary literary sources for more of his deserving American colleagues.) Seen as a whole, these texts shed new light on the wide range of Inness's intellect, his presciently modern attitude to art, and his investment in many foundational ideas of nineteenth- and early-twentieth-century American cultural history.

I extend my many thanks to Michael Quick for sharing the bibliography from his forthcoming George Inness catalogue raisonné and for answering several factual questions regarding Inness's life and work. Mr. Quick also kindly sent me his transcription of Inness's lecture "The Logic of the Real Æsthetically Considered," delivered in Boston in 1875 and recently discovered in the *Boston Daily Advertiser* by Gerald L. Carr.

I would also like to thank all of the representatives of collections containing documents by Inness for permission to publish their materials: Judy Throm and Wendy Hurlock Baker, Archives of American Art, Smithsonian Institution, Washington, D.C.; Susan Snyder, The Bancroft Library, University of California, Berkeley; Bethany Engstrom, Farnsworth Art Museum, Rockland,

Maine; R. A. Friedman, The Historical Society of Pennsylvania; Leslie A. Morris and Peter X. Accardo, Houghton Library, Harvard University; Mark D. Mitchell, National Academy Museum, New York; Maurita Baldock, The New-York Historical Society; AnnaLee Pauls, Rare Books and Special Collections, Princeton University Library; and Andrew Martinez, Rhode Island School of Design. My special thanks to Anne Bentley, Curator of Art/Acting Registrar, Massachusetts Historical Society, for locating the letter to Thomas B. Clarke that contains Inness's statement on *Sunset in the Woods* (1891) and to Toni Liquori, Media Coordinator/Rights and Reproductions, for helping to secure photographs of works from the Montclair Art Museum.

I thank Rita Lascaro for her characteristically elegant book design and George Braziller for his steadfast support. As always, my deepest appreciation goes to my husband, Richard L. Bell, for his endless supply of sound advice, humor, and encouragement.

A Note on the Transcriptions

George Inness did not feel a pressing need to follow prescribed rules of grammar. When writing letters, he rarely used apostrophes and occasionally, in haste, omitted parts of words. He especially hated periods, often ending sentences with a calligraphic flourish and starting a new one without capitalizing the first letter of the first word. To reproduce such sentences as written would have created an editorial minefield. Therefore, when transcribing such texts, I left five blank spaces between the sentences and added essential corrections in brackets. The intention was to retain the feel of Inness's writing style and, simultaneously, produce legible copy. Abbreviations (e.g., "recd" for "received") and British spellings (e.g., "elabourate" and "favour") have been retained; strikethroughs have been retained when legible. Periods have not been added after such common abbreviations as "Mr" and "Feb"; // signifies a line break in the original manuscript that, for spatial considerations, had to be omitted in the transcription. When a word is first misspelled (e.g., "Snedecors" for "Snedecor's"), it is followed by "[*sic*]"; each subsequent misspelling of that word is printed without the "[*sic*]." When the word is misspelled in a different way (e.g., "Snedicor" for "Snedecor"), "[*sic*]" again follows the misspelled word on the first occasion only. The typography of previously printed texts was retained when it did not distract from legibility. I have added brief prefatory remarks in brackets to establish the context of the documents or to clarify obscure references. Finally, the selection of illustrations is unique to this edition.

FIG. 1. George Inness, *Leeds in the Catskills, with the Artist Sketching*, c. 1868, oil on canvas, 47¹/₂ x 71³/₄", Courtesy of the Berkshire Museum, Pittsfield, Massachusetts, Gift of Zenas Crane.

FIG. 2. Thomas Cole, *View from Mount Holyoke, Northampton, Massachusetts, after a Thunderstorm (The Oxbow)*, 1836, oil on canvas, 51¹/₂ x 76", The Metropolitan Museum of Art, New York, Gift of Mrs. Russell Sage, 1908 (08.228).

GEORGE INNESS:
ARTIST, WRITER, PHILOSOPHER

George, my love for art is killing me, and yet it is what keeps me alive.
—Inness to his son, George Inness, Jr.[1]

THE PLACE WAS THE TOWN OF LEEDS, in Greene County, New York, on the west bank of the Hudson River, and the time was about 1868. Two years later, Frederic Edwin Church would begin to construct Olana, his stunning home in the nearby city of Hudson. Catskill, a haven for Hudson River School painters, was fewer than four miles to the southeast. The weather in New York City was especially hot that summer, and so, in July, George Inness arranged for his wife, Elizabeth, and their children to spend it with him in Leeds. In a letter to a patron, the lawyer Thomas B. Carroll, Inness declined Carroll's offer to join him on a trip northwest to the St. Lawrence River, preferring to continue uninterrupted the "course of study" in which he was engaged. The prosaic tone of Inness's response to Carroll accords with the modesty of his self-portrait in a painting from this period, *Leeds in the Catskills, with the Artist Sketching* (c. 1868) (FIG. 1). Here, the diminutive figure of Inness sketches on a sloping hill under a small umbrella. Facing him are the mountains of the Catskill High Peaks. Although the location had inspired countless artists before him, it was perhaps to Thomas Cole that Inness alluded, for Cole likewise presented himself, sketching near an artist's umbrella, in *View of Mount Holyoke, Northampton, Massachusetts, after a Thunderstorm — The Oxbow* (1836) (FIG. 2).[2]

If we based our understanding of Inness only on this unassuming self-portrait, we would not, in a sense, see the whole picture, for the image of Inness as a temperate Hudson River School painter hardly accords with first-hand literary descriptions of Inness *as a painter*. One such account was recalled by J. Francis Murphy, an attentive student of the Barbizon School who would later become a leading Tonalist. At one point, probably during the late 1870s, Murphy joined Inness, Inness's son George Inness, Jr., and Bruce Crane on a sketching trip to the Catskills.[3] According to Murphy, the artists began the morning by assembling their canvases, brushes, and boxes of paints and then set off in a wagon to

find a suitable location in which to work. When they reached the desired setting, each one chose a favorite spot and began his composition. Late in the day,
a nor'easter materialized and sent the shivering painters back to their wagon.
Inness, however, was missing. "I know where the old man is; I'll get him,"
Murphy volunteered. Murphy climbed up a steep slope and "found Inness
backed up against a ledge of rock which partly protected him from the wind. His
coat was off, his face was streaked with color where he had brushed away the
perspiration with paint-smeared fingers, he was painting like mad at a gorgeous
sunset—and he refused to budge until he had finished his sketch."[4]

When contrasted to the self-portrait in *Leeds in the Catskills*, Murphy's
account presents Inness in a far more vivid light. We now see him battling the
elements, refusing to compromise his intentions to nature's capricious behavior.
He had a job to do and was not prepared to let a minor climatic event sway him
from the goal of completing his work. This sense of devotion to his art—this
willingness to make all kinds of sacrifices to the cause of painting—intrigued,
perplexed, bemused, frustrated, and often inspired Inness's friends and colleagues. They became deeply interested in his artistic practices, preoccupations,
struggles, ideas, even his appearance. Many sought to observe him while he
painted. They attempted to engage him in conversations on diverse topics, from
the technical to the theoretical; as it happened, they listened to him discourse
more than they conversed. Later, they studiously recorded his comments and
their observations in articles and essays. As these recollections have never been
assembled for publication, one of the primary functions of the present volume is
to offer all of the most important essays on Inness, written mainly during his
lifetime and shortly after his death, in a single volume.[5] Although they are
clearly biased to varying degrees by the intimacy of friendship or by the partial-
ity that accompanies profound admiration, these invaluable accounts present
Inness to us anew. They complement and enrich knowledge derived from viewing his paintings. Together, they help to construct a multivalent, humanistic
framework in which to revisit and reevaluate Inness's extraordinary contribu-
tions to American cultural history.

As suggested above, Inness loved to learn and express his ideas. A few
astute editors recognized this feature of his personality and interviewed him
for their newspapers and journals. Inness's four interviews—for *Harper's New
Monthly Magazine* in February 1878, for *The Art Journal* and the New York
Evening Post in 1879, and for the *New York Herald* in 1894—together constitute one of our most vital sources of information on his thinking.[6] Moreover,

outside of tending to his family and painting, one of Inness's favorite activities was studying and writing about art, literature, philosophy, science, and spirituality. It seems that only family members and close friends knew that he viewed painting and writing as wholly integrated, complementary activities, for few of his many manuscripts made it into print during his lifetime. Therefore, a second and equally important purpose of this book is to rectify this oversight by reprinting all of Inness's interviews and extant writings—his essays, speeches, poems, and letters.[7] These primary documents help us to reconstruct the scope and character of Inness's intellectual life. They challenge the insular view of Inness as an impulsive, even careless painter, driven only by instinct, and suggest that he tempered his impulse toward spontaneity in painting by becoming one of the most analytical, inquisitive artists of his generation.

To be sure, Inness's son had undertaken a similar venture when he wrote *Life, Art, and Letters of George Inness*, published by the Century Company in 1917. In this primarily biographical volume, the author included many of his father's letters and excerpts from some philosophically minded essays. From this volume, we have excerpted the letters and essays, as well as anecdotes containing quotations by Inness, leaving behind the useful but more prosaic biographical passages. The volume was limited in that it did not contain the interviews or all of the letters and essays, not even those published during Inness's lifetime; moreover, it has long been out of print. The time had come, therefore, for a more complete presentation of Inness's ideas and for an anthology of reflections on his life and work written by those who knew him.

> *While looking at the Claude which hangs next to one of the Turners in the National Gallery—and which knocks the Turner all to pieces—I seemed to be in the presence of a great, earnest mind.*
> —Inness, in "A Painter on Painting"[8]

The capacity for independent study and for representing nature's forms and effects generally remains accessible to artists; more challenging is developing an understanding of compositional structures and techniques. Had Inness remained in his hometown of Newburgh, New York, he would have found few opportunities, during the early nineteenth century, to obtain an artistic education. However, his family moved to New York City, then to Newark, New Jersey, and back to New York in 1831. According to his friend and biographer, the art critic George Sheldon,

Inness worked "off and on for two years,"[9] presumably during the early 1840s, at the New York engraving firm of Sherman & Smith and, shortly thereafter, at N. Currier (later Currier & Ives).[10] There, he would have learned the fundamentals of compositional organization by studying paintings by the old masters, notably Claude Lorrain. Inness, Jr., tells us that his father's first major artistic revelation came when he compared reproductions of these paintings to nature. Referring to the compositions in the prints, he observed, "There was a power of motive, a bigness of grasp, in them. They were nature, rendered grand instead of being belittled by trifling detail and puny execution."[11] He expressed "power of motive" and "bigness of grasp" in such early paintings as *The Juniata River* (1856) (FIG. 3), where he used typical Claudian features—the detailed foreground, the framing element of two banks of trees, the placid body of water and staffage figures (a man and cattle) in the middle ground, and low-lying mountains in the distance—to create an expansive, commanding view of the countryside. The schematic Claudian structure, used in concert with the careful delineation of forms and the judicious alternation of light and shade across the setting, endowed *The Juniata River* with an inviting sense of spatial breadth and depth. In all, the painting signaled an important achievement for a nascent American artist.

Despite its title, *The Juniata River* could represent almost any pastoral setting. Inness's use of the Claudian structure suggests that the work was as much a carefully honed studio composition as a representation of the landscape of central Pennsylvania. Although, during the 1850s, Inness was still learning and experimenting with compositional formats, he developed an idiosyncratic habit of treating famous subjects as an afterthought. There are exceptions: his two crystalline renditions of the Delaware Water Gap, both painted in 1857 (private collection; Montclair Art Museum, New Jersey) and his view of St. Peter's, Rome, also of 1857 (New Britain Museum of American Art, Connecticut), for example. Still, when painting the Roman aqueduct about 1852, he relegated the famous structure to a tiny, almost inconsequential detail in the distant landscape (High Museum of Art, Atlanta). This tendency was unusual at the time, for during the 1850s and 1860s American artists habitually returned from trips to the western states and territories with detailed sketches for paintings of Yosemite and returned from Europe with meticulous representations of the Colosseum, the Roman Forum, and the Parthenon. Inness's interest would come to reside, instead, in the challenge of pictorially expressing his emotional reactions to a setting, be it famous or anonymous, and in stimulating emotional reactions from his viewers.

FIG. 3. George Inness, *The Juniata River*, 1856, oil on canvas, 37 x 55", The Haggin Collection, The Haggin Museum, Stockton, California.

Indeed, Inness would, in image and word, become a vocal advocate for creating original works of art that would, as he put it, not "instruct" or "edify" his viewers but "awaken an emotion"—any kind of emotion—in them.[12] An opportunity to champion this cause came in 1878 when the painter and decorative artist John La Farge published an article in the New York *Evening Post* outlining the superiority of engraving over painting.[13] Inness strongly disagreed; he saw engraving as a reproductive art form. In his response to La Farge, entitled "A Plea for the Painters" and included in the present collection, he expounded on the greater challenge of creating unique works of art. He argued that the painter is superior to the engraver for three reasons. First, possessing the "creative impulse," the painter has to devise a means to convey that impulse in "the most rapid way." Second, he has to "represent distances, spaces, etc., directly from nature." Third, he has to "be a colorist—the most difficult thing in the world," for color, according to Inness, was "the soul of painting. . . ." Ultimately, he stated, "the presence of the creative power is always acknowledged to be the quality essential to great art."[14]

In many ways, Inness's paintings function as tangible manifestations of these three ideas. For example, we see evidence of the rapid expression of the "creative impulse" in *The Coming Storm* (1878) (FIG. 4), a work painted on the cusp of his late landscape period (c. 1878–94). Here, his dynamic brushwork brilliantly captures summer's refulgent, capricious activity. A storm approaches and transforms the landscape. The swirling, grayish strokes in the sky reflect the artist's vigorous application of thinned paints, as do tiny daubs—highlights—on the tree on the foreground coulisse. Golden yellow streaks on the verdant middle ground suggest light gently emerging through fissures in the thick rain clouds and help to create the illusion of spatial expansiveness. Speed, energy, intensity; a formidable sense of three-dimensionality; and the sensitive selection of naturalistic colors together identify *The Coming Storm* as a self-contained arena for Inness's intuitive reactions to nature and an expression of his desire to "awaken an emotion" in his viewers—for this one, the uneasy anticipation of chaos. For these reasons and others, it reflects his highest artistic ideals.

⬥•⬥•⬥

> *When asked by a fellow artist how he could suggest so much of nature with little more than a "rub of color," Inness replied, "I have a method of handling my brush that is all my own."* —Elliott Daingerfield[15]

Progressive artists inevitably struggle with and reinvent the creative process for themselves. When we read Inness's reflections on this subject, then compare these ideas to the tangible evidence of his paintings, and finally read eyewitness accounts of him at work we begin to see how closely affiliated his aesthetic outlook and practices were to his inventive predecessors. For example, according to his son, Inness thought Titian was "the greatest colorist that ever lived" and, perhaps in homage to him, spent a summer at Pieve di Cadore, the Venetian artist's birthplace.[16] The sense of admiration is hardly surprising, as Inness and Titian both dilated the communicative potential of broad, gestural brushwork, each one developing an efficient system, in their late periods, of representing complex forms as concisely as possible. In *La carta del navegar pitoresco* (1660), Marco Boschini tells us that, according to Palma il Giovane, Titian "blocked in his pictures with a mass of colors, which served . . . as a bed or foundation for what he wished to express; and upon which he would then build. I myself have seen such underpainting, vigorously applied with a loaded brush. . . . And in this way with four strokes of the brush he was able to suggest a magnificent figure."[17] Among many observers, the painter Elliott Daingerfield played the role of Palma to Inness's Titian. His equally vivid descriptions—many are reproduced here—echo the language of Palma's account as they convey the speed and confidence with which Inness worked. "What a delight it was to watch [Inness] paint when in one of those impetuous moods which so often possessed him," Daingerfield declared. "With a great mass of color he attacked the canvas, spreading it with incredible swiftness, marking in the great masses with a skill and method all his own, and impossible to imitate; here, there, all over the canvas, rub, rub, dig, scratch, until the very brushes seemed to rebel, spreading their bristles as fiercely as they did in the days of yore along the spine of their porcine possessor."[18] In another first-hand account, this one written by Arthur Turnbull Hill—son of George Waldo Hill, a Brooklyn dentist, amateur painter, and friend of Inness's—we can almost feel the "energy of [Inness's] attack upon a canvas, . . . the rapidity and accuracy of his drawing and brushwork and the amount of space he would cover in a few moments. . . ." According to Hill, after Inness had, on one occasion, "plunked" down a whole tube of white paint on his palette, then he "began that rapid brush-work—that scrubbing, rubbing, spreading of the paint across the canvas without

FIG. 4. George Inness, *The Coming Storm*, 1878, oil on canvas, 26 x 39", Albright-Knox Art Gallery, Buffalo, New York, Albert H. Tracy Fund, 1900.

FIG. 5. Thomas Cole, *Aqueduct near Rome*, 1832, oil on canvas, 44½ x 67⁵⁄₁₆", Mildred Lane Kemper Art Museum, Washington University, St. Louis, Missouri, University purchase, Bixby Fund, by exchange, 1987, WU 1987.4.

seeming to lift the brush from its surface. . . . The whole thing was done without, so to speak, stopping to take breath; other colors, black, blue, orange, had followed in quick succession after the white, and in a few moments the color scheme of the picture was completely changed."[19]

As both Titian and Inness grew older, the challenge of refining imagery became decreasingly important to them. In his *Harper's* interview of 1878, Inness conveyed his ideas on this subject as he discussed the value of painting rapidly *and* concisely. "The reality of every artistic vision lies in the thought animating the artist's mind," he observed, and continued, "Consequently we find that men of strong artistic genius, which enables them to dash off an impression coming, as they suppose, from what is outwardly seen, may produce a work, however incomplete or imperfect in details, of greater vitality, having more of that peculiar quality called 'freshness,' either as to color or spontaneity of artistic impulse, than can other men after laborious efforts—a work which appeals to the cultivated mind as something more or less perfect of nature."[20] Inness traveled abroad twice during the 1850s: to Rome and Florence in 1851–52 and to Rome and Paris from

FIG. 6. George Inness, *Old Aqueduct, Campagna, Rome*, 1871, oil on paper mounted on board, 8³⁄₄ x 13", Montclair Art Museum, Montclair, New Jersey, Gift of Mrs. Eugene G. Kraetzer, Jr., 1953.38.

1853 to 1854. During his third trip to Italy (1870–74), he put into practice his ideas on the concise expression of forms. He returned to the subject of the Roman aqueduct, this time painting it from a closer vantage point. Again, he may have been thinking of Cole, who had treated the subject some forty years earlier (FIG. 5). Cole's refined pictorial style, which allowed him to represent the tiny cracks and delicate hues of the eponymous aqueduct, brought him substantial critical acclaim for this painting.[21] In *Old Aqueduct, Campagna, Rome* (1871) (FIG. 6), Inness characteristically neglected details of the aqueduct and featured the humble shepherds and their flock in the foreground. In a stunning example of pictorial expressionism, he twisted and daubed curls of grayish-ocher paint to incarnate sheep and flocks of grazing sheep along the rocky terrain. In a sense, by employing a "method of handling [his] brush" that had not yet fully entered into the pictorial vocabulary of American artists, Inness demonstrated "the creative process" that, seven years later, he would champion in his New York *Evening Post* article, "A Painter on Painting." These bold, convincing gestures echoed, remarkably, the objectives of Titian; with them (and with kindred examples from the

1870s and later), Inness essentially fulfilled the Venetian painter's promise to suggest, "with four strokes of the brush, . . . a magnificent figure."

Evoking the stance of Gustave Courbet, who famously refused art instruction to a group of students ("every artist should be his own teacher," Courbet told them), Inness resisted the didactic, doctrinaire aspects of teaching art.[22] He did, however, take the American-born British painter Mark Fisher under his wing while he lived in Medfield, Massachusetts, in the early 1860s.[23] A bit later, in 1864, he accepted an invitation to offer some informal art instruction at Eagleswood Military Academy in Perth Amboy, New Jersey, where he stayed until 1867. Run by Marcus Spring and his wife, Rebecca Buffum Spring (both Quakers) under the aegis of the social reform community The Raritan Bay Union, Eagleswood offered instruction in a variety of subjects, including physical fitness, English, foreign languages, mathematics, sciences, and natural philosophy, as well as drawing and painting. The Springs commissioned a home, christened "Eagleswood Eyre," to be built for Inness and his family (FIG. 7). There, he offered art lessons to his "pupils," including Louis Comfort Tiffany, Carlton Wiggins, and James Steele MacKaye.[24] The Springs' son-in-law, MacKaye would later

FIG. 7. George Inness's home and studio, Eagleswood Eyre, at Eagleswood, Perth Amboy, New Jersey (from 1864–67), photograph, 1889, George Inness file, Le Brun Library, Montclair Art Museum, New Jersey.

become a well-regarded actor. Tiffany described Inness's approach as follows: "Inness did not give instruction in painting; his way was to criticize or appreciate the work of a young artist from time to time. Perhaps the disquisitions into which he launched were sometimes confusing, for they were likely to carry the mind of the learner far afield. But he had a good deal of William Morris Hunt's inspirational quality. He set high ideals before the student."[25]

Inness would periodically accept invitations to examine the work of younger painters. On these occasions, he found himself more willing to demonstrate technique than to explain it. The artist and writer Frederick Stymetz Lamb offered an account, also reprinted here, of one such artists' convention. Lamb highlighted the physical intensity of Inness's work and the intimacy of Inness's relationship to paint's materiality. According to Lamb,

> All of the young men were anxious to understand Inness' method
> of painting. The eventful day arrived, a Sunday, when Inness could
> spare the time. . . . When Inness arrived he rushed at once to the
> studies and started to give his theories of painting. . . . He spoke of
> color combination, showed methods of brush work and finally set
> aside both brush and palette. Taking his thumb he drew the color
> together with a few marvelous sweeps—as was often his habit—
> then excitedly seizing his friend by the lapel of his coat, he
> explained the reason at the same time leaving beautiful color com-
> binations on the Sunday coat![26]

Although the intimacy of Inness's relationship to paint was unusual for artists of his generation, it became more commonplace toward the turn of the century. It would, of course, become a hallmark of modern art. In this regard, Albert Pinkham Ryder extended Inness's legacy. He shared Inness's enthusiasm for the act and process of painting. In an interview with Adelaide Louise Samson, published in 1905 in *Broadway Magazine* as "Paragraphs from the Studio of a Recluse," Ryder recalled struggling during his fledgling efforts to paint. He found that he could neither "imitate the canvases of the past" nor represent nature accurately without becoming "lost in a maze of detail." Abandoning both options, he returned to studying nature and, in a moment of revelation, saw the world around him more concisely; he saw it, specifically, as "three masses of form and color—sky, foliage and earth—the whole bathed in an atmosphere of golden luminosity." He described what he did next:

> I threw my brushes aside; they were too small for the work in hand.
> I squeezed out big chunks of pure, moist color and taking my
> palette knife, I laid on blue, green, white and brown in great
> sweeping strokes. As I worked I saw that it was good and clean and
> strong. I saw nature springing into life upon my dead canvas. It was
> better than nature, for it was vibrating with the thrill of a new cre-
> ation. Exultantly I painted until the sun sank below the horizon,
> then I raced around the fields like a colt let loose, and literally bel-
> lowed for joy.[27]

For Inness and Ryder, art emerged from the irrepressible force of personal necessity, from a need to explore, through the creative process, the reality of nature, or the self, or a combination of both, a new reality that resided beyond the familiar, beyond tradition, beyond history.[28] To be sure, the products of their exploration differ considerably. If visible brushwork constitutes one of the hallmarks of Inness's late landscape paintings, Ryder's extensive revisions would often erase all traces of spontaneity; in its stead, Ryder deposited an aura of serene mysticism within the fossilized layers of paint (FIG. 8). Still, both artists established a new depth of engagement with painting, and both held that inspiration resides neither in subject matter nor in predetermined artistic formulas but in the unique relationship that an artist develops with his materials. These perspectives made Inness and Ryder two of the period's most inventive and influential artists.

There are scores of his canvases about, most of them unfinished and kept as studies. But you feel that no man could paint these things were he not both a psychologist and a poet.
　　　　　　　　　—An anonymous visitor to Inness's studio in 1894[29]

As Romantic painters, Inness and Ryder sought to intensify the experience of viewing paintings by linking them to complementary or corresponding ideas in poetic form. In so doing, they extended the long tradition of *ut pictura poesis* ("as with painting so with poetry") and enriched the legacy of the American painter-poet that began with Washington Allston.[30] Inness and Ryder occasionally wrote poems to accompany their paintings, especially when the works went on exhibition. In a review of the 1878 Annual Exhibition at the National Academy of Design, an anonymous critic for the *New York Herald* noted that Inness inscribed "long poetical quotations" on "large tablets," which he placed next to his paintings.[31] According to art historian William Innes Homer, Ryder inscribed a poem on a tablet or, when he exhibited the painting, had the poem printed in the exhibition catalogue.[32] For both artists, poems were, in Homer's words, a "suggestive accompaniment" to paintings and deepened the aesthetic experience. Moreover, Inness was known to have written a poem to accompany the work of another artist: "The Whirlwind," a sculpture by his son-in-law, Jonathan Scott Hartley (see pages 124–25, below). Although it seems that the majority of Inness's poems were independent entities, they may well have been inspired by his paintings or by aspects of his paintings. Finally, a leitmotif of Inness's poems is their spiritual overtones, a subject that deserves further study. Here, we have reproduced Inness's extant poems, including those from George Sheldon's 1882 profile of Inness for *Harper's Weekly Magazine*.

From the reminiscences and recollections included in the present volume, we gain insight into still other aspects of Inness's artistic practices. We learn, for example, that, like Ryder, he constantly reworked his paintings. According to his son, Inness would "take a canvas before the paint was really dry, and, being seized with another inspiration, would paint over it."[33] Sheldon tells us that often Inness painted "fifteen hours a day." Having spent a great deal of time in Inness's studio, he could account for "the dozen or more canvases" that he would see there and could describe how Inness "worked as the humor seized him, going from one to another with palette and maul-stick, and always standing when painting."[34] The account of

FIG. 8. Albert Pinkham Ryder, *Pegasus (The Poet on Pegasus Entering the Realm of the Muses)*, early to middle 1880s, oil on wood panel, 12 x 11³/₈", Worcester Art Museum, Worcester, Massachusetts, museum purchase, 1919.33.

Inness working on several paintings simultaneously is, again, surprisingly similar to Palma's account (via Boschini) of Titian, which tells us that by "operating on and re-forming these figures, [Titian] brought them to the highest degree of perfection . . . and then, while that picture was drying, he turned to another."[35] By remaining engaged in multiple projects simultaneously, Titian and Inness challenged the academic practice of beginning and completing individual paintings in sequence. Furthermore, by keeping several works "in progress" at once, both artists allowed the trajectory of each painting's development to be guided at least in part by such internal forces as mood and inspiration, that is, by the demands of their unique pictorial practices.

Primary accounts also reveal that Inness was not content to limit his compulsion for repainting to his own work. According to the landscape painter and illustrator A. T. Van Laer, Inness left a memorable impression when he visited the studio of the American painter Walter Clark. Clark was absent but a painting remained on his easel. Having studied the composition, Inness saw room for improvement and so made the rather extraordinary decision to rework it. His stealthy mission accomplished, Inness "quietly" exited the room and, as Van Laer

FIG. 9. George Inness, *The Coming Storm*, c. 1879, oil on canvas, 27¼ x 41¾", Addison Gallery of American Art, Phillips Academy, Andover, Massachusetts, Gift of Anonymous Donor, 1928.25.

wryly observed, left "Mr. Clark the happy possessor of a very fine Inness."[36] "It was almost impossible," he added, "for Inness to look at things from any standpoint but his own."[37] On another occasion, recounted in his son's biography and reprinted here, Inness found himself in need of a canvas—any canvas, even a used one. He located a suitable candidate, which happened to contain a scene of several large oxen. Inness did not know—or, worse, did not care—that his own son had painted it and exhibited it, to some critical acclaim, at the National Academy of Design. Inness, Jr., eventually noticed that his work was missing but neglected to ask his father about it. Several years later, he found himself examining one of his father's paintings, subsequently titled *The Coming Storm* (c. 1879) (FIG. 9), at his sister's home. In the raking light, he discerned the outline of his large oxen beneath layers of fresh paint. It was not until 1984, when *The Coming Storm* was X-rayed (FIG. 10), that the son's oxen fully emerged beneath the father's stormy landscape.

While George Inness, Jr., tolerated his father's excesses, Inness himself paid a high price for his chronic dissatisfaction. Reworking his compositions would occasionally bring dramatic success, but looming ahead was the constant threat of dramatic ruin. The artist and art critic Arthur Hoeber tells us that, on the one hand, Inness could paint a brilliant landscape, such as *A Gray, Lowery Day* (c. 1877; Davis Museum and Cultural Center, Wellesley College, Massachusetts), in no more than twenty-four hours. On the other hand, he writes, "[T]he amount of work [Inness] destroyed was appalling. He was just as likely, at a second painting, to completely change the scheme of a beautiful start and, finally, in despair, to scrape out all he had done."[38]

Thomas B. Clarke (see below, FIG. 38) was one of Inness's leading patrons, his agent, and the recipient of numerous letters from the artist, all of which are reprinted here. One day, while trying to explain to Clarke why he had reworked a painting that a client had already purchased, Inness confessed a sense of dismay over his perennial discontent; he even invoked spiritual forces as a resolution to his chronic problem. He said, "Clarke, if I could only learn to leave a thing alone after I feel that I have what I want! It has been the curse of my life, this changing and trying to carry a thing nearer to perfection. After all, we are limited to paint. Maybe, after we get to heaven, we shall find some other medium with which to express our thoughts on canvas."[39]

FIG. 10. X-Ray of George Inness's *The Coming Storm*, c. 1879, taken by the Williamstown Regional Art Conservation Laboratory, Inc., #84-092, Addison Gallery of American Art, Phillips Academy, Andover, Massachusetts, Gift of Anonymous Donor. All rights reserved.

Along with Inness's compulsive need to repaint came his insistence on retaining aesthetic and proprietary control over his work and his disdain for the exigencies of the art market. The letters and documents in this volume provide ample evidence of how he reacted to pressures from the art world, namely, to the overriding tendency of art critics, dealers, and collectors during the 1850s and 1860s to value famous scenes painted in a high degree of finish—features that he tended to avoid in his own work. By the late 1870s, he had seen the careers of Church, Albert Bierstadt, and Pre-Raphaelite painters on both sides of the Atlantic all flourish. He had seen how pictorial refinement and exactitude—a sense of pictorial finish—generated commercial success for these artists and a broader market for their work than for paintings deemed "hastily painted and carelessly composed,"[40] or some variation thereof, as his often were. In 1868, he distinguished between his larger, more suggestive landscapes, which he knew were difficult to sell, and his "small elabourate pictures" for which, he wrote to his client Thomas B. Carroll, he could "always get a prise [sic]."[41] By the end of the 1870s, Inness declared that, in his view, the commercial situation remained essentially unchanged: detailed paintings of well-known subjects sold. "It is mercantile work that is finished," he stated in his *Harper's* interview of 1878, "and finish is what the picture-dealers cry for."[42] When discussing the art market with his son, he advised, "Never paint with the idea of selling. Lose everything first, George." He added, "Be honest; somebody's going to find it out."[43] Inness's associations of pictorial finish with commercialism, with the art market, and with insincerity were some of the most persistent themes of his life; they are represented throughout the documents in the present collection.

The texts included here confirm another facet of Inness's aesthetic outlook, that is, his insistence on maintaining proprietary control over his work. He felt, essentially, that his paintings were his property regardless of whether or not he had sold them, and that he could rework them—always, of course, with an eye toward improvement—whenever they reentered his field of vision. Inness, Jr., elaborated on his father's position:

> My father had the idea firmly established in his mind that a work of art from his brush always remained his property, and that he had the right to paint it over or change it at will, no matter where he found it or who had brought it, or what money he may have received for it. Wherever he found his pictures after they had left

his studio he criticized, and would in most violent language declare the thing was "rot," that the sky was false or the distance out of key, and in a very matter of fact way would say "Just send it around to the studio to-morrow and I'll put it into shape."[44]

Not surprisingly, this attitude regularly generated problems. Hoeber, for example, described how Inness would often render "quite unrecognizable" the paintings that collectors brought to him for "some little repainting."[45] The parties involved were then faced with the task of determining which version—the old or the new—was superior. Naturally, Inness reserved for himself the exclusive right to assess the merits of his work and to determine when a painting could, once again, leave his easel. His son recounts the story of a gentleman from New York who, during the late 1870s or early 1880s, visited Inness's studio and purchased a painting—purchased it, but, unfortunately, neglected to take it with him. The client had hardly left the studio before Inness began to "tickle . . . up" the painting to carry out a thought. He then

> kept on "tickling it up" until the canvas was an entirely different picture, and one that, I regret to say, had lost rather than gained in the process of tickling.
>
> The next day the gentleman came to the studio to see his picture, and, finding it unrecognizable, insisted that this canvas was not his.
>
> "Yes, it is," replied Inness. "I have changed it just a little to give it snap."
>
> "Why, the picture's ruined," said the purchaser, "and I refuse to take it."
>
> "Very well," answered my father; "you couldn't have it now at any price. Your money cannot buy my art. I give you what I choose, and whether you like it or not is a matter of indifference to me. What right have you to tell me what you like or what you do not like? I am the only one capable of judging my own work."[46]

The case of the New York gentleman suggests that Inness repudiated the unspoken authority that clients wield over artists. He sought to reverse the power of the client/artist relationship and to return to the artist the right to dictate the identity and prospect of his work. He saw collectors as no more than temporary custodians of artworks; essentially, of course, he was correct. In his view, money mattered little and whatever authority it possessed could easily be annulled by the will of the artist.

Inness was hardly alone in wanting to uphold his right to rework his paintings. Paul Valéry reminds us that Edgar Degas, who had much to say on the subject of "finish" and artists' rights, adopted a kindred attitude. Valéry stated, "I think [Degas] believed that such a work [one done after innumerable sketches and then "a series of operations"] could never be considered finished. He could not conceive of an artist seeing one of his paintings after a lapse of time, without wanting to work on it again. Occasionally he would even carry off paintings that had hung for a long time on the walls of friends' rooms, taking them back to his lair, from which they rarely reappeared. A few of his intimates were driven to hiding the paintings of his they possessed."[47] Valéry added that "the need to take back pictures [Degas] considered unfinished, never left him. He kept by him numerous paintings he intended retouching, finding them unworthy of leaving his studio in their to him unfinished state."[48]

Inness's insistence on maintaining aesthetic and proprietary control over his work was idealistic, and such idealism had its limits, even for Inness. Documents in this collection reveal that, when it came to his paintings and career, he could be vigorously pragmatic. Attentive to his standing in the art world, Inness sprinkled letters to his patrons and potential patrons with healthy doses of self-confidence, letting them know, for example, that he would send them nothing but his finest. Writing to A. D. Williams in August 1872, he identified *Lake Nemi* (1872) (FIG. 11) as "one of my very best, as I intended it should be, and I am happy to say was so looked upon by all who saw it at my studio."[49] In a letter to Isaac Bates in 1878, he held one of his compositions to be "as fine in sentiment as anything I ever did and I think more masterly."[50] He also kept a watchful eye on the art market. In 1893, when Clarke was serving as his agent, Inness sent him two paintings, one entitled *Afterglow—Southern Florida* and the other *A Breezy Day, Vicinity of Montclair*. "I want these pictures to net me $800.00 cash, which framed at $1250 leaves you 450.00 or one third and fifty dollars over," Inness wrote. "I think that three of this size, of good quality, can be sold more easily than one 30 x 45. . . . " Knowing that he could entice more collectors with smaller, less expensive paintings, he told Clarke that he would send him only pictures of this reduced size because "our clients will be more extended and receipts greater for both of us in the end." He safeguarded his elevated status— by then, widely accepted—in the art world and proscribed situations in which

FIG. 11. George Inness, *Lake Nemi*, 1872, oil on canvas, 30 x 45", Museum of Fine Arts, Boston, Gift of the Misses Hersey, 49.412, © 2003 Museum of Fine Arts, Boston.

he would be compared with other artists. When encouraged to send his paintings to the World's Columbian Exposition of 1893 in Chicago, he resisted at first because, as he put it, "I will not exhibit at all . . . if obliged to compete."[51] Ultimately, he relented and fifteen of his paintings, nearly all from Clarke's collection, were exhibited, one more than Winslow Homer.

As an artist whose work challenged the prevailing ideals of the American art establishment during the 1850s and 1860s and who, consequently, struggled to support himself and his family until his mid-fifties, Inness cast a skeptical gaze on art associations. By that time—that is, by the late 1870s—he had been affiliated with the National Academy of Design for about fifteen years, having been elected an Associate Member in 1853 and an Academician in 1868, but he did not allow his affiliation to prevent him from criticizing the Academy's standards for the election of new members. In his interview with the New York *Evening Post* in 1879, he reflected on the Academy's shrinking authority and bluntly censured it for privileging cronyism over talent. He stated, "The most mediocre artistic ability on the part of a candidate for admission, if accompanied by the wit to keep his nose clean and his shoes well brushed, or still better, by business, social or political talents, with enough money for a 'spread' once in a while, are of more weight than any show of true artistic instincts." In place of the Academy, he suggested instituting several smaller societies of which "all the members have one general aim tending to the development of some distinct artistic sympathy." Membership in these smaller associations would be restricted to twenty artists each, thirty at the most. Each society would hold exhibitions that would attract, as Inness put it, "a certain class of minds who could purchase any picture toward which they might feel inclined with a confidence that they were obtaining something representative of an idea; something which would secure a more and more perfect expression with the increase of time, instead of, in a year or so, going 'out of fashion.'"[52] (Inness left unresolved the problem of selecting works that would represent a single "idea" and neglected to explain how artists would be admitted to the rather small groups. Moreover, he seemed untroubled by the patronizing tone of his hope that such exhibitions would attract "a certain class of minds" and not, say, the general public.) In fact, it was not only toward the Academy that Inness expressed displeasure; he disliked art associations in general. In a letter of 13 January 1881 to the painter J. Carroll Beckwith, reprinted here, he offered his resignation from the rival of the Academy, the more progressive Society of American Artists, stating that he wanted to leave the responsibilities of the organization "wholly to the younger artists," although it is just as likely that he resigned to avoid either sacrificing time away from his studio or offending his fellow Academicians.[53] Inness's investment in politics led him in another, related direction. He had been an ardent abolitionist and, later in life, a follower of the political economist and social reformer Henry George. He particularly admired George's idea of a single tax system and made public his devotion to the cause and to workers' rights in general in an article entitled "Unite and Succeed," published in *The American Federationist*, the literary voice of the American Federation of Labor. Four years earlier, Inness delivered an address honoring Henry George when he visited New York. We have reprinted both of these texts in the present volume.[54]

Mr. Inness's nature is a deeply religious one.   —George Sheldon[55]

The documents in this collection illuminate, although they do not entirely clarify, another dominant feature of Inness's life and work: his devotion to religious ideas. Although his rather ordinary upbringing predicted neither the breadth of his artistic achievements nor the depth of his intellectual curiosity, it did signal his early engagement with religion. According to his son, Inness was "brought up on religious discussion. His mother was a devout Methodist, his aunt, who later became his stepmother, was an equally devout Baptist. His uncle, his mother's brother, was a stanch Universalist, and was as uncompromising in his beliefs as the other members of the family; hence religious discussion became the principal topic of conversation, or, I should say, argument, in the homecircle."[56] It is likely that Inness's exposure to different religions, his early sense of social displacement within artistic circles, and his burgeoning intellectual curiosity all contributed to his commitment to religious study during the 1860s.

In the 13 July 1867 issue of *Harper's Weekly*, an anonymous writer profiled the nature of Inness's interest in religion: "If [Inness] had not possessed an intense love of form and a wondrous sense and power of expression of color, he would have been a preacher or a philosopher in another way, for he has a deep religious nature and an extraordinarily analytical philosophical mind. In his religious faith he is a disciple of SWEDENBORG, and believes that all material objects in form and color have a spiritual sig-

FIG. 12. Emanuel Swedenborg as assessor of mines, 1734, frontispiece to Swedenborg's *Principia*, engraving by Johann-Martin Bernigeroth, the Younger, after a portrait by Johann Wilhem Stör, Swedenborg Image Archive.

nificance and correspondence."[57] The *Harper's Weekly* article marked the first occasion in which the names of Inness and Swedenborg were publicly affiliated. Inness had probably been exposed to the writings of the eighteenth-century Swedish scientist-turned-mystic Emanuel Swedenborg (FIG. 12) since 1851. That summer, Inness rented studio space on the Via Sant'Apollonia in Florence directly above the American artist William Page. In addition to being a skilled portraitist, Page was a well-known adherent to Swedenborgian doctrine. Page may have introduced Inness to some basic principles of the doctrine, such as correspondence theory, the doctrine of influx, and the spiritual significance of numbers and colors, principles to which Inness subsequently alluded in many of the articles, poems, and letters reprinted here.

Indeed, 1867, the year of the *Harper's* profile, was an especially active one for Inness on the Swedenborgian front. In the early fall, he had read a sermon entitled "The Ribband of Blue" written by the Reverend Dr. Jonathan Bayley, a British Swedenborgian minister. In it, Bayley performed Swedenborgian exegesis on Numbers 15:38-39, a biblical passage that encourages "the children of Israel" to make "fringes in the borders of their garments throughout their generations," and to put on this fringe "a ribband of blue." For Bayley, the garment was a metaphor for religion clothing the soul and the blue fringe an allusion to the fact that God concerns himself with even the "lowest," or ostensibly insignificant, parts of human beings. Bayley then turned to the issue of color, for in Swedenborgian doctrine colors correspond to spiritual principles. The blue of the ribbon signified "truths of faith" (a variant of the concept of "true blue"). He further suggested that the specific shade of blue was "Techeleth," or warm blue, that is, blue tinged with red, where red signified "truths of love." According to Bayley's reading, then, the cloth and its blue, heavenly fringe would mean that "all our truth ought to be softened and warmed by love."[58] Inness agreed with the majority of Bayley's explanation but disagreed with his interpretation of the specific shade of blue on the ribbon. In his reply, entitled "Colors and Their Correspondences," originally published on 13 November 1867 in the *New Jerusalem Messenger*, the leading Swedenborgian newspaper of the day, and reprinted here, Inness offered a slightly different perspective on the subject, one based on his experiences as an artist. He argued that the shade of blue would contain not only blue and red (which, when blended, create purple, the color of secular royalty) but also yellow, which signified truths of outward life or, put another way, the love of man. For Inness, the combination of all three colors in the ribbon—the blue of truth with red (the love of God) and yellow (the love of man)—made it even more intensely spiritual.[59]

In order to have written his article in 1867, Inness must have already dedicated several years of research to Swedenborgian doctrine; to be sure, he would continue this field of study for the rest of his life. He secured his commitment to the faith in Brooklyn, New York, on 4 October 1868. On that day, the Reverend Dr. John Curtis Ager—a pastor, writer, translator of Swedenborg's texts, and a friend of the artist's—baptized Inness and his wife in the Swedenborgian Church of the New Jerusalem, formerly located at Monroe Place and Clark Street.[60] In their recollections of Inness, many of his friends alluded to the character of his interest in Swedenborg's writings. In

February 1895, Sheldon wrote that "Swedenborgianism interested [Inness] as a metaphysical system, especially in its science of correspondences; but he never formulated for himself a theological creed, because, as he said, a man's creed changes with his states of mind, and the formulation made to-day becomes useless to-morrow."[61] The painter and, during the 1870s, the American consul to Rome David Maitland Armstrong left another tantalizing clue to Inness's engagement with the concept of the spiritual significance of colors. In his 1920 memoir, he recalled meeting Inness once in the White Mountains, probably during the late 1870s, where the two artists "spent several hours talking together." Actually, it seems that Armstrong listened while Inness talked "about a theory he had of color intertwined in the most ingenious way with Swedenborgianism, in which he was a devout believer. Toward the latter part of the evening," Armstrong recalled, "I became quite dizzy, and which was color and which religion I could hardly tell!"[62] In his eulogy for Inness, also reprinted here, the Reverend Ager referred to Swedenborg as one of Inness's primary intellectual and spiritual resources. He described how, in the Swede's writings, Inness "found the basis for his theories of art. He found there the true solution for all the problems of expression."[63] Taking into consideration the strong bias with which Ager undoubtedly approached the topic, his remarks nevertheless echo the general tenor of commentaries on the relationship by many who knew Inness personally.

Inness's commitment to Swedenborgian doctrine has been the subject of numerous scholarly studies, and there is insufficient space here to offer a thoroughgoing analysis of the subject.[64] Still, by way of introduction, it should be noted that Inness appears to have been drawn to Swedenborg's writings primarily for their broad, metaphysical nature, for the ways in which they present an elaborate, scientific vision of the relationships between the natural and spiritual realms. Science, in fact, resided at the heart of Swedenborg's work, even his most spiritual theories. As a young man, Swedenborg revealed an early talent for scientific research.[65] He studied with the astronomers John Flamsteed and Edmond Halley and invented several new scientific systems, including prototypes for a submarine and an airplane.[66] He authored studies on geology and chemistry; later, he studied anatomy at the School of Surgery and Dissection in Paris and at the Anatomical Theater in the University of Padua. Using his research in anatomy and physiology, he wrote *Economy of the Animal Kingdom* (1740–41) and *Soul's Domain* (1744–45), in which he employed pragmatic, scientific methods in his Cartesian search for the "seat" of the human soul.[67] These studies reflect Swedenborg's pursuit of common ground between the otherwise conflicting epistemological systems of science and religion.

The events that permanently secured Swedenborg's reputation for his followers—and undermined it for skeptics—occurred in 1743. That year, Swedenborg began to experience a series of "vastations," or crises of selfhood.[68] Over a twenty-one month period in 1743–44, he recorded his visionary experiences in his *Journal of Dreams* and *Spiritual Diary*.[69] At first, the experiences consisted of a general awareness of his involvement in a process greater than himself and beyond his control. As the epiphanic incidents continued, they gradually assumed a religious guise. Beginning in the spring of 1744, he experienced theophanies, that is, visions of God or Christ.[70] Swedenborg soon abandoned his scientific work and dedicated his remaining twenty-seven years to describing his revelatory spiritual experiences, to Bible study, and to theological and metaphysical writings.

Having felt that he gained direct experience of the divine, Swedenborg based much of his spiritual writings on the principle that a spiritual world resides beyond the range of the bodily senses but within a realm of the most substantial being and reality. This spiritual world is not above the natural world in space but is an interior world within the natural—akin, for Swedenborgians, to the soul's relationship to bodily organs.[71] The relationship between the interior and exterior realms is correspondential in that every thing and every quality from the natural world first possesses a spiritual identity, a correspondence at the level of the soul.[72]

Swedenborg presented the essence of this idea in *Arcana Coelestia* (*Heavenly Secrets*) (1749–56), his first major theological publication and an exegetical study that sought to reveal the inner, spiritual meaning of each passage from Genesis and Exodus.[73] Its premise is that the Bible was written in an ancient and esoteric "language of correspondences," so that every term used within it corresponds to a spiritual idea. To decipher the correspondence is to unveil long hidden "treasures of knowledge." One Swedenborgian used especially dramatic language to describe the powers of correspondence: "Correspondence is a torch by the light of which we may explore the now darkened and buried temples of ancient knowledge, which modern enterprise has exhumed for our inspection. As the skilful geologist from a single tooth or bone, which he finds imbedded in the solid rock, or from a foot print impressed upon the sand which is now hardened into stone, is able to restore the whole animal form; so from the relics of antiquity, by aid of the science of correspondence, we may yet be able to restore the whole body of ancient philosophy."[74]

Correspondences divulged the internal meaning of Scripture by unveiling the transcendent meaning, or spiritual essence, of the literal words.[75] Likewise, they provided an understanding of the essentially spiritual identity of all facets of the natural realm. As we have seen, it was by adhering to the science of correspondences that Inness and the Reverend Bayley could analyze the spiritual identities of the colors referenced in the passage on the "ribband of blue" in Numbers and could interpret the text in general as a divine message proclaiming God's concern for the most seemingly inconsequential aspects of human life.

In *Arcana Coelestia*, Swedenborg included as interchapter material several reports of his spiritual experiences; he later published an expanded version of these accounts in *Heaven and its Wonders, and Hell* (widely known as *Heaven and Hell*) (1758). In this more illustrative version of his metaphysics, he provided meticulous descriptions of the three, interdependent regions of the afterlife: the celestial, the spiritual, and the natural (or "spiritual-natural") realms. Following the principle of correspondences, these three regions accord with the three major parts of the human body (the body, head, and extremities) as well as three regions of the mind, which are graded according to the degree to which they accept spiritual truths.[76] "Spiritual influx," another major component of his metaphysical doctrine, is the force of Divine Good, of life, that flows into the receptacles, or vessels, of man and nature. The degree to which this force of spiritual truth is manifested corresponds to the degree to which the individual is charitable, or expresses his faith and love of God through charitable works. In *Heaven and Hell*, Swedenborg presented a third component of his doctrine: the idea that space and time in the spiritual realm do not exist as we know them through their fixed coordinates in nature. Liberated from restrictions of place and duration, they are measured by "inward states" and through "changes of state," by which he meant changes of thought.[77] Swedenborg harnessed this distinction when he explained how he could experience the spiritual realm: his body remained in one place while his spirit journeyed to spiritual communities.

Inness conveyed his understanding of the Swedenborgian principles of "spiritual truths," charity, and influx through his paintings and writings. As his daughter Helen ("Nell") Hart Inness was preparing for her forthcoming marriage to the sculptor Jonathan Scott Hartley, Inness took the occasion to offer some fatherly reflections on this new stage of her life, a time when he felt that her "spiritual faculties" were "beginning to unfold." In a letter, reprinted here, he explained his belief, derived from Swedenborg, that "[e]very individual man or woman born into this world is an offshoot of that Infinite Mind or Spirit which we call God. God creates in us sensation, and through it we are made conscious of the world we live in." In Swedenborg's *True Christian Religion*, his summary of the doctrines of the New Church, we recognize a kindred passage, which reads, "Man is a receptacle of God, and a receptacle of God is an image of God; and as God is love itself and wisdom itself, and man is a receptacle of these. . . . [M]an is man from his being able to will what is good and understand truth wholly as if from himself, and yet with the ability to know and believe that he does so from God; for as man knows and believes this, God puts His image in man. . . . "[78]

Inness alluded to Swedenborgian influx when he explained to Nell that, eventually, we find our world to be "a continual changing state, but a state which forms the basis of all our knowledges." This state is continually changing, he added, "because our spirits individualized here, or born, created as distinct from the Infinite, gradually recede from natural surroundings into what each one eventually becomes, viz., the embodiment of his or her own love or desires." Here, Inness is again echoing Swedenborg on the subject, in that the Swedish mystic held that "the state of man's life is continually changing, from infancy even to the end of life, and afterwards to eternity. . . . The reason why the changes of state of these two lives or faculties [the body and spirit] are perpetual with man, from infancy to the end of his life, and afterwards to eternity, is that there is no end to knowledge, less to intelligence, and still less to wisdom; for in their extent there is infinity and eternity, from the Infinite and Eternal from whom they are."[79]

As mentioned above, Inness's understanding of Swedenborgian doctrine infiltrated his poetry as well. In "The Pilgrim," he described the power of the sun as the source of divine energy and truth. He conveyed his Swedenborgian belief, rooted in (but not identical to) Platonic philosophy, that the visible world is a poor reflection of a more real, more authentic reality in the spiritual realm. He described the sun as the source of an "Ever-flowing, all-pervading good, // Eternal, real, yet to the mind // That seeks to see, // Forever the unknown; for // What is seen is not reality."[80] In *Arcana Coelestia*, Swedenborg wrote, "memory-knowledges [factual knowledge] are in a light nearly the same as that in which is the sensual of man's sight [physical sight], and this light is such that unless it is enlightened within by the light which is from truths [spiritual light], it leads into falsities, especially into those derived from the fallacies of the senses; and also into evils from falsities."[81] In another poem, entitled "Exaltation," Inness encourages the reader to "Sing joyfully! // A real world to see" for "God all space fills."[82] Here, he is referring directly to the Swedenborgian principle that God exists in a space distinct from space in the natural realm, in a spiritual space that is without length, breadth, and depth. This spiritual space is, in Swedenborg's mystical language, "space without space and time without time."[83] Such visionary ideas undoubtedly resonated deeply with Inness. According to his son, during one especially fervent period of painting when Inness had "dabbed and smeared" for "a quarter of an hour" to "bring a composition out of chaos," he finally exclaimed in frustration, "Oh, to paint a picture, a sunset, without paint! To create without paint!"[84]

Inness's landscapes, especially those from his late period, are by no means straightforward pictorial representations of Swedenborgian principles—neither of the science of correspondence nor divine influx; the artist would not have converted his theological beliefs into his artistic practices so simplistically or overtly. However, as these examples have shown, Swedenborgian doctrine contributed to the long and complicated process of shaping Inness's intellectual, familial, and spiritual life. As an artist who had been "brought up on religious discussion" and who possessed a "deeply religious nature," he endeavored to find forms of artistic expression for his spiritual beliefs. Convinced, as he was, that "God is always hidden" and that "beauty depends upon the unseen—the visible upon the invisible," he would instinctively have veiled his beliefs within his own artistic techniques and systems of representing nature.

What George Inness most enjoyed, in his hours of ease, was talking and writing on metaphysical subjects like the Darwinian hypothesis of evolution, and the distinction between instinct and reason.
—George William Sheldon[85]

The theme of the artist-as-amateur philosopher has maintained a long and provocative history in Western art. Delacroix and Johann Wolfgang Goethe, Cole and Asher B. Durand, Mark Rothko and Philip Guston are among the many artists who have needed to express their ideas about art both pictorially and philosophically. Inness, Jr., observed that, during the latter part of his father's life, he wrote and discoursed constantly on theological subjects: "He was full of theories of art, religion and ethics, and would talk theory and preach theory to all who would listen to him. It made no difference whether they agreed with him or ever understood; he kept right on talking theory. I have seen him pin a man to a chair and pound his ideas into him for hours at a time until he and his listener were both exhausted."[86] Musa Mayer's description of her father's need to expound on philosophical topics sounds a kindred bell. For Mayer, Guston "was a great teacher because he was a great talker. He loved a freewheeling exchange. When an idea excited him, he would often hold forth, dominating conversation. Personal revelations, speculations on art and literature, or on any field of human inquiry—science, metaphysics, politics, psychology—all of it interested him. He wore out his friends, keeping them up until all hours in marathon dialogues that would eventually become monologues as their stamina failed to match his."[87] Inness and Guston felt a pressing need to understand the artistic theories and ambitions of earlier artists, to understand the criteria of successful works of art in different cultures, and to set the trajectory of art into its philosophical context. In short, for both artists, philosophical inquiry undergirded and enriched their work as painters.

There is little doubt that metaphysics preoccupied Inness throughout his adult life. He was driven by existential questions on the nature of life, the self, and the afterlife. He explored his ideas on these subjects in talks, in manuscripts, and extemporaneously to friends and colleagues. For example, in 1875, he delivered a lecture at the Boston Art Club entitled "The Logic of the Real Æsthetically Considered,"[88] a transcription of which, recently located, has been reprinted in the present volume. According Sheldon, Inness avidly studied nineteenth-century Irish and English philosophy, both ecclesiastical and utilitarian; he "would wade through a treatise of Archbishop Whately's or John Stuart Mill's, and industriously record the more notable of his animadversions."[89] In his final interview, given to the *New York Herald* and published posthumously, Inness concisely summarized his metaphysical outlook: "I am seventy years of age, and the whole study of my life has been to find out what it is that is in myself; what is this thing we call life, and how does it operate."[90]

By his own account, Inness wrote "piles upon piles" of manuscripts on metaphysical subjects, although, as noted, none of these texts has survived intact.[91] The art dealer Alfred Trumble described how Inness wrote the texts for himself with no intention of publishing them. He remarked,

When [Inness] was not endeavoring to paint it [art] he was writing it, not with any special idea of giving it to the public, but for the purpose of more closely examining and expounding it for himself. After a long day's labor in his studio, he would refresh himself with a long night at his desk. After a day of disappointment at his easel, through failure to secure upon the canvas that subtle spirituality which he saw, or rather felt, in his subject as its soul, he would turn for fresh enlightenment and inspiration to his manuscripts, and seek in them the clue which he had lost.[92]

Inness's critics, friends, and family members described him as "devoted to mystical speculations,"[93] as needing help in solving his "deep metaphysical problems"[94] and his "metaphysical theories."[95] In furnishing Trumble with details for a biography that accompanied the 1895 executor's sale of the artist's work, James A. Inness wrote, "I have alluded to my brother's metaphysical labors. These were taken up more as a relaxation after excessive efforts in the field of art, than as a regular pursuit. However, he was at all times fond of discussion on social and theological problems, and at one time told me that in his early days, if his health had permitted, he would have become absorbed in metaphysical studies."[96] Sheldon summarized Inness's involvement in philosophy when he observed, "From theology to metaphysics, also, the passage is easy; and Inness is a metaphysician too."[97] The character of Inness's "metaphysical labors" has never been fully defined. Sheldon described one of Inness's manuscripts, "The Mathematics of Psychology," as "a contribution to the philosophy of numbers . . . a veritable *scientia scientiarum* [literally, "knowledge of knowledges," or, more loosely, "warehouse of knowledge"]" and elaborated on Inness's interest in numerology.[98] In another essay, John C. Van Dyke, professor of the history of art at Rutgers College during the late nineteenth century, also referenced Inness's study of the spiritual significance of numbers when he stated, "In his theory of the unities everything in the scheme entire dropped into its appointed place. He could show this, to his own satisfaction at least, by the symbolism of numbers, just as he could prove immortality by the argument for continuity."[99]

Several members of Inness's circle referred to the intimate relationship between his art and his intellectual research. In 1882, Charles DeKay wrote, "In the mind of Inness, religion, landscape, and human nature mingle so thoroughly that there is no separating the several ideas. You may learn from him how the symbolization of the Divine Trinity is reflected in the mathematical relations of perspective and aërial distance. . . . He not only believes what he says, but he tries to carry out in his pictures this interrelation of art and religion."[100] Daingerfield described how Inness was always "intensely interested in philosophical research when considering questions relative to art or religion, the two subjects which lay at the core of his deepest sympathies. . . . "[101] Van Dyke even placed art subservient to Inness's intellectual pursuits. He believed that Inness "certainly thought that his views about life, faith, government, and ethics were sound and applicable to all humanity. Art was only a part of the universal plan.... All his life he was devoted to mystical speculations. He had his faith in divination, astrology, spiritualism, Swedenborgianism; and he was greatly stirred by all social questions."[102] Likewise, the English decorative artist and art critic Charles Caffin portrayed an intertwined relationship among Inness's art, philosophical research, and theological beliefs. For him, Inness "may have been guided" in his late paintings "by his study of Swedenborg's writings, but, on the other hand, it is as likely that the craving within himself after the psychical and spiritual, which propelled him toward that study, determined also the final purpose of his art."[103]

Although we have grown accustomed to investigating commonalities between art and philosophical systems—Gothic architecture and scholasticism, Georges Seurat's paintings and the Bergsonian *durée*, Piet Mondrian's paintings and Theosophy, for example—Inness's self-described investigation of metaphysical subjects and his recurrent affiliations with "metaphysical labors" and "metaphysical studies" were unusual for a nineteenth-century American landscape painter. They were hardly unusual, however, in the context of mid- to late nineteenth-century intellectual history, a time of concerted and widespread investigation of metaphysical ideas. It is hoped that, with this publication and others, Inness will continue to be investigated not only as an artist but as a contributor to our understanding of Gilded Age intellectual history as well.

<hr />

Some artists . . . like a short brush to paint with, and others a long brush; some want a smooth canvas, and others a rough canvas; some a canvas with a hard surface, and others a canvas with an absorbent surface; some a white canvas, and others a stained canvas. Deschamps [sic], *you know, bought old pictures and painted over them; his canvas was a painting before he touched it . . . .*
—Inness, in "A Painter on Painting"[104]

As we have seen, Inness's early landscape paintings, such as *The Juniata River* (1856), reveal his attentiveness to the compositional formats of the old masters. Paintings from the late 1850s and 1860s brought to fruition his admiration for the freedom of brushwork and intimate settings seen in Barbizon landscapes, to which Inness was exposed during a second trip to Europe that brought him to

France in 1853. The texts included here confirm that Inness was, indeed, an avid student of the history of art. For example, while discussing the appearance of grass in sunlight during an interview, apparently conducted outside, with Sheldon in 1882, he remarked on the artistic problem of how to "keep the local color of that grass and those trees, and yet preserve their tone," and stated that Rousseau "is about the only man I know who solved it."[105] Inness's interviews also reveal that he studied the types of brushes artists used, whether or not they liked to paint over smooth or rough canvases, over white or stained ones, or over previously painted surfaces. He studied types of quick-drying or slow-drying oils used for varnishing. He discussed different theories on how to teach art—whether or not to provide explicit instruction or to leave students to fend for themselves with only sporadic advice and commentary from their teacher.

He discussed the works of a wide range of artists, including Michelangelo, Titian, Correggio, and Claude; the Barbizon painters Constant Troyon, Corot, Rousseau, and Daubigny; Thomas Couture; the landscape painter Felix Ziem, the Academic painters Gérôme, Pierre-Auguste Cot, and Meissonier; the Romantic painters Delacroix, Turner, and Allston; and Marie François Firmin-Gerard. In his undated "Letter on Impressionism" and in his final interview, "His Art His Religion," he misjudges Impressionism, referring to it as a "fad" and one of several artistic "shams." His disdain makes sense when we contrast the Impressionist's aim of capturing the changing effects of light on a scene at specific temporal moments with Inness's desire to represent anonymous locations during extended cosmological events—sunrise, moonrise, and sunset. And yet, there is much that links Inness with Impressionism, namely, their mutual interest in aligning aesthetics with scientific principles—secular ones in the case of Monet, spiritual ones for Inness.

Finally, this volume features a prosaic but intriguing aspect of Inness's life that complements the texts on metaphysics and allusions to Swedenborgian doctrine: Inness's appearance (FIGS. 13–16). For example, we learn from a friend, the painter Darius Cobb, that Inness "was of medium height, and spare in build.... He seemed charged with electricity; and as his expressive face confronted me, with the dark eyes throwing their intense light through his glasses into mine, I was drawn to him at once."[106] According to his friend Frederick Lamb, "In personal appearance Inness was slim, wiry, giving the impression of height, dark in color with strong features, piercing black eyes and hair worn slightly long.... If we look for a parallel in the American type, we would be forced to say 'Yankee,' although, perhaps, we would prefer to say Lincoln." And later: "Inness the man

FIG. 13. Napoleon Sarony, *George Inness*, late 1870s, albumen print, 6 x 4³/₈", Culver Pictures, New York.

FIG. 14. George Gardner Rockwood, *George Inness*, before 13 July 1867, carte-de-visite photograph, 4¹/₂ x 2¹/₂", Courtesy of Picture History.

FIG. 15. *George Inness at Niagara Falls,* c. 1884, photograph, image courtesy of the American Art Association records, 1853–1924, Archives of American Art, Smithsonian Institution, Washington, D.C.

FIG. 16. George Inness, Jr., *George Inness Sketching Outside his Montclair Studio*, c. 1889, oil on canvas board, 14 1/2 x 15 1/4", Montclair Art Museum, Montclair, New Jersey, Museum Purchase; Acquisition Fund, 1945.109.

was a fascination: simple and direct, clear of thought, quick of action, he was yet intensely human, and human with the simplicity which is the simplicity of a great mind."[107] Maitland Armstrong described Inness as "a small, nervous man, with ragged hair and beard, and a vivacious, intense manner, an excellent talker and much occupied with theories and methods of painting, and also of religion."[108] When S. C. G. Watkins, a dentist, first met Inness in Montclair, New Jersey, where the artist spent the final seventeen years of his life, he was taken aback. Inness appeared at his office covered with dust, perspiring freely, with his hair in disarray. The doctor's assistant seemed perplexed but soon realized that Inness was "not a common working man or tramp, so she allowed him to remain in the reception room." After formal introductions were made, Watkins concluded that Inness "was unusual and yet of a high type, beyond the ordinary." [109]

From the texts in this collection, we may construct our own interpretation of the life, ideas, aspirations, struggles, and accomplishments of George Inness. We may enrich the established view of Inness as one of the most inventive painters of his generation, impressive as that appellation may be. We may now consider his body of work as an expression of his panoramic interests—in ecclesiastical and utilitarian philosophy, in the scientific-mystical doctrines of Swedenborg, in the social politics of Henry George, in writing and discoursing on aesthetics and the machinations of the art world, and in working his way through art history. We may follow the roots of those interests to Inness's artistic, social, and intellectual environments and explore resonances between his ideas and those of his predecessors, contemporaries, and successors. Ultimately, each facet of Inness's intellectual life shaped his metaphysical outlook, determined the trajectory of his engagement with landscape painting, and helped him to understand his life and work anew each day. They are the challenges that kept him, and continue to keep him, so fully "alive."

Notes to "George Inness: Artist, Writer, Philosopher"

1. George Inness, Jr., *Art, Life, and Letters of George Inness* (New York: The Century Co., 1917), p. 101.

2. Nicolai Cikovsky, Jr., first connected the two paintings in *George Inness* (New York: Harry N. Abrams, Publishers, 1993), p. 54.

3. In 1878, Inness painted at least two landscapes with references to Greene County, New York, in their titles. See LeRoy Ireland, *The Works of George Inness: An Illustrated Catalogue Raisonné* (Austin: University of Texas Press, 1965), #861: "Sunburst, Green [*sic*] County, N.Y.," signed and dated 1878, and #862: "Landscape, Greene County," signed and dated 1878.

4. Murphy's account is reprinted in George Chambers Calvert, "George Inness: Painter and Personality," *The Bulletin of the Art Association of Indianapolis, Indiana,* The John Herron Art Institute 13:5-8 (November 1926): 45.

5. William Gerdts discusses the recollections in "Some Reminiscences of George Inness," in *George Inness: Presence of the Unseen, A Centennial Commemoration* (Montclair, NJ: Montclair Art Museum, 1994), pp. 13–17.

6. "A Painter on Painting," from *Harper's New Monthly Magazine* 56 (February 1878): 458–61, was reprinted in Nicolai Cikovsky, Jr., and Michael Quick, *George Inness* (Los Angeles County Museum of Art, 1985), pp. 205–09.

7. In a letter to the Montclair Art Museum (7 May 1956), Rose Inness Hartley, one of Inness's granddaughters, explained that the artist's personal effects were destroyed in a house fire in 1942 (George Inness file, Le Brun Library, Montclair Art Museum, NJ). A descendant of Inness's confirmed that the effects, including Inness's library and drawings, were destroyed "in a house fire during the 1940s" (Conversation with the descendent, 23 February 1998).

8. Inness in "A Painter on Painting," op. cit., p. 460.

9. G. W. [George William] Sheldon, "George Inness," *Harper's Weekly Magazine* 26:1322 (22 April 1882): 246. Hereafter: Sheldon 1882. George Sherman and John Calvin Smith operated the firm of Sherman & Smith. In 1841, they designed and engraved plates for the *New York Mirror*. See Mantle Fielding, *Dictionary of American Painters, Sculptors & Engravers*, ed. Glenn B. Opitz (New York: Apollo Books, 1995), p. 847.

10. Nathaniel Currier operated his businesses at 152 Nassau Street and 2 Spruce Street in New York from 1838 to 1856. He joined James Merritt Ives in 1857 to become Currier & Ives, which was in business until 1901. As a young man, Inness would have been a shop hand, employed to copy the designs of other artists. Although Currier & Ives commissioned artists to create original lithographs—such as William Morris Hunt's *Stag in the Moonlight* (1857)—Inness, in the early to mid-1840s, had not yet established himself in the art world. By 1860, however, his status had changed. That year, Currier & Ives reproduced his *Delaware Water Gap* (1857; Montclair Art Museum) as *View on the Delaware: 'Water Gap' in the Distance* (1860, lithograph, $16^5/_{16}$ x $22^1/_2$", Library of

Congress, Washington, DC). See *Currier & Ives: A Catalogue Raisonné: A Comprehensive Catalogue of the Lithographs of Nathaniel Currier, James Merritt Ives, and Charles Currier, including ephemera associated with the firm, 1834–1907*, introduction by Bernard F. Reilly, Jr. (Detroit: Gale Research Company, 1984), #6957.

11. Inness, Jr., op. cit., pp. 14.

12. Inness in "A Painter on Painting," op. cit., p. 458.

13. John La Farge, "A Plea for the Engravers: Letter from the Artist La Farge," *[New York] Evening Post* (20 March 1878): 3.

14. George Inness, "A Plea for the Painters: A Letter from the Artist Inness," *[New York] Evening Post* (21 March 1878): 2.

15. Elliott Daingerfield, "George Inness, N.A., An Appreciation," in *Catalogue of the Loan Exhibition of Important Works by George Inness, Alexander Wyant, Ralph Blakelock* (Chicago: Moulton & Ricketts, 1913), n.p. [p. 7].

16. Inness, Jr., op. cit., p. 75.

17. Marco Boschini, *Breve instruzione premessa a Le ricche minere della pittura veneziana* (1674) in *La carta del navegar pitoresco*, Anna Pallucchini, ed. (Venice and Rome: Istituto per la Collaborazione Culturale, 1966), p. 711: "Tiziano . . . abbozzava it suoi quadri con una tal massa di Colori, che servivano (come dire) per far letto, o base alle espressioni, che sopra poi li doveva fabricare; e no ho veduti anch'io de' colpi risoluti, con pennellate massiccie di colori, . . . e con queste massime di Dottrina faceva comparire in quattro pennellate la promessa d'una rara figura. . . . " Translated by David Rosand in his "Titian and the Critical Tradition," David Rosand, ed., *Titian: His World and His Legacy* (New York: Columbia University Press, 1982), p. 24.

18. Elliott Daingerfield, "A Reminiscence of George Inness," *Monthly Illustrator* 3:2 (March 1895): 262–64.

19. Arthur Turnbull Hill, "Early Recollections of George Inness and George Waldo Hill," *New Salmagundi Papers. Series of 1922* (New York: The Library of the Salmagundi Club, 1922), pp. 110–11.

20. Inness in "A Painter on Painting," op. cit., p. 461.

21. Exhibited at the National Academy of Design in 1833, Cole's *Aqueduct near Rome* was engraved by James Smillie the same year and, according to Eleanor Jones, became "one of the most popular images by an American artist in Italy." See E. Jones, "Thomas Cole: *Aqueduct Near Rome*," in Theodore E. Stebbins, Jr., *The Lure of Italy: American Artists and The Italian Experience, 1760–1914* (Museum of Fine Arts, Boston, in association with Harry N. Abrams, Publishers, New York, 1992), pp. 260–61.

22. See Gustav Courbet, Letter from the *Courrier du dimanche*, 25 December 1861, in Pierre Courthion, ed., *Courbet raconté par lui-même et par ses amis* (Geneva: Pierre Cailler, 1950), II, pp. 205–07.

23. See Inness, Jr., op, cit., pp 40–41.

24. Ibid., p. 68.

25. Tiffany quoted in [Charles DeKay], *The Art work of Louis Comfort Tiffany* (Garden City, NY: Doubleday, Page, 1914), p. 78. See also Doreen Bolger Burke, "Louis Comfort Tiffany and his Early Training at Eagleswood, 1862–1865," *American Art Journal* 19:3 (1987): 29–39.

26. Frederick Stymetz Lamb, "Reminiscences of George Inness," *The Art World* 1:4 (January 1917): 252.

27. Albert Pinkham Ryder, "Paragraphs from the Studio of a Recluse," reprinted in William Innes Homer and Lloyd Goodrich, *Albert Pinkham Ryder: Painter of Dreams* (New York: Harry N. Abrams, Publishers, 1989), p. 186.

28. Inness and Ryder have been affiliated since Charles DeKay's article on Ryder, the first devoted solely to the artist, in the *Century Magazine*. See Henry Eckford [Charles DeKay], "A Modern Colorist: Albert Pinkham Ryder," *Century Magazine* 40 (June 1890): 250–59. DeKay saw Ryder as one of the preeminent colorists of his day and, for this reason, ranked him with William Morris Hunt, Inness, Homer Dodge Martin, and La Farge. Collectors who owned Inness's paintings, notably Thomas B. Clarke, often owned several works by Ryder as well. On Clarke, see H. Barbara Weinberg, "Thomas B. Clarke: Foremost Patron of American Art from 1872 to 1899," *American Art Journal* 8:1 (May 1976): 52–83.

29. Anonymous interviewer in "His Art His Religion. An Interesting Talk with the Late Painter George Inness on His Theory of Painting," *New York Herald* (12 August 1894): 4:9.

30. For Allston's poems, see Washington Allston, *The Sylphs of the Season, with other poems* (Boston: Cummings and Hilliard, 1813) and Washington Allston, *Lectures on art, and poems*, ed. Richard Henry Dana, Jr. (New York: Baker and Scribner, 1850). See also *Thomas Cole's Poetry: The Collected Poems of America's Foremost Painter of the Hudson River School*, ed. Marshall B. Tymn (York, PA: Liberty Cap Books, 1972).

31. "Fine Arts. National Academy of Design," *New York Herald* (31 March 1878): 7. Unfortunately, neither the quotations nor the tablets have survived.

32. Homer and Goodrich, op. cit., p. 150. All of Ryder's poems are reprinted in Homer and Goodrich, op. cit., pp. 211–18. For example, the poem that he wrote to accompany *Toilers of the Sea* (c. 1883–84, oil on wood panel, 11½ x 12", The Metropolitan Museum of Art, New York) reads, "'Neath the shifting skies, // O'er the billowy foam, // The hardy fisher flies // To his island home." It was published in the catalogue of the Seventh Annual Exhibition of the Society of American Artists, 26 May–21 June 1884; Ryder also inscribed lines of the poem on a label attached to the back of the painting.

33. Inness, Jr., op. cit., p. 117.

34. George William Sheldon, "Characteristics of George Inness," *The Century Illustrated Monthly Magazine* 49 (February 1895): 533.

35. Marco Boschini, op. cit.: "Così, operando e riformando quelle figure, le riduceva nella più perfetta simmetria che potesse rappresentare il bello della Natura e dell'Arte; e doppo, fatto questo, ponendo le mani ad altro." Translated by Rosand in "Titian and the Critical Tradition," op. cit.

36. A. T. Van Laer, "George Inness," *Arts for America* 5 (February 1896): 20.

37. Ibid.

38. See Arthur Hoeber, "A Remarkable Collection of Landscapes by the Late George Inness, N.A.," *International Studio* 43 (April 1911): 37.

39. Quoted in Inness, Jr., op. cit., pp. 192, 195.

40. "Art Gossip," *Cosmopolitan Art Journal* 4:4 (December 1860): 183.

41. George Inness to Thomas B. Carrol[l], 8 August 1868, Misc. Mss. I, George Inness letters, Folder 10F1, Manuscripts Division, Collection of The New-York Historical Society.

42. Inness in "A Painter on Painting," op. cit.

43. Inness quoted in Inness, Jr., op. cit., pp. 131–32.

44. Inness, Jr., op. cit., p. 140.

45. Hoeber, op. cit.

46. Inness, Jr., op. cit., pp. 190–91.

47. Paul Valéry, *Degas. Dance. Drawing,* trans. Helen Burlin (Paris: A. Vollard, 1936; New York: Lear Publishers, 1948), p. 40. Although his implication is clear, Valéry never precisely defined what Degas meant by a "series of operations."

48. Ibid, p. 58. The question of the power of the unfinished work came to a head, of course, in the cases of *Whistler v. Ruskin* and *Whistler v. Eden.* Linda Merrill examines the first case in exemplary detail in *A Pot of Paint: Aesthetics on Trial in Whistler v. Ruskin* (Washington, DC, and London: Smithsonian Institution Press, 1992). For a thorough study of the latter trial, see Albert Elsen, "The Artist's Oldest Right?" *Art History* 2:2 (June 1988): 217–30.

49. George Inness to A. D. Williams, Albano, 13 August 1872. From transcribed copy. Object file for *Lake Nemi*, Department of the Art of the Americas, Museum of Fine Arts, Boston.

50. George Inness to Isaac Bates, 25 October 1878, Rhode Island School of Design Archives, Isaac Comstock Bates Scrapbook of Artist Correspondence, 1877–1889.

51. All quotations in this letter are from George Inness to Thomas B. Clarke, Tarpon Springs, Florida, 23 January 1893, Rare Books and Special Collections, Princeton University Library, Call #C0140, General Mss. Misc., Box I [Inness], folder AM12814.

52. Inness quoted in "Strong Talk on Art," *[New York] Evening Post* (3 June 1879): [3].

53. George Inness to J. Carroll Beckwith, 13 January 1881, George Inness manuscript file, National Academy Museum Archive, New York.

54. For an exploration of Inness's involvement with the ideas of Henry George, see Leo G. Mazow, "George Inness: Problems in Antimodernism," PhD diss., University of North Carolina, Chapel Hill, 1996. See also Mazow, "George Inness, Henry George, the Single Tax, and the Future Poet," *American Art* 18:1 (spring 2004): 58–77.

55. G.W. [George William] Sheldon, "George Inness," in *American Painters: Eighty-three Examples of their Work Engraved on Wood* (New York: D. Appleton & Company, 1879), p. 31.

56. Inness, Jr., op. cit., pp. 20–21.

57. "American Artists. George Inness," *Harper's Weekly: A Journal of Civilization* 11:550 (13 July 1867): 433.

58. Reverend Dr. Jonathan Bayley, *The Ribband of Blue. A Sermon.* New Jerusalem Tracts (New York: New Swedenborgian Publishing House, 1866; reprint New York: E. Hazzard Swinney, 1872), p. 14.

59. George Inness, "Colors and Their Correspondences," *New Jerusalem Messenger* 13:20 (13 November 1867): 78–79. For a thorough analysis of Bayley's text and Inness's article, see Sally M. Promey, "The Ribband of Faith: George Inness, Color Theory, and the Swedenborgian Church," *American Art Journal* 26:1–2 (1994): 45–65, where Inness's article was first reprinted on p. 46.

60. The documents concerning the date and place of the Inness baptisms were first published in Promey, ibid., pp. 55-57. Several of Ager's translations from Swedenborg's Latin editions are still in print, namely *Heaven and Hell* (1758), *Divine Love and Wisdom* (1763), and *True Christian Religion* (1771), published by the Swedenborg Foundation, West Chester, Pennsylvania.

61. George William Sheldon, "Characteristics of George Inness," op. cit., p. 530.

62. [David] Maitland Armstrong, *Day Before Yesterday: Reminiscences of a Varied Life*, edited by his daughter Margaret Armstrong (New York: Charles Scribner's Sons, 1920), p. 199.

63. "Homage to George Inness," *New-York Times* (24 August 1894): 8; reprinted, with slight variations, in Inness, Jr., op. cit., pp. 217–19.

64. See Nicolai Cikovsky, Jr., "The Life and Work of George Inness," PhD diss., Harvard University, 1965 (subsequently published by Garland Publishing, Inc., 1977); Nicolai Cikovsky, Jr., *George Inness* (New York: Praeger Publishing, 1971); Cikovsky, Jr., and Quick, op. cit.; Robert Jolly, "George Inness's Swedenborgian Dimension," *Southeastern College Art Conference Review* 11:1 (1986): 14–22; Mary Phillips, "The Effect of Swedenborgianism on the Later Paintings of George Inness," in Erland J. Brock, gen. ed., *Swedenborg and His Influence* (Bryn Athyn, PA: The Academy of the New Church, 1988), pp. 427–37; Cikovsky, Jr., *George Inness*, op. cit.; Promey, op. cit.; Michael Quick, "George Inness: The Spiritual Dimension," in *George Inness: Presence of the Unseen*, op. cit., pp. 29–32, 34; Eugene Taylor, "The Interior Landscape: George Inness and William James on Art from a Swedenborgian Point of View," *Archives of American Art Journal* 37:1–2 (1997): 2–10; *George Inness: The 1880s and 1890s.* Essay by Leo G. Mazow, with commentaries by Rachael Ziady DeLue (Annville, PA: Lebanon Valley College, 1999); Rachael Ziady DeLue, "George Inness, Landscape Representation, and the Struggle of Vision," PhD diss., Johns Hopkins University, 2000; Adrienne Baxter Bell, *George Inness and the Visionary Landscape* (New York: George Braziller, Publishers, and the National Academy of Design, 2003); Rachael Ziady DeLue, *George Inness and the Science of Landscape* (Chicago and London: University of Chicago Press, 2004); Adrienne Baxter Bell, "George Inness: Painting Philosophy," PhD diss., Columbia University, 2005; Michael Quick, *George Inness: A Catalogue Raisonné* (New York and London: Rutgers University Press, 2006).

65. The basic studies of Swedenborg's life and work include Signe Toksvig, *Emanuel Swedenborg: Scientist and Mystic* (New Haven: Yale University Press, 1948); Inge Jonnson, *Emanuel Swedenborg* (New York: The Swedenborg Society, 1971); Cyriel Sigstedt, *The Swedenborg Epic: The Life and Works of Emanuel Swedenborg* (London: The Swedenborg Society, 1981); and George F. Dole and Robert H. Kirven, *A Scientist Explores Spirit: A Biography of Emanuel Swedenborg, with Key Concepts of his Theology* (West Chester, PA: Chrysalis Books, 1997). The most comprehensive examination of Swedenborg's influence in America remains Margaret Beck Block, *The New Church in the New World* (New York: Swedenborg Publishing Association, 1964). A useful collection of essays on Swedenborg is Robin Larsen, ed., *Emanuel Swedenborg: A Continuing Vision* (New York: Swedenborg Foundation, 1988).

66. In *Visionary Scientist: The Effects of Science and Philosophy on Swedenborg's Cosmology* (West Chester, PA: Swedenborg Foundation Publishers, 1969), Inge Jonsson describes how Swedenborg's spiritual perspective was rooted in his early scientific projects and how closely it resonated with emerging Enlightenment views of science and spirit.

67. Emanuel Swedenborg, *Economy of the Animal Kingdom*, trans. Augustus Clissold, 2 vols. (Philadelphia: Swedenborg Scientific Association, 1955); originally published as *Oeconomia Regni Animalis in transactions divisa, quarum haec tertia de Fibra, de Tunica Arachnoidea, et de Morbis Fibrarum agit, anatomice, physice, et philosophice perlustrata* (Amsterdam, 1740); Emanuel Swedenborg, *Soul's Domain Thoroughly Examined by Means of Anatomy, Physics, and Philosophy*, widely referred to as *Soul's Domain*, trans. J. J. G. Wilkinson, 2 vols. (London: William Newbery, 1843; Bryn Athyn, PA: Swedenborg Scientific Association, 1960); originally published as *Regnum Animale, Anatomice, Physice, et Philosophice Perlustratum* (The Hague, 1744).

68. In *The New Church in the New World*, Block described Swedenborg's experiences as "strange dreams and phantasies, tremors, prostrations, trances, sweatings, and swoonings" and how, during these episodes, Swedenborg "alternated between moods of deepest gloom and states of ecstatic joy" (Block, op. cit., p. 11). See also Carolyn A. Blackmer, "Psychological Basis of Swedenborg's Spiritual World Experiences," *Studia Swedenborgiana* 1:3 (January 1975): 27–52.

69. Emanuel Swedenborg, *Journal of Dreams*, commentary by W. Van Dusen, ed. (from the Swedish) by G. E. Klemming, trans. J. J. G. Wilkinson, ed. W. R. Woofenden (New York: Swedenborg Foundation, 1977, 1986) and *The Spiritual Diary of Emanuel Swedenborg, being the record during twenty years of his supernatural experience*, trans. Professor George Bush, MA, and the Rev. James F. Buss, 5 vols. (London: James Speirs, 1883–1902).

70. On one such occasion, he claimed that the Lord appeared to him and explained that His task was to "explain to me the spiritual meaning of Scripture." See *The Spiritual Diary of Emanuel Swedenborg*, ibid., nos. 58–59.

71. This idea is further explained in "Lessons in the Science of Correspondence. 1: What is Correspondence?" *New Jerusalem Messenger* 12:37 (27 March 1867): 154.

72. In *The New Church in the New World*, Block identified "the science of correspon-

dence"—a means to see reality through symbols, "a technique for discovering hidden meanings"—as the main contribution of the Swedenborgian New Church. "In place of the literalism to which other churches are bound in their attempts to find fresh interpretations of the Scripture to present-day needs," Block explained, "the New Church offers an inner sense,—a whole world of metaphysical truth awaiting investigation. In place of the pietism and other-worldliness to which the more Catholic branches of the church are tending in their reaction to modern materialism, the New Church offers a far saner philosophy in the belief that the two worlds, through separate and distinct, are yet mutually interdependent, and that the highest form of life of the material plane, the fullest and richest, is at the same time the highest form of spiritual life" (Block, op. cit., pp. 399–400). As in her profile of Swedenborg, Block's description of the New Church emphasized the way in which church doctrine intertwines mystical ideas with rational methods.

73. Emanuel Swedenborg, *Arcana Coelestia, the Heavenly Arcana Contained in the Holy Scripture or Word of the Lord Unfolded, Beginning with the Book of Genesis: together with wonderful things seen in the world of spirits and in the heaven of angels*; trans. and ed. by Rev. John Faulkner Potts (New York: The Swedenborg Foundation, 1928–38); originally published as *Arcana Coelestia, quae in Scriptura Sacra, seu Verbo Domini sunt, detecta: Sequuntur quae in Genesi[;] Hic quae in Capite Decimo Sexto: Una cum Mirabilibus Quae visa sunt In Mundo Spirituum, et in Coelo Angelorum* (London, 1749–56).

74. "Lessons in the Science of Correspondences. 3: Is Correspondence a Science?" *New Jerusalem Messenger* 12:41 (10 April 1867): 163.

75. In *Arcana Coelestia*, Swedenborg treated the creation story of Genesis not as literally true but as true in the internal, or spiritual, sense, that is, as a representation of our spiritual character. The first dawning of light corresponds to our ability to see truth in our minds. The water vapors, as clouds in the sky above the seas, show the separation and distinction between the waters above (heavenly truths) and the waters below (truths about natural things). Truth and water form a correspondential relationship because both satisfy human needs: our thirst for knowledge and our physical sensation of thirst. For Swedenborg, the Bible records not only the history of Israel but also an image of the spiritual growth of all human beings, from leaving the garden, being redeemed from Egypt, wandering in the wilderness, and finding a home in Canaan, a place in Jerusalem. For Swedenborgians, "The Bible as a whole, and not only the parables of Jesus, could function as a series of psychodramas leading to spiritual awareness." See Dorothy Harvey, "Swedenborg and the Bible," in Larsen, ed., *Emanuel Swedenborg*, op. cit., p. 371.

76. Emanuel Swedenborg, *Heaven and Hell*, rev. trans. by George F. Dole, intro. by Colin Wilson (West Chester, PA: Swedenborg Foundation, 1976); originally published as *De Coelo et ejus mirabilibus, et de Inferno, ex auditis et visis* (London, 1758). See Part 5 ("There are Three Heavens").

77. Ibid., Part 18 ("Time in Heaven") and Part 22 ("Space in Heaven"); see also Part 23 ("Heaven's Form").

78. Emanuel Swedenborg, *The True Christian Religion Containing the Universal Theology of*

The New Church Foretold by the Lord in Daniel VII. 13, 14; and in Revelation XXI. 1, 2 (New York: The American Swedenborg Printing and Publishing Society, 1910); originally published as *Vera Christiana Religio, continens universam Theologiam Novae Ecclesiae, a Domino apud Danielem cap. vii. 13, 14, et in Apocalypsi cap. xxi. 1, 2, praedicta. Ab. Emanuele Swedenborg, Domini Jesus Christi servo* (Amsterdam, 1771), no. 48, parts 7, 5.

79. Emanuel Swedenborg, *The Delights of Wisdom Pertaining to Conjugial Love*, trans. Samuel M. Warren, rev. trans. Louis H. Tafel (New York: The American Swedenborg Printing and Publishing Society, 1910), no. 185.

80. George Inness, "The Pilgrim," typescript, LeRoy Ireland papers, Archives of American Art, Smithsonian Institution, reel 95, frame 1034.

81. Emanuel Swedenborg, *Arcana Coelestia*, op. cit., vol. 8, no. 6004.

82. George Inness, "The Pilgrim," typescript, LeRoy Ireland papers, op. cit., reel 95, frame 1036.

83. Swedenborg, *The True Christian Religion*, op. cit., no. 30.

84. Inness, Jr., op. cit., pp. 130–131.

85. George William Sheldon, "Characteristics of George Inness," op. cit., p. 530.

86. Inness, Jr., op. cit., p. 61.

87. Musa Mayer, *Night Studio: A Memoir of Philip Guston* (New York: Da Capo Press, 1997), p. 78.

88. "The Logic of the Real Æsthetically Considered," *Boston Daily Advertiser* (12 April 1875): 4.

89. George Sheldon, "Characteristics of George Inness," op. cit., p. 530. Sheldon refers to the English theologian and political economist Richard Whately and the British philosopher and political economist John Stuart Mill. It is clear, from a passage in Inness's unpublished manuscript "The Mathematics of Psychology," which Sheldon reprinted in "George Inness" (see below, pages 181–83), that Inness read Mill's *A System of Logic Ratiocinative and Inductive: Being a Connected View of the Principles of Evidence and the Methods of Scientific Investigation*, ed. J. M. Robson (1843; Toronto: Toronto University Press, 1973). Inness cited, almost verbatim, a passage from Mill's book in which he summarized Whately's belief that "syllogizing, or reasoning from generals to particulars, is not, agreeably to the vulgar idea, a peculiar mode of reasoning but the philosophical analysis of the mode in which all men reason, and must do so if they reason at all." (Mill, p. 187, citing Whately's *Elements of Logic* [London, 1826, 1840]). Inness, for his part, challenged Mill's equation of brute instinct with reason, or with the capacity to use past experience as a barometer of future experience. He distinguished "animal instinct" from the "spiritual principle, or the rational faculty." In other words, Inness added a spiritual dimension to Mill's analysis of the concept of reason. Inness may also have read Whately's *The Practical Nature of the Doctrines and Alleged Revelations Contained in the Writings of Emanuel Swedenborg* (1839).

90. Inness quoted in "His Art His Religion," op. cit., p. 4:9.

91. Ibid.: "I have written piles upon piles of manuscripts on it [the relationship between art

and theology], and my method is to take these piles and re-write them in a very condensed form. Gradually this grows and is 'boiled down,' and all the first essays destroyed."

92. Alfred Trumble, *George Inness, N.A., A Memorial of the Student, the Artist, and the Man* (New York: The Collector, 1895), p. 13.

93. John C. Van Dyke, "George Inness," *Outlook* 73:10 (7 March 1903): 536.

94. Inness, Jr., op. cit., p. 105. In describing the relationship between his father and his mother, Inness, Jr., recalled, "He depended on her for everything, from the arranging of his necktie to the solving of his deep metaphysical problems."

95. Trumble, op. cit., p. 13.

96. Quoted in ibid., p. 23.

97. Sheldon 1882, p. 246.

98. Ibid.

99. Van Dyke, op. cit.

100. Henry Eckford [Charles DeKay], "George Inness," *Century Illustrated Monthly Magazine* 24:1 (May 1882): 63.

101. Elliott Daingerfield, "Introduction," in *Fifty Paintings by George Inness* (New York: privately printed, 1913), p. 5.

102. Van Dyke, op. cit., pp. 535–36.

103. Charles H. Caffin, "Some American Landscape Painters," *Critic* 45:2 (August 1904): 126.

104. Inness quoted in "A Painter on Painting," op. cit., p. 458.

105. Inness quoted in Sheldon 1882, p. 244.

106. Stanwood Cobb, "Reminiscences of George Inness by Darius Cobb" (c. 1894), *Art Quarterly* 26 (summer 1983): 236.

107. Lamb, op. cit., p. 251.

108. Armstrong, op. cit.

109. S. C. G. Watkins, "Reminiscences of George Inness, the Great Painter, as I Knew Him," in *Reminiscences of Montclair* (New York: A. S. Barnes and Company, 1929), pp. 107–8.

INTERVIEWS

"A Painter on Painting"

(FEBRUARY 1878)

[This interview for *Harper's New Monthly Magazine* was the first Inness gave and is the most widely quoted. In it, he describes his philosophy of art, reflects on the strengths and weaknesses of other artists, including Jean-Baptiste-Camille Corot, J. M. W. Turner, and Washington Allston, expounds on the problems of finishing paintings, and describes his highest ideal: to paint "the civilized landscape."]

"SOME ARTISTS," SAID MR. GEORGE INNESS, as he leaned over to relight his cigar (I was conversing with the landscape painter)—"some artists like a short brush to paint with, and others a long brush; some want a smooth canvas, and others a rough canvas; some a canvas with a hard surface, and others a canvas with an absorbent surface; some a white canvas, and others a stained canvas. Deschamps [*sic*], you know, bought old pictures and painted over them; his canvas was a painting before he touched it; and I should say that if a man wished to paint as Delacroix painted, an old picture would suit him as well as a new canvas to put his scene on. On the other hand, Couture painted only over a fresh, clean canvas, slightly stained, while Troyon evidently preferred a plain white surface, because he and Couture used transparent washes of color, through which the original surface of their canvases could often be seen. But Delacroix painted solid all through, and his quality, unlike that of Troyon, Couture, Ziem, and other artists, does not depend upon the transparency of the color. Some artists use quick-drying oils for varnishing, and others slow-drying oils. Most artists prefer to paint in a north room, because there the light is more equable—the sun does not come in. But Mr. Page likes a south room, although I don't know why. You see, there are no absolute rules about methods of painting."

"Principles, I suppose, are the things that should be looked after."

"Yes, principles—a few of them, that's all. Pupils can't be taught much by an artist. I have found that explanations usually hinder them, or else make their work stereotyped. If I had a pupil in my studio, I should say to him as Troyon once said in similar circumstances, 'Sit down and paint.' Still, now and then, I should tell him a principle of light and shade, of color, or of *chiar-oscuro*, and criticise his work, showing him where he was right and where he was wrong, as if I were walking with him through a gallery of pictures, and pointing out their faults and their merits. The best way to teach art is the Paris way. There the pupils—two, three, or more—hire a room, hire their models, and set up their easels. Once or twice a week the master comes in, looks at their work, and makes suggestions and remarks, advising the use of no particular method, but leaving each pupil's individuality free. If a young man paints regularly in the studio of his teacher, he is apt to lose spontaneity and vitality, and to become a dead reproduction of his teacher. Van Marcke suffered, I think, from this cause. He painted within arms-length of Troyon, and he has become a sort of inanimate Troyon."

"What is it that the painter tries to do?"

"Simply to reproduce in other minds the impression which a scene has made upon him. A work of art does not appeal to the intellect. It does not appeal to the moral sense. Its aim is not to instruct, not to edify, but to awaken an emotion. This emotion may be one of love, of pity, of veneration, of hate, of pleasure, or of pain; but it must be a single emotion, if the work has unity, as every such work should have, and the true beauty of the work consists in the beauty of the sentiment or emotion which it inspires. Its real greatness consists in the quality and the force of this emotion. Details in the picture must be elaborated only enough fully to reproduce the impression that the artist wishes to reproduce. When more than this is done, the impression is weakened or lost, and we see simply an array of external things which may be very cleverly painted, and may look very real, but which do not make an artistic painting. The effort and the difficulty of an artist is [*sic*] to combine the two, namely, to make the thought clear and to preserve the unity of impression. Meissonier always makes his thought clear; he is most painstaking with details, but he sometimes loses in sentiment. Corot, on the contrary, is, to some minds, lacking in objective force. He is most appreciated by the highly educated artistic taste, and he is least appreciated by the crude taste. He tried for years to get more objective force, but he found that what he gained in that respect he lost in sentiment. If a painter could unite Meissonier's careful reproduction of details with Corot's inspirational power, he would be the very god of art. But Corot's art is higher than Meissonier's. Let Corot paint a rainbow, and his work reminds you of the poet's description, 'The rainbow is the spirit of the flowers.' Let Meissonier paint a rainbow, and his work reminds you of a definition in chemistry. The one is poetic truth, the other is scientific truth; the former is aesthetic, the latter is analytic."

"You do not, then, think highly of Meissonier?"

"I do, and I do not. Meissonier is a very wonderful painter, but his aim seems to be a material rather than a spiritual one. The imitative has too strong a hold upon his mind; hence, even in his simplest and best things, we find the presence of individualities which should have been absent. That idea which came fresh into his mind from the scene that he saw had in it nothing of self. Why should he not have conveyed it in its original freshness and purity, unalloyed by the mixture of those individualities? Even in his greatest efforts there is not that power to awaken our emotion which the simplest works of a painter like Deschamps possess. There every detail of the picture is a part of the vision which impressed the artist, and which he purposed to reproduce to the end that it might impress others; and every detail has been subordinated to the expression of the artist's impression. Take one of his pictures, 'The Suicide'—a representation of a dead man lying on a bed in a garret, partly in the sunlight [FIG. 17]. All is given up to the expression of the idea of *desolation*. The scene is painted as though the artist had seen it in a dream. Nothing is done to gratify curiosity, or to withdraw the mind from the great central point—the dead man; yet all is felt to be complete and truly finished. The spectator carries away from it a strong impression, but his memory is not taxed with a multitude of facts. The simple story is impressed upon his mind, and remains there forever.

"Contrast such a work with a Meissonier. Here the tendency seems to me to be toward the gratification of lower desires, and you see long-winded processions and reviews; great historical compositions; you see horses painted with nails in their shoes, and men upon them with buttons on their coats—nails and buttons at distances from the spectator where they could not be seen by any eye, however sharp or disciplined. Meissonier's *forte* lies in his power of representing one, two, or three figures under circumstances where they can be controlled by a single vision; and his best works are small pieces, like his 'Chess-Players,' for instance. But this very power of his, when used in representations like his great historic subjects, is a fault. Indeed, all historic subjects have in them necessarily more or less of what belongs to the literary mind. Their successful treatment depends upon a general ability to represent, and not so much upon great ability to imitate. By the greater intensity of mind, which removes him from external things to the thorough representation of an idea, Deschamps surpasses Meissonier. Gérôme is worse than Meissonier, and in the same way. So is

FIG. 17. Alexandre-Gabriel Decamps, *The Suicide*, c. 1836, oil on canvas, 15³/₄ x 22", The Walters Art Museum, Baltimore, Maryland, Purchase by William T. Walters, 1876/8.

Detaille; so are the multitudes of their school. It is the same story all through. Deschamps's mind is more perfectly governed by an original impulse, and it obeys more perfectly the laws of vision."

"Who are the best landscape painters?"

"As landscape painters, I consider Rousseau, Daubigny, and Corot among the very best. Daubigny, particularly, and Corot, have mastered the relation of things in nature one to the other, and have attained in their greatest works representations more or less nearly perfect. But in their day the science under-lying impressions was not fully known. The advances already made in that sci-ence, united to the knowledge of the principles underlying the attempts made by those artists, will, we may hope, soon bring the art of landscape painting to perfection. Rousseau was perhaps the greatest French landscape painter; but I have seen in this country some of the smaller things of Corot which appeared to me to be truly and thoroughly spontaneous representations of nature, although weak in their key of color, as Corot always is. But his idea was a pure one, and he had long been a hard student. Daubigny also had a pure idea, and so had Rousseau. There was no affectation in these men: there were no tricks of color."

"Is Turner as great a painter as Mr. Ruskin pronounces him?"

"Parts of Turner's pictures are splendid specimens of realization, but their effect is destroyed by other parts which are full of falsity and clap-trap. Very rarely, if ever, does Turner give the impression of the real that nature gives. For example, in that well-known work in the London National Gallery which presents a group of fishing boats between the spectator and the sun (the sun in a fog) we find that half of the picture, if cut out by itself, would be most admirable. Into the other half, however, he has introduced a dock, some fishermen, some fishes: an accumulation of small things impossible under the circumstances to unity of vision. Frequently, as in this case—in fact, almost continually—the sun is represented as before us, and objects are introduced for the purpose of conveying Turner's ideal of effects in all sorts of false lights, as though there were half a dozen different suns shining from various positions in the heavens. Of course all this may appeal—as probably he intended it should—to foolish fancies, which are only sensuous weaknesses, and not the offspring of profound feeling. His 'Slave-Ship' is the most infernal piece of clap-trap ever painted. There is nothing in it. It has as much to do with human affections and thought as a ghost. It is not even a fine bouquet of color. The color is harsh, disagreeable, and discordant. Turner was a man of very great genius, but of perverted powers—perverted by love of money, of the world, or of something or other. His best things are his marines, in which appear great dramatic power. Constable was the first English painter of the modern landscape idea; and the French school to which Troyon, Corot, Daubigny, and others I have mentioned belong was founded upon him. These Frenchmen learned from Constable, and improved upon him. But in Turner the dramatic predominated—the desire to tell a story. His 'Wreck,' for example, contains little figures in boats, and other details which are incompatible with the distance, and which prevent that impression which comes to the spectator from a vision of nature. The greater of the French artists would have given to that boat and those figures only a general appearance of more or less complex forms suitable to convey the sense of weight and the sense of distance. While looking at the Claude which hangs next to one of the Turners in the National Gallery—and which knocks the Turner all to pieces—I seemed to be in the presence of a great, earnest mind. The picture, to be sure, manifests some childishness that resulted from a certain lack of artistic knowledge; but the general impression is of something out-doors. The canvas is as fresh as if painted yesterday, and all seems air and light, while the Turner, on the contrary, is a mere make-up of fancies. I think the general estimate that any true artist must form before the works of Turner is that he was a very subtle scene-painter. He stands alone, it is true, and I do him all reverence; but his genius was not of the highest order."

"You prefer French art?"

"Among the French artists, undoubtedly, have been found the best works of art. Delacroix, for example, was one of the greatest of them. His 'Triumph of Apollo,' on a ceiling of the Louvre, is a most sublime story. It really signifies, I think, the regeneration of the human soul. An enormous serpent represents the sensual principle; the smoke from its mouth, forming the whole base of the picture, represents all ideas of darkness and gloom, and, as it spreads and rises, assumes monstrous forms, which are the evil consequences of natural lusts. Above is Apollo, the sun-god, standing in the brilliant light, his chariot drawn by horses which are intelligences, and surrounded by various divinities which drive down the monstrous forms that are rising. It is a splendid allegory, painted with immense power, but, of course, with no attempt to realize nature, to represent what we see. Yet it is a true story, both ideal and descriptive. Nevertheless, many of Delacroix's pictures are bad—broken, confused, and presenting the appearance of efforts to describe what can not be described, to realize what he never saw, and could not have seen, but what he only heard. Hence arises the confusion, though the realization in parts is wonderful. Firmin-Girard (to take a more modern instance) seems to have gone from a higher to a lower degree of description. His description was first of heaven; it is now of the world. The 'Flower Market' is painted in a thoroughly worldly spirit—a 'Market' for a market—and dollars were apparently demanded according to the number of people and things described. Such a picture is not a description of any thing significant, of any thing worth describing. Here is an example of a man who, apparently from the lack of success in a higher sphere, has given himself up to pander to wealth and popularity; for in a sale last winter of pictures in the Kurtz Gallery there was an earlier work of his—a small pastoral description, which belonged to another world. I noticed it among all the paintings in the room. Its singular beauty and tenderness arrested my attention. It seemed to carry the spirit of conjugal love almost into the reality of nature. No appreciative mind could look at it without being possessed by the gentlest emotions, and without being excited to the purest desires. Every thing around it, in comparison, seems to be animated by the spirit of lust and of the world. Yet the picture was not generally appreciated. Scarcely any body stopped before it, and at the sale it went for a song. It is a great misfortune for Firmin-Girard that he should not have held his own."

"Was Washington Allston a great painter?"

"Washington Allston's 'Vision of the Bloody Hand' was, excepting Deschamp's 'Suicide,' the most significant picture, in my opinion, in the Johnston collection [FIG. 18]. In the *technique* of color and form it is inferior, and the spectator received, in consequence, a disagreeable impression of woodenness. But the story is given with the simple earnestness of the 'I saw' of inspiration. Allston's misfortune was that the literary had too strong a hold upon his mind, creating in him ideas which were grandiose. By the literary I mean the influence upon us of what we have heard or read of things we have not seen. In 'Belshazzar's Feast,' by the same artist, we perceive a powerful feeling overwhelmed in a mass of literary rubbish. Who cares for Belshazzar or his feast, unless we can meet him on 'Change, and he asks us to dinner? The story of *Mene, Mene, Tekel, Upharsin* is a

FIG. 18. Washington Allston, *Spalatro's Vision of the Bloody Hand*, engraved frontispiece after a lost painting of 1831, for Clara Erskine Clement Waters, *A Handbook of Legendary and Mythological Art* (New York: Hurd and Houghton, 1871), Princeton University Library, New Jersey.

story of today, and if Allston had freed his head from the clouds of literary fancy, and taken notice of the facts before his eyes, he would not have struggled (his picture bears most evident marks of a struggle) with the impossible. The powerful emotion which the vision of Belshazzar, really seen, would have evoked, forcing the spectator to overlook or disregard impertinent vessels of gold and of silver and all the paraphernalia of external circumstance, should and might have found in Allston an admirable translator, for when not trammelled by the ghosts of other men's fancies he worked well and nobly. We see this in his portrait of Benjamin West, in the Boston Athenæum, in the knock-down argument of an individual character. How real seems that portrait alongside of Stuart's pink fancy of Washington! and what a piece of bosh, by contrast, is the 'Portrait of Benjamin West, Esquire' (I believe he wasn't 'Sir'd'), 'President of the Royal Academy,' by Sir Thomas Lawrence! Things that were can be properly represented only in things that are."

"What is the tendency of modern art buyers?"

"Our country is flooded with the mercantile imbecilities of Verboeckhoven and hundreds of other European artists whose very names are a detestation to any lover of truth. The skin-deep beauties of Bouguereau and others of whom he is a type are a loathing to those who hate the idolatry which worships waxen images. The true artist loves only that work in which the evident intention has been to attain the truth, and such work is not easily brought to a fine polish. What he hates is that which has evidently been painted for a market. The sleekness of which we see so much in pictures is a result of spiritual inertia, and is his detestation. It is simply a mercantile finish. Who ever thinks about Michael Angelo's work being finished? No great artist ever finished a picture or a statue. It is mercantile work that is finished, and finish is what the picture-dealers cry for. Instead of covering the walls of his mansion with works of character, or, what is better, with those works of inspiration which allure the mind to the regions of the unknown, he is apt to cover them with the sleek polish of lackadaisical sentiment, or the puerilities of impossible conditions. Consequently the picture-dealer, although he may have, or may have had, something of the artistic instinct, is overwhelmed by commercial necessity. The genuine artist sometimes supposes that he suffers because his love is not of the world. But let him beware of such a fancy. It is a ghost. It has no reality. Our unhappinesses arise from disobedience to the monitions within us. Let every endeavor be honest, and although the results of our labors may often seem abortive, there will here and there flash out from them a spark of truth which shall gain us the sympathy of a noble spirit."

"What is the true use of art?"

"The true use of art is, first, to cultivate the artist's own spiritual nature, and secondly, to enter as a factor in general civilization. And the increase of these effects depends upon the purity of the artist's motive in the pursuit of art. Every artist who, without reference to external circumstances, aims truly to represent the ideas and emotions which come to him when he is in the presence of nature, is in process of his own spiritual development, and is a benefactor of his race. No man can attempt the reproduction of any idea within him, from a pure motive or love of the idea itself, without being in the course of his own regeneration. The difficulties necessary to be overcome in communicating the substance of his idea (which in this case is feeling, or emotion), to the end that the idea may be more and more perfectly conveyed to others, involve the exercise of his intellectual faculties; and soon the discovery is made that the moral element underlies all, that unless the moral also is brought into play, the intellectual faculties are not in condition for conveying the artistic impulse or inspiration. The mind may, indeed, be convinced of the means of operation; but only when the moral powers have been cultivated do the conditions exist necessary to the transmission of the artistic inspiration which is from truth and greatness itself. Of course no man's motive can be absolutely pure and single. His environment affects him. But the true artistic impulse is divine. The reality of every artistic vision lies in the thought animating the artist's mind. This is proven by the fact that every artist who attempts only to imitate what he sees fails to represent that something which comes home to him as a satisfaction—fails to make a representation corresponding in the satisfaction which it produces to the satisfaction felt in his first perception. Consequently we find that men of strong artistic genius, which enables them to dash off an impression coming, as they suppose, from what is outwardly seen, may produce a work, however incomplete or imperfect in details, of greater vitality, having more of that peculiar quality called "freshness," either as to color or spontaneity of artistic impulse, than can other men after laborious efforts—a work which appeals to the cultivated mind as something more or less perfect of nature. Now this spontaneous movement by which he produces a picture is governed by the law of homogeneity or unity, and accordingly we find that in proportion to the perfection of his genius is the unity of his picture. The highest art is where has been most perfectly breathed the sentiment of humanity. Rivers, streams, the rippling brook, the hill-side, the sky, clouds— all things that we see—can convey that sentiment if we are in the love of God and the desire of truth. Some persons suppose that landscape has no power of communicating human sentiment. But this is a great mistake. The civilized landscape peculiarly can; and therefore I love it more and think it more worthy of reproduction than that which is savage and untamed. It is more significant. Every act of man, every thing of labor, effort, suffering, want, anxiety, necessity, love, marks itself wherever it has been. In Italy I remember frequently noticing the peculiar ideas that came to me from seeing odd-looking trees that had been used, or tortured, or twisted—all telling something about humanity. American landscape, perhaps, is not so significant; but still every thing in nature has something to say to us. No artist need fear that his work will not find sympathy if only he works earnestly and lovingly."

E., "Mr. Inness on Art-Matters"

(1879)

[The title of this interview for *The Art Journal* only hints at the wide range of topics that Inness covers. Here, he examines the ethics of sensuality in art and life and explains that "the great spiritual principle of unity" is the "fundamental principle of all Art." He expounds on Native American, Egyptian, Greek, and Christian art and criticizes what he feels to have been the damaging influence of science on art since the seventeenth century. He refers, somewhat surprisingly, to the French psychiatrist and theorist Valentin Magnan, whose influential redefinition of mental degeneration excised religion and mysticism as potential sources of the illness. Magnan's adherence to an essentially positivist, secular approach to medicine appears to have motivated Inness's attack.]

"CONSIDERABLE INTEREST SEEMS TO BE TAKEN AT PRESENT," said Mr. George Inness, "in the subject of the nude in Art. It is a subject on which many artists hold views much more conservative than they are given credit for."

"The popular opinion," I replied, "seems to be that artists as a class do not recognise the presence of morality or immortality in a picture or statue."

"Yet, undoubtedly, some pictures and statues are immoral in their tendency. I don't think that the 'Venus' of Titian is the purest form of Art. Titian's object in painting it was not necessarily a licentious one, but was probably to exhibit his marvellous power of imitating flesh. This was a false motive, and the consequence is that the sense of nakedness predominates over the ideas of form, *chiaro-oscuro* and color. Had these ideas been equally operative in his attempt to produce a piece of realism, what I should call the extra-sensuous would not have been the great feature of the picture. Had he been governed by these ends he would probably have chosen his subject differently. As for such representations as 'Leda and the Swan,' 'Danae,' 'Venus and Adonis,' &c., they certainly are beyond the pale of toleration. No modern artist would publicly exhibit such subjects. It seems to me, moreover, that thousands of fashionable imported figure-pieces, in which laces and furbelows direct attention to forbidden charms by concealing them, are scarcely less objectionable. You know the canvases that I mean. They come from France, from Spain, from Italy, and adorn hundreds of parlours in every city in Christendom."

Persons who know Mr. Inness would not accuse him of bigotry on any subject, least of all on a practical matter of Art. I listened with some interest, therefore, to the further exposition of his views.

"What, then," I asked, "is the test of pictorial impurity?"

"The point I start from," he replied, "is the motive of the artist. If his motive is pure, his work will convey pure ideas. This rule is simple, and can be verified. It is of universal application. Test it for yourself."

"Yet, doubtless, it would not commend itself to every moral philosopher."

"Specialists in morals are not authorities on Art. Art is above any ideas that moralists possess—just as religion is above any such ideas. Religion is not governed or controlled by moral ideas. It creates moral ideas. In like manner true and pure Art creates good taste. Good taste cannot be created from ideas about good taste. It originates in artistic inspirations which are above such ideas. Now, good taste may be called the guardian of morality in Art-matters; it prevents a painter from painting what is morally offensive. The man with a fine artistic instinct would hate, detest, putting anything impure on his canvas—he couldn't bear the sight of it; it would be antagonistic to his feelings. When objectionable pictures are painted, depend upon it they are done with intent—an intent that is abhorrent to a fine artistic instinct. The best safeguard, after all, is an ideal presentation of one's subject. All art in which the ideal predominates is pure. It is excess of realism in Art that makes Art-works disgusting. Here is a pencil-sketch of my own—a young girl about to slip into a brook from the overhanging trunk of a tree. She is disrobed, and proposes to take a bath. I did it with the purest kind of motive, feeling that it was a thing of beauty, and knowing that in no other way could I convey the sentiment which I wanted to convey. I shall put it on canvas, keeping the background cool and sweet, and trying to idealise the subject as much as possible. It seems to me that this subject, so treated, is as pure and beautiful as any other. If I should put coarse realism into it, it would be horrible. Moreover, I paint the girl at a distance of thirty or forty feet, which gives at once a subdued effect. The reason for doing so is that the mind does not receive the full impression of any object looked at, unless the object is at a distance three times its own length or height. For example, a man six feet high should be painted as if he were eighteen feet off from the spectator. If he is in the midst of accessories, a proportionate distance should be allowed in addition;

else you get a linear impression only, and produce a work more or less literary or descriptive. You can't receive the full impression of a large object that is just under your nose. It must be distant from you at least three times its own length. This is the law of true realism. Take ———'s *genre* pictures, for example. They are literal transcripts from the model who stands almost beside him. They are too sensuous. They are not Art. The artist must never forget that in nude figure-painting, when the ideal is ignored, the tendency is inevitably to the lustful. The nude human form should never be painted for its own individualities—there is no use in so doing—but from a desire to represent beauty in form. Otherwise the result is invariably something shocking to modesty. We don't need to contemplate individualities and peculiarities of the male or female figure, unless we are anatomists or surgeons. Who ever drew an objectionable inspiration from the sight of a beautiful Greek statue? Mere nudity is not necessary for immodesty. The pictures in such a journal as the *Police Gazette* are not pictures of the nude. A woman's stocking, the arrangement of her dress, the attitude of her figure, the expression of her face—any of these, and much less than any of them, is enough to vitiate and degrade an illustration. We all know very well

FIG. 19. *Aphrodite of Melos (Venus de Milo)*, c. 150–125 BCE, Parian marble, 6'10", Musée du Louvre, Paris.

what such things are produced for. But who supposes that Michael Angelo or Flaxman was prompted by objectionable motives in the production of their masterpieces of sculpture?"

"But those works were free from the snare of colour."

"That is true enough. But recall scores of great paintings of the nude in the European galleries. How many of them are as pure as the 'Venus' of Milo [FIG. 19]? Take, for example, Titian's fine picture, 'Sacred and Profane Love,' in the Borghese collection at Rome. Assuredly here are no traces of improper intent.

Nor is the influence of the presentation to be found fault with. Hundreds of similar cases might be adduced. Has anybody ever wished to see them destroyed?"

"Is Gérôme's 'Phryne' objectionable?"

"Gérôme is by no means a representative of the purest artistic principles. If that picture had been painted in accordance with those principles, nobody in the world would criticise it. Gérôme is too realistic with regard to form. He does not idealise enough. His treatment of form is literal, literary, descriptive, rather than ideal. He falls into the error of the *genre* painter I mentioned a moment ago. His 'L'Almée?' Well, a simple-minded artist would have given us the picturesque and no more; for that would be the impression which such a scene would naturally make. If a painter is to hunt through all the details of such a scene, and note all the seductions of the dance, with the intention of particularising them, the best plan will be to drop Art, and write objectionable books. 'The Sword-Dance?' It is a bad picture, I know, but I forget all about it."

"What's to be said of a work like Lefebvre's 'La Cigale?' "

"It is silly— neither nature nor good Art. Correctness of linear design it may possess, but further than that it has no beauty at all; it has neither colour, distance, air, space nor *chiaro-oscuro*—none of the elements that make a work of Art beautiful or desirable. As for its morality, it is perfectly negative. There was not artistic power nor motive enough in the man to create anything when he did that. Cot's 'Spring' ('Le Printemps')? Well, as far as form is concerned, it is very beautiful, and that is all I think about it.

"Objectionable?"

"No. I think when we get to heaven we'll all have plenty of spring-times like that—if we love our wives. I think if the work was artistically better, that the sentiment it was intended to convey would be better and purer. One trouble about some nude pictures is that they present the form at the expense of atmosphere, distance, and space. Hence the mind of the spectator is occupied in excess with the particularities of the form."

"But some people will have it that artists, as a class, are not shining lights morally."

"An artist has as good a right to be considered sensitive to the claims of morality as any other person. But I think he has a tendency to detest professional moralists; and in this respect he resembles the old theologians, who held that morality doesn't save a man. That, however, is not to say that he goes into the bad practices of some old theologians. The most immoral people I know in the world," continued Mr. Inness, slyly, "are journalists and magazine editors. I think, in general, that singleness and sincerity of artistic aim will never go far astray. If the artist obeys his inspiration, and goes straight ahead to give it to the world, he is not likely to miss the mark. The half-dressed French toilet-scenes, and all trumpery of that kind, do not impress you as having been done from a desire to present what is truly beautiful. I should like to ask any intelligent person if Mr. Loop's recent studies of the nude, in the Academy exhibitions, suggest anything of evil, and if they are not on a much higher moral plane than those importations of frivolous Frenchwomen *en déshabille?* Because some works of Art are immoral in their tendency, it would not be fair to condemn the whole profession of artists. The practices of some clergymen are very far from meritorious, but you would not found upon them a sweeping generalisation. Not every clergyman is carried away by the temptation to seek, not spiritual truth, but the establishment of those moral surroundings that will support him in the exercise of his authority. Nobody condemns the Catholic Church, for example, because at the time of the Reformation the power of the priests seemed to be exercised independently of moral considerations."

"It has been objected by one writer that 'God has clearly shown us that the human body is to be covered.'"

"In the Book of Genesis it is recorded that, after Adam had sinned, God helped him to cover himself. But I do not see what this has to do with the subject of pictorial representations. In many parts of the world people's dress is very meager. I cannot suppose that God is angry with the inhabitants therefor. As for the recently-expressed opinion that the tolerance of vulgar pictures in some quarters is due to the influence of 'a sickening cant about high Art,' this is a mistake; in fact, such works are always looked upon by artists as a low form of Art. One chief complaint of artists is, that a part of the public run after things that are not high Art at all. I never heard a human being call such pictures high Art. I admit at once," continued Mr. Inness, "that many figures-pieces in private and public collections do not subserve the interests of spiritual culture. Yet, their presence in hundreds of cathedrals and churches, in the Old World and in the New, is evidence that they have been supposed to possess this function. If the Protestant Church does not continue to employ the means that the Catholic Church did and does to excite the imagination (which I hold to be the life of the soul), it still often teaches sensuous ideas with respect to God, whom the great Master of Life himself has told us is a spirit. The fact is, that the human mind of necessity exists and acts on a sensual basis; without its passions it would not be what God has created it. These passions exist, and always must exist. Man's effort should be to learn how to use them, not how to stifle them. Dam them up at one point, and they will overflow at another. Still, as I have said, the motive of the artist should be taken into consideration, and it must not be forgotten that many figure-pieces, to which objection might at first be made by some specialists, were conceived and executed as representations of what is not sensuous, but spiritual; or, to express the same thought in other words, were conceived and executed as representations not of the physical but of the ideal."

"Then you believe that the opinion of an artist in matters of ethics should count for as much as his opinion in matters of aesthetics?"

"Why not? The artist finds constantly that the very necessity of his Art-life is the cultivation of his moral powers. The loss of these is the loss of all artistic power. He knows this, and he feels it. Of course, on specific points of casuistry, there are differences of judgment. There are things which one man thinks to be of the most vital importance morally, but which to another man quite as good, pure, just, and honourable, are of no importance whatever. The discrepancy is due to the influence of education."

"In his late work on 'The Renaissance in Italy,' Mr. Symonds asserts that 'the spirit of Christianity and the spirit of figurative Art are opposed, not because such art is immoral, but because it cannot free itself from sensuous associations. It is always bringing us back to the dear life of earth, from which the faith would sever us. It is always reminding us of the body which piety bids us to forget. Painters and sculptors glorify that which saints and ascetics have mortified. The masterpieces of Titian and Correggio, for example, lead the soul away from compunction, away from penitence, away from worship even, to dwell on the delight of youthful faces, blooming colour, graceful movement, delicate emotion. When the worshipper would fain ascend on wings of ecstasy to God the infinite, ineffable, unrealised, how can he endure the contact of those splendid forms in which the lust of the eye and the pride of life, professing to subserve devotion, remind him rudely of the goodliness of sensual existence? As displayed in its most perfect phases, in Greek sculpture and Venetian painting, Art dignifies the actual mundane life of man; but Christ, in the language of uncompromising piety, means everything most alien to this mundane life—self-denial, abstinence from fleshly pleasure, the waiting for true bliss beyond the grave, seclusion even from social and domestic ties.'"

"It is all very pretty and very nice," responded Mr. Inness; "but I want to ask the moralist if he is going to create heaven by his morality; in other words, if he expects to create spiritual states by means of moral ideas. The world is full of sensuous beauty. Would you destroy it? Why did God create it? Could the human spirit rise unless it had power through the body of gratifying passion? What is the vital difference between the teachings of Christ and the teachings of Buddha? The latter says, 'Abstract yourself from the world.' The former says, 'Be in the world, and be not of it.' The teaching of the Bible is that God has created good and has created evil, and that the duty of man is to choose between them. To destroy man's appetites and the power to gratify them would be to destroy the power of choosing between heaven and hell. If we are to rise spiritually, we must have the opportunity of choosing not to gratify these appetites. The truth is, that the moralist preaches to himself and to his class. I acknowledge no class. I object to the pretensions of the moralist because it is his aim to rule mankind by external force, whereas the force that conquers is the force within—the spiritual force. Here is where my belief in God comes in. Mr. Symonds's mistake is in assuming that the meaning of Christ's teachings about self-denial, abstinence from physical pleasure, and so on, lies in the letter rather than in the spirit. Christ never said anything that need lead an artist to be ashamed of, or sorry for, creating or enjoying sensuous form. The lily of the valley is sensuous form; Christ bids us consider it. Art is representative of spiritual principles—it is founded upon laws which are analogous to the laws of life. The great spiritual principle of unity, for example, is the fundamental principle of all Art. The great spiritual principle of harmony—harmony in form, harmony in colour, the general harmony arising from the relation of things to one another, and the relation of parts to parts—must be considered, and, as far as possible, realised by every artist in his work. No man can be in the pursuit of studies such as these without finding it necessary to refer back constantly to the principles of his own constitution as a human being, of his relation to life and to society. There is quite as much reason, therefore, to believe that the artist may be of as salutary service in the make-up and development of humanity as the merchant, the tailor, the carpenter, and the editor."

"Still," said I, "it is objected that even at its best Art is never more than simply not immoral; that, by the very conditions of its being, its character is sensuous."

"I acknowledge that it is the mission of Art to appeal to the mind through the senses. But there are a great many arts besides the art of painting. There is the art of writing, for instance. In that art the great endeavour is so to personalise things as to make the appeal as nearly as possible analogous to that which is addressed to the senses. Now, I am far from supposing that the art of painting is religion. I do not suppose that the art of writing is religion. I do not suppose that the art of mercantile manœuvring is religion. I do not suppose that religion itself, in any form that has yet come into the world, is absolute truth. Not that it does not contain absolute truth; its truth is to be perceived by the wise, by those who have understanding. The best that can be said of anything that is not religion—anything whatever, no matter what—is that it is not immoral, that is, that it is not bad. I do not suppose that progress in spiritual things is to be made by the pursuit of any secular occupation merely for the love of the occupation itself. The man who acknowledges that all he receives, all he sees, all he knows, is the direct gift of that Divine Personality which is Being itself, is in the way to reap spiritual benefit from everything that he puts his hand to. He will become greater, better, nobler, as he grows older. He will learn to love the good, and to forget his follies."

"It is often said that the story a picture tells is the literary, not the artistic, part of the work. Is this distinction well grounded?"

"It is not, for the reason that it is in contravention of that law of duality which reigns everywhere. No truth can exist separate from the good that it exerts. In every picture there is a story, of course. One story is told well; another not. One makes a great deal of a little; another makes a great deal that is useless. A story told by a *littérateur* must obey the laws of literary art. A story told by a painter must obey the laws of pictorial art. The painter tells his story with the pathos of his colour, with the delicacies of his *chiaro-oscuro*, with the suggestions of his form. These are elements which the artist perceives in Nature, and which are superior to literary art, because they create it. For of what value is a mere bald enumeration of the things that one sees? That which inspires with a human sympathy what is told, making it appeal from man to man, is a subtle essence which exists in all things of the material world, and which addresses eloquently, through the senses, the human consciousness, creating an intellectual perception of niceties of relation, of peculiarities of condition, and constituting an atmosphere about the bald detail of facts. These elements the artistic mind is continually engaged in endeavouring to give men sensuous apprehension of, and thus to speak to them of that which is unseen—of that which the Spirit of God working in it reveals. It therefore is not precise to say that the story is not an artistic quality of a work of Art; for the two are so intimately connected that they are as the soul and the body in the man, which form one personality. The reason why the artist is often induced to say that the story is nothing, is because he unconsciously perceives the possibility of the Creative Spirit's making something out of nothing—as the old theology would say, but which I should prefer to call the power of creating all things from Himself.

"The evils of sensuality," continued Mr. Inness, "are not the greatest evils among men, great though they be. If we believe that the true happiness of man consists in his spiritual elevation, and in his communion with the Divine Personality, we must believe that what tends only to the degradation of the *propria persona* of the individual is not the greatest evil; because from that he may rise to acknowledge his own weakness, and to rest himself upon the strength of the Infinite. If this be so, the greatest evil among men is that which puts man in direct antagonism to such noble ideas, and consequently separates him further and further from conscious conjunction with the Divine Personality and his own soul's rest. And that evil is the love of the world. The founder of Christianity considered a Magdalene to be in a more hopeful condition than a mammon-hunter. In general, let us beware of the assumption that everything which comes through education is absolute truth. For it is pretty well understood that our natural instincts—so, at any rate, all theologians have taught us—tend to evil. Now, we may say that the reaction against this tendency to evil induces reason. But what causes the reaction? If must be something that has been inducted into us as truth. So that our reasoning against the gratification of our appetites is not a natural instinct. Now, shall we assume that, because we have been indoctrinated in ideas which have been considered by others as truth, and perhaps accepted more or less absolutely as such by ourselves, we are to test those truths entirely by our reason? Our reason is evidently formed not entirely from the truths, although the truths have been the active force, while natural instincts have been the basis. Consequently I contend that no man can tell me from his reason, or from the moral ideas built upon it, what is the great positive good for myself or for another. All he can tell me is what is relatively good, i. e., good according to my relations to him, and according to his social surroundings. I conceive, therefore, that I can receive no idea of the absolute good, but as a truth of faith, or as the working of some power within me which I believe to be good, and in which I consequently trust. My own experiences have taught me that, in all that are called inspirational ideas, I find truth. In the story of the divine man, known to the world as Jesus Christ, I am taught not that if I look upon a woman as a thing of beauty will my soul shrivel; but that if I lust after her. Specialists in morals may find that they lust incontinently after everything beautiful. I have the same passions as other men. I thank God I do not."

"Is it true that Art originated in the love of imitation?"

"The generally received opinion that Art originated in the love of imitation is an error analogous to that greater one which attributes the origin of religions to the external observation of Nature merely. Art really originated in the desire to communicate intelligence, this desire expressing itself in the representation of natural forms. That this is the true view is evident from the fact that among primitive peoples these representations of natural forms were and are produced not with the aim to make them as like the originals as possible, but to impart some information. Take, for example, the American Indians. With them a carelessly-drawn circle serves to represent a man's head; a carelessly-drawn oval, his body; four simple strokes, his arms and legs. In all primitive representations of natural forms we shall find the same indifference to likeness or portraiture. The aesthetic love of form was a new and distinct development of the sympathetic life of man. Previous to this love, was the intellectual principle, which was the first outgrowth of man's sympathetic life, and which expanded with the expression of ideas by forms, and again with the expression of ideas by sounds. These ideas were ideas of consciousness—the soul expressed and reëxpressed what it was conscious of—and they acted as moral forces. Among the Egyptians, the earliest historic race, these ideas regulated the love of form by certain prescribed rules that originated, doubtless, in religious scruples. Among the Greeks these ideas were free from the influence of religious scruples, but were subjected to the influence of the Hellenic conception of the heroism of the soul in its combat with matter. This conception, acting as a moral force, restrained the charms of the senses, and represented natural forms so as to convey ideas of the heroic, and of the beautiful which grew out of the heroic. As the Greek mind became degraded, the ideal hero and the beauty of virtue ceased to be controlling forces. The worship of living men began, and with it came individual portraiture, the imitation of individual forms, the decline of Art. Christian Art, like the founder of Christianity, was born in a manger. Unlike the Art of primitive peoples, it was produced by no intellectual desire, nor by the love of Nature in any imitative sense. It grew from a sympathy for the sufferings of humanity. Unlike the Art of Greece, it was inspired, not by the heroism that combats opposing matter, but by the divine resignation that submits to it. It grew and changed, however, as the ideas of the founder of Christianity were profaned by the love of power; and, gradually clothing itself in the graces and beauties of the Greek mind, it received the impress of natural reality. This change continued, until, in Holland, we find Art imitating natural objects more closely than ever before or since. Lower than this, Art could not go. Great and many were the attempts, both in the world of thought and in the world of Art, to get back to the early Christian source of inspiration—sympathy for human suffering, love for one's fellow-man. But the forms once vital were now dead. The time of a new epoch had come—the epoch of the scientific mind, which began in the last century, and is still in progress. The development of this scientific mind is a reaction against the assumptions of ecclesiastical dogmatism. But love for one's fellow-men has grown for eighteen centuries, and is strong. The weaker love, born of speculative thought, must yield to it. Science is unable to conceive of spirit; it ignores the reality of the unseen; and the tendency of Art has been to follow in the train of science, for Art is but the concrete expression of the era in which it is formed."

"What is to be said of pre-Raphaelitism?"

"The doctrine called pre-Raphaelitism was a true outgrowth of the scientific tendency of the new age. It was false as a philosophy, though necessary as a reactionary force. It carried the love of imitation into irrational conditions. Objects were painted without regard to their distances; and in England, where it took its strongest hold, the most frightful conglomerations were produced under the assumption of absolute accuracy. Science gives no true image of humanity. Its man is a machine, reasoned from sensation. The true end of Art is not to imitate a fixed material condition, but to represent a living motion. The intelligence to be conveyed by it is not of an outer fact, but of an inner life. Therefore, the knowledge how to get the mastery of sensuous impressions is the kind of knowledge that the painter needs. The pre-Raphaelite worker, who would enter into the higher sphere of Art, must first learn to see that his work of imitation has no life in it; that all attempts at imitation are puerile. Art requires the knowledge of principles. You must suggest to me reality—you can never show me reality."

"Do you take much stock in Impressionism?"

"Impressionism has now become a watchword, and represents the opposite extreme to pre-Raphaelitism. It arises from the same skeptical scientific tendency to ignore the reality of the unseen. The mistake in each case is the same, namely, that the material is the real. It was supposed by the founders of the Impressionist school that the æsthetic sense could be satisfied by what the eye is impressed with. The Paris Impressionists a few years ago had so nearly succeeded in expressing their idea of truth, that only flat surfaces, the bounds of which represented, at some points, defined forms, appeared on their canvases. Everything was flat. But God's truth is only made more evident by such error, and the exhibited folly serves to restrain further attempts. Science now teaches that it is the inexperienced eye that sees only surfaces, and the efforts of Magnan and others to reduce their aesthetic culture to zero was wonderfully attained. Since their day, the aim of the Impressionist has been to be governed more by feeling."

"Yet knowledge is power?"

"It is an old saying that knowledge is power. Properly understood, this is undoubtedly true, but its constant repetition tends to give the truth undue prominence, leading many minds to accumulate what proves to be a burden rather than a blessing. Suppose that instead of saying, 'Knowledge is power,' we say, 'Knowledge is the basis of power.' That would be absolutely true, and besides exceedingly significant. Or, to change the figure, knowledge is the seed which, in order to be useful, must be covered up, and die within the warm soil of human affection. It is good to have such seed, if we plant it. An artist may study anatomy, geology, botany—any science that helps the accuracy of his representations of Nature; but the quantity and the force of his acquisitions must be subjected to the regulating power of the artistic sentiment that inspires him. Otherwise his pictures will be anatomical platitudes, scientific diagrams, geographical maps, instead of living men and significant landscapes. When the love of learning is separated from the love of use, it obtrudes itself at the expense of beauty. This is a chronic trouble in the studios. So many pictures speak of labour, and constraint on the part of the painter—so few, of ease and freedom! He who is daily giving us beautiful representations has loved what he has painted, and his love has been wisdom to him. Delight in one's subject begets a higher knowledge respecting it than the knowledge of muscles, ligatures, tissues, or Silurian rocks; higher, as wisdom is higher than knowledge. 'Get wisdom,' says the royal sage of Israel. He does not say, 'Get knowledge.' Were our affections pure, that is, free from worldly considerations, they would in all cases lead us to the attainment of that knowledge which would best develop the best that is in us. You cannot stretch your genius beyond the bounds of its own wisdom, without losing virility and life."

"What is Art?"

"Art is a representation of life in the form of a new and distinct potency. The greatness of Art is not in the display of knowledge, or in material accuracy, but in the distinctness with which it conveys the impressions of a personal vital force, that acts spontaneously, without fear or hesitation. The results of intellectual caution are antagonistic to the human element, and are also scientifically incorrect. This vital, creative force does not act according to law. It creates law, while in the process of expansion. Accordingly, a man of science will often discover, in a work of Art, principles of which the artist was wholly unconscious.

Much has been said of the comparative difficulties of various branches of Art. But difficulties have nothing to do with the matter. 'Eat what thy soul loveth.' The real difficulty is in bringing the intellect to submit to the fact of the indefinable—that which hides itself that we may see it. The intellect naturally desires to define everything. It cannot define God; therefore it cannot trust him. Art is a subtle essence. It is not a thing of surfaces, but a moving spirit, harmonising the discordant by rejecting the excess of the sensuous cravings of the intellect. Like the humanity of God, it is personal only to love; unknown to the worldling; a myth to the searching intellect."

"Strong Talk on Art"

(3 JUNE 1879)

[The summary directly below was published with the interview in the New York *Evening Post*.]

Mr. George Inness, the Artist, Discusses, with Characteristic Force, the National Academy (of which he is a member), the Society of American Artists (of which also he is a Member) and Art Associations in General.

"THE NATIONAL ACADEMY IS CRITICISED BY SOME, Mr. Inness."

"Yes, you can scarcely pick up a newspaper whose art-articles are not strictures, more or less severe, not only upon it, but also upon the other art associations of the city—the Metropolitan Museum and the Society of American Artists, for example. The history of these institutions has been in consequence a conflict rather than a development."

"And the reason of this is—?"

"Because they are founded upon ideas that prevail in countries whose social conditions and forms of government are different from ours. The spirit of the American people is antagonistic to the exclusive assumption of rights by any self-constituted body."

"How, then, shall artists associate most favorably for their own commercial good and for the growth of their own distinctive ideas?"

"That is the question; for I think it but sensible to assume that a national art can arise only out of the development of individual artistic tastes, modified by the effect of association."

"You are not satisfied with the National Academy?"

"No. It was founded by artists who were essentially English in their culture, and was naturally modelled by them upon the Royal Academy of London; in fact was, as far as could be, that institution over again. The hope was, no doubt, that it would prove as lasting. But one element in our national purpose appears to have been overlooked. The ambition of the Academy through its forty members to represent the national art instincts of the country was soon to find a check in the democratic spirit instilled in us from our birth. This spirit has led to an increase to nearly one hundred members with as many associates. With this increase of members there has been a corresponding increase of discordant elements and less directness of aim."

"But why is newspaper criticism so often unfavorable?"

"The real cause of the denunciation so often let loose upon this institution is that the latter's use is nowhere obvious, except as a picture mart, or as a school inferior in its results to what might be done by the self-combined efforts of natural art instincts when the consciousness of progress decides the choice of masters."

"On what principles should art associations be organized?"

"The first thing to be understood in the investigation of the difficulties in the way of art associations with us is the true relation which the art instinct bears to the human one of universal freedom. The desire to give freedom to each individual of the race is not a conception

FIG. 20. Daniel Huntington, *George Inness*, n. d., oil on canvas, 20 x 16", National Academy Museum, New York.

of the lowest type of mind, but, on the contrary, of the highest. Now, art professes to perform a service between the lowest and the highest type of mind. Consequently the moment its instincts are made subservient to democratic control they begin to degrade, and art's distinctive purpose in the elevation of the race is lost. No culture, no wealth, no righteousness, whose possessor does not consider himself as but a factor in this divine operation of freeing the race can ever promote to the least extent the development of an art which shall represent the national aim of our people."

"What then was the mistake of the National Academy?"

"The National Academy made this mistake: it assumed that the pomaded culture of royal prerogative should represent our national art; and consequently it took a title by which no one body of artists, however select, could possibly be truly described. Philadelphia or Boston had just as good a right as New York to represent her Academy as the National Academy of Design. But further, this body so designating itself cannot assume to represent the artistic instincts even of New York city. Its pretensions even to do this are disputed. So conflicting already are its aims that it is about impossible for genius or even brilliant talents to enter its building unless favored by conditions, either moral or social, with which art has nothing to do. The most mediocre artistic ability on the part of a candidate for admission, if accompanied by the wit to keep his nose clean and his shoes well brushed, or still better, by business, social or political talents, with enough money for a 'spread' once in a while, are of more weight than any show of true artistic instincts."

"How, then, shall art associations be formed so as properly to do their business?"

"In its very nature art is restrictive and exclusive. A mind of thorough artistic instincts can do its best only where its surroundings are sympathetic with itself. All outside issues, and all influences that do not cherish art tend to dissipate such instincts. How then shall associations be formed to further the requisite purposes? I answer by the organization of small societies in each of which all the members have one general aim tending to the development of some distinct artistic sympathy. Assuming to represent nothing but themselves, these societies should never be so large that the smallest business capacity would not be sufficient to qualify its officers, thus making the clear evidence of artistic instinct and sympathy with the peculiar sentiment of each society the main qualification for membership. Twenty members should suffice for each society; certainly there should not be more than thirty. About these societies there naturally would spring up constituencies which would enable each one, that had sufficient vitality, to hold a reasonably good exhibition, upon which would depend its continued existence. By such an arrangement each exhibition would become a matter of especial interest to a certain class of minds who could purchase any picture toward which they might feel inclined with a confidence that they were obtaining something representative of an idea; something which would secure a more and more perfect expression with the increase of time, instead of, in a year or so, going 'out of fashion.' As at present constituted the National Academy of Design has at least three times the number of members proper to form an harmonious society capable of developing a distinct artistic sentiment."

"Some of the newspapers sneer at what they call 'the Hudson River school.'"

"Certain members of the National Academy of Design have been stigmatized, I know, as the Hudson River school. But if they have artistic vitality really sufficient to form a society devoted to the development of scenic landscape, why should there not be such a school? If the sentiment is a pure one and free from any but purely artistic motives the school would certainly become an acknowledged power. It is true that scenic art can never assume to be a representative of the higher forms of mind—in other words, of the deeper principles of human nature—and must always attain its cohesive principles or what makes it act from what is more abstract and poetic though more humble as to outward pretensions. Yet it may become a very beautiful representation of one of the various forms of culture which lead mankind from the lower into the higher types of life. The deep pathos of the soul which descends to be crucified in the flesh is best represented in the simplest and humblest forms of nature. Yet the scintillations of that divine contest are emblemed in all the glories of the outer world."

"The ideal future of art then, is—?"

"In the past art has presented only ideas of truth. In the future it must be the expression of social sympathies—the deepest social sympathies, those which Christianity has awakened in the heart of civilization. Art, as a whole, would then taken [*sic*; take] a course representative of the culture of the day. Each art sentiment would have its own philosophy, growing with its growth, and criticism would eventually become established upon distinct ideas that would be more or less clearly represented at the several exhibitions. The works of each body would be judged from its own point of view, and the spicy insolence of self-constituted critics would no longer be considered a necessity. The confusion produced by viewing large unclassified exhibitions would be another evil done away with. As our art societies increased large exhibitions might be organized at certain periods representing the state, and these might eventually increase to a great national exhibition, all being classified by each society's being represented separately, the hanging being attended to by delegates from each society, but the general exhibition not being controlled by artists, farther, at least, than that their suffrages might be demanded for the election or appointment of commissioners. This of course must be a thing of the future, but in a city so large as New York funds which may now be used only in heaping up confusion might be used to form the nucleus of a general exhibition in which order, harmony and satisfaction might be made to rule, and the distinctive use of art as an element of social, and consequently national harmony, become a self-evident truth."

"What is the position of the Society of American Artists?"

"So far the society has been chiefly a clique. Like most new organizations it possibly embraces discordant elements yet to be sifted out. It must harmonize and crystallize itself. Whether or not, out of its present elements, it can make an ideal society like that which I have described remains to be seen. No such society can exist that is not composed of members of a reasonable degree of efficiency. All must be at least fair producers, otherwise the stronger will naturally desire to associate themselves with those who will in some reasonable degree keep pace. But the National Academy of Design assumes to bestow upon its members an honor and right to consideration above other artists by force of the toy magical letters 'N. A.' This in itself forms an attraction to superficial minds who have as much time to spend outside of their art as in it."

"Should an artist ever consult the popular taste?"

"The true artist paints for 'values.' A tree in a landscape is to him not a dark green mass, but so much color against so much sky. He studies things not for themselves but for their relations one to the other. He never paints his picture in details but all together. The trouble with him is that he is apt to overlook the necessities of the public. He admires too much what is suggested, rather than what is realized, by values. Thus he gets into a false state, and is satisfied with daubs. The ideal method is to unite the exterior and the interior truths. The humblest spectator should be satisfied. Have your read 'L'Assommoir'? It is the most remarkable novel of the day. Do you know what I am going to do? I am going to try to please *Gervaise*—she deserves some pleasure. But, in doing so, I hope to show her truths that she never saw before."

"His Art His Religion. An Interesting Talk with the Late Painter George Inness on His Theory of Painting"

(12 AUGUST 1894)

[A representative of the *New York Herald* conducted this intimate interview at Inness's home in Montclair, New Jersey. It sheds light on the artist's preoccupations toward the end of his life; in fact, it was published nine days after his death in Bridge-of-Allen, Scotland. One of the most intriguing parts of the conversation highlights Inness's struggle to unite "feeling" with the principles of the "science of geometry" in his art and then to apply those principles to his study of theology. Ultimately, Inness describes his art *as* theology "resolved . . . gradually into a scientific form," a development that had become "so very interesting" to him. The headings are original to the text.]

Greatest Landscapist of the Day.

The Artist Did Not Believe in Medals and Rewards and Thought Impressionism a Sham.

THERE ARE SOME FAMOUS PAINTERS, but away far back in the past, who are said to have made of their art a religion, and in doing so they elevated both before the eyes of the whole world. Such men as Michael Angelo, Murillo, Raphael, Leonardo for instance. But these painted in a time when religious subjects were almost the only ones, outside of mere portraiture, for which wealthy patrons could be found.

The Church was the wealthiest of all of these patrons, and the only one which has lived to preserve these masterpieces for the delight of future generations. It may be said, therefore, that the motive in these grand and enduring works of art was partly accidental.

It has remained for a painter of modern days, of our time and country, to literally make of his art a religion, and to work out with his brush a theory of theology sufficient to satisfy his keen analytical mentality. And not in mere allegorical human figures has he found and conveyed his conceptions, but he has gone direct to nature, and from that source slowly gathered his theories of nature's God and the great hereafter.

That man was George Inness, probably the most powerful landscape artist of his time, the news of whose death was recently cabled from Scotland, and whose loss is deeply deplored in artistic circles.

Where Inness Lived for Twelve Years.

In close proximity to the little town of Montclair, N. J., on a hillock, distinguishable at a distance for its giant elms and lordly pines, stands the cottage which for twelve years or so was the painter's home [FIG. 21]. Last year he gave this cottage to his daughter, the wife of J. Scott Hartley, the sculptor, and at a little distance to the south built for himself and wife a new cottage. It was on its

FIG. 21. George Inness's Home, 151 Grove Street, Montclair, New Jersey, from 1885–94, photograph, n.d. (before 1912), Local History Collection, Montclair Public Library, Montclair, New Jersey.

porch that he stood one bright, breezy day not long ago, soon after his return from his painting trip to St. Andrews, gazing upward with affection in to the dark, thick foliage of his great pines on the broad lawn, with its burning patch of what the children call Prince's features, and opening his lungs with big sighs of contentment. He was a man of medium height, with evidently no thought to throw away on mere matters of dress. His gray, soft hat covered a mass of tousled dark hair, in which there were but a few streaks of gray, although he was then reaching to his seventieth year. His beard was of the typical Uncle Sam type, growing very sparsely on the cheeks and luxuriantly on the chin. There was a gleam of welcome in the large, bright eyes behind the old fashioned spectacles, and I was ushered into the cottage.

Filling the back of the mantel over the quaint open fireplace stood a bas-relief in marble representing his two children, Julia and George, riding hobby horses, and near by was an excellent bust of the painter, made by Mr. Hartley [FIG. 22].

The furnishing is quaint, but there is nothing about the rooms suggestive of the successful artist—little bric-a-brac or collections of curious objects. There are a number of pictures on the walls, nearly all landscapes, and probably all from the same brush, though few are signed. They are interesting from the fact that they show the master hand of Inness at various epochs of his art. There is one, a coast scene in Cornwall, a boat grounded in the foreground, another tossing in the distance on the angry waves, and a group of figures at the left in the dark shadow of the beetling cliff. This was his work some thirty years ago.

Could See Faults in his Work.

"Yes, I can see the fault in that now. It is too much a picture of the boat," he remarked. "I am going to enlarge it and give it more foreground. You see, my theory is that there should be no figure below the line of consciousness, because in art—but come with me into the studio [FIGS. 23a, 23b]. I can explain it better there."

At a quick, nervous gait he led the way to a frame building back of his old cottage, nearly

FIG. 22. Jonathan Scott Hartley, *Bust of George Inness*, 1891, bronze, 24 x 15½ x 11⅝", Montclair Art Museum, Montclair, New Jersey, Gift of William T. Evans, 1915.55.

covered with vines and creepers. Its interior comprises two large, bare and lofty rooms.

There are scores of canvases about, most of them unfinished and kept as studies. But you feel that no man could paint these things were he not both a psychologist and a poet.

"Take a cigar," says Mr. Inness, adding, "I smoke a good many, but I cannot tell bad from good."

"When did I first begin to paint pictures?" he repeated, with the slightest shade of annoyance in his tone, as if it were a waste of time to talk of anything except in the abstract. "Well, I was about eighteen when I started out to be an artist.

Sold his First Picture to the Old Art Union.

"The first picture I painted was a little one that was bought by the old Art-Union. I cannot remember exactly what it was and would like to see it now. About 1850 there was a picture of mine of St. Peter's at Rome. It was painted in Paris. That was bought by a man in England. I painted a smaller one, which was sold to a New Yorker. Young George Williams, of the firm of Williams &

FIG. 23a. George Inness's studio (north-west side), 151 Grove Street, Montclair, New Jersey, from 1885–94, photograph by W. H. Crocker, c. 1890, Local History Collection, Montclair Public Library, Montclair, N.J.

FIG. 23b. George Inness's studio, 151 Grove Street, Montclair, New Jersey, photograph, c. 1910, Miscellaneous Photographs Collection, Archives of American Art, Smithsonian Institution, Washington, D.C.

Stevens art dealers, Broadway, saw this and commissioned me to paint the same thing, only larger for $250. That was a good price. I remember seeing the picture in their window as I passed down Broadway, and it struck me as a piece of art, though I don't know how it would look to me now. I was very much surprised when Doll (Doll & Richards, Boston), who was a partner of Williams, told me that that picture sold for $1,300 to some Englishman, for that was then a tremendous price.

Could Not Make a Living In America.

"Of course I had all sorts of ups and downs, and never could make a living in my own country; I had to go abroad to do that. While here I did all sorts of jobs and was often switched from art. Here, for instance, is a picture I made of Scranton, Pa., done for the Delaware and Lackawanna Company, when they built the road [*The Lackawanna Valley*, c. 1855, National Gallery of Art, Washington, D.C.]. They paid me $75 for it. Two years ago, when I was in Mexico city, I picked it up in an old curiosity shop. You see I had to show the double tracks and the round house, whether they were in perspective or not. But there is considerable power of painting in it, and the distance is excellent."

"But, Mr. Inness, you have now personally no grounds for complaint on that score?"

"Perhaps not, I am bought now," he said modestly, and then assertively: "But see the years that have passed! Even to-day our wealthy men are not our supporters—not my supporters. We are growing in art, I suppose, as in every-thing else. We are not sufficiently assertive. There is a great deal taken on assertion.

"Americans are afraid to admire an example of native art. This is more espe-cially true at home. I did well when abroad from Americans who came there. I never could make a living in my own country.

Did Not Think Much of French Art.

"Mind you," he continued, "there is an immense deal of fine art in these French exhibitions, but there is also very much that is preposterous. To obtain recognition, however, it must be French. Of the many pictures the French send over here I have seen nothing very good. Of Cazin, whom the Americans are now fussing about, I have seen nothing remarkable, though some pretty pictures."

"But, you are not opposed to exhibitions, Mr. Inness?"

"Yes, I am; to competitions in art and the awarding of medals and all that sort of thing. These exhibitions are not made with sufficient care. They are too much of a jumble, so that the pictures exhibited continually conflict with one another. When it comes to the awards, they are well enough in a school where the mas-ter has certain methods and ideas of his own because he can judge which pupils come nearest to those methods and ideas. But the artist comes out as an indi-vidual. Who is going to judge of his work when it is acknowledged that some who have proved the greatest have not been recognized at all during their life-times? No, the awarding of a medal to a work of art is reducing art to a sphere of mechanics. Every artist has his own feeling, and if he develops it may be a great master in his way, yet the other schools, the men with other methods and ideas, will not recognize the merit of his work."

"But can this matter of feeling be explained in words?"

"I think so. I have made a thorough and complete theory of it. I am seventy years of age, and the whole study of my life has been to find out what it is that is in myself; what is this thing we call life, and how does it operate. Upon these questions my ideas have become clearer and clearer, and what I hold is that the Creator never makes any two things alike or any two men alike. Every man has a different impression of what he sees, and that impression constitutes feeling, and every man has a different feeling.

"Now, there has sprung up a new school, a mere passing fad, called Impressionism, the followers of which pretend to study from nature and paint it as it is. All these sorts of things I am down on. I will have nothing to do with them. They are shams.

"The fact came to my mind in the beginning of my career. I would sit down before nature and under the impulse of a sympathetic feeling put something on canvas more or less like what I was aiming at. It would not be a correct portrait of the scene, perhaps, but it would have a charm. Certain artists and certain Philistines would see that and would say, 'Yes, there is a certain charm about it, but did you paint it outdoors? If so, you could not have seen this and that and the other.' I could not deny it, because I then thought we saw physically and with the physical eye alone. Then I went to work again and painted what I thought I saw, calling on my memory to supply missing details. The result was that the picture had no charm—nothing about it that was beautiful. What was the reason? When I tried to do my duty and paint faithfully I didn't get much; when I didn't care so much for duty I got something more or less admirable. As I went on I began to see, little by little, that my feeling was governed by a certain principle, which I did not then understand as such."

"But these are merely scientific formula," he went on. "Every artist must, after all, depend on his feeling, and what I have devoted myself to is to try and find out the law of the unit; that is, of impression. Landscape is a continued repetition of the same thing in a different form and in a different feeling. When we go out-doors our minds are overloaded; we don't know where to go to work. You can only achieve something if you have an ambition so powerful as to forget yourself, or if you are up in the science of your art. If a man can be an eternal God when he is outside, then he is all right; if not, he must fall back on science."

Nature Is No Impressionist.

"But is it not possible, Mr. Inness, to establish a measuring point in art?"

"Not in a broad, general sense. The worst of it is that all thinkers are apt to become dogmatic, and every dogma fails because it does not give you the other side. The same is true of all things, art, religion and everything else. You must find a third, as your standpoint of reason. That is how I came to work in the science of geometry, which is the only abstract truth. The diversion of the arc of consciousness and so on, which I have already mentioned.

"And no one can conceive the mental struggles and torments I went through before I could master the whole thing. I knew the principle was true, but it would not work right. I had constantly to violate my principle in order to get in my feeling. This was my third. I found I was right, and went on in perfect confidence, and I have my understanding under perfect control, except when I overwork myself, when I am liable to get wriggley, like anybody else."

"Then what do you do?"

"Shut myself up with my books and write, applying the principles I have found true in art to pure reasoning on the subject of theology.

"That is what you see in my pictures and ask me to explain. That is the feeling, you see, and the sentiment. I have always had it, but have not always understood the principles which govern it. People ask me why I keep on, old as I am, for I am seventy, and I say simply because of a principle beyond me, that goes on outside of me in developing higher and higher forms of truth. Of course this development must depend in a measure on physical strength and power. I find my great trouble is to watch that I do not overwork myself.

"How many pictures have your painted?" was asked, as the eye rambled over the scores of unfinished canvases which cover the lofty walls of this barnlike studio.

"I don't know. I have destroyed more than I have sold, in the hope of doing something better. I cannot always get just the effect I want. There are really not many of my pictures in existence."

"And when you grow weary of painting, Mr. Inness?"

"Then I take to theology. That is the only thing except art which interests me. In my theory, in fact, they are very closely connected. That is, you may say it is theology, but it has resolved itself gradually into a scientific form, and that is the development which has become so very interesting to me. I have written piles upon piles of manuscripts upon it, and my method is to take these piles and rewrite them in a very condensed form. Gradually this grows and is 'boiled down,' and all the first essays destroyed."

It was evident that this recluse, groping for years among the eternal paradoxies [*sic*] of nature, working out her secrets with his skilful brush, had developed a system of theology and a theory of the mainsprings of feeling and inspiration that were to him vivid and all-sufficing.

WRITINGS

*Letters to Family Members, Letters on Art,
Essays, Speeches, and Poems*

Letters to Elizabeth Hart Inness (1855–84)

[Inness's letters to his wife (FIG. 24), first printed in George Inness, Jr., *Life, Art, and Letters of George Inness*, are among his most personal. Here, we bear witness to his emotions—his expressions of deep affection for her, their children, and grandchildren, and his regret at having to be apart from them. And yet, we see how he needed private time, undistracted by family and business concerns, to concentrate fully on painting. Moreover, many of the letters provide insight into a rarely discussed and insufficiently explored aspect of Inness's work: his representations of human figures.]

FIG. 24. Mrs. George Inness (Elizabeth Hart Inness), photograph, c. 1862, reproduced in George Inness, Jr., *Life, Art, and Letters of George Inness*, p. 59.

Scranton, [Pennsylvania], Sept., 1855

My dearest wife:

Above all things in the world I would love to see you. I have to think of you the more that I am in trouble. I left my baggage at St. John's and walked to Stroudsburg. The scamp never sent it. I left for Scranton with the promise from the stage proprietor that it should be sent to me the next day. It has not come, and I shall now be at expense to get it. I had to buy a shirt and other things, so that my money is almost gone. Send me ten dollars. I fear I shall need it. You will have to wait until I can send you money or until I return. There is no other way.

I kiss you a thousand times, my Love, and will hasten to you as soon as possible. Kiss my little ones for me. I will write you a long letter soon.

Your affectionate husband, // GEORGE INNESS.

Liverpool, Feb. 13, 1873

My Dear Wife:

I have just received your two letters and hasten to answer a few lines before leaving for the boat. Do not worry about me, as I am well provided for and am all right. I presume that you have received the letter I wrote from London.

I shall be quite as well satisfied if the $1,000 is not sent, if you have enough, until I can reach Boston, as it will leave me free to make other arrangements if desirable. Williams will probably be desirous of making overtures to me, and in case the money is paid I shall feel delicate in working from one party to another. As soon as I reach Boston I will find out how things are and telegraph you money.

Give my love to all and believe me your

Affectionate husband, // Fear nothing, // GEORGE.

———

Sunday, Milton, July, 1881

My darling wife:

I was glad to get your two letters, as I had wondered why I had not heard from you more frequently. I begin to feel lonely without you, but there is no help for it. What I determine upon I must hereafter carry out resolutely or I shall accomplish nothing. I will no longer have any unfinished work in my wake to bother me.

My picture still needs about three days, I think, but if I can improve it after that I shall not hesitate to use the time. I think you will be somewhat surprised when you see it. The old man seems to strike people as wonderful. The boy's face also is considered very fine, although he is not yet finished, particularly the figure and hands, which have a great deal to do with the faces. The old man's eyes, just peering out from under the rim of his hat against a glowing twilight sky, have a most weird and striking effect. The hands are very thorough and strong in character, and the whole picture is exceedingly mellow and rich with the light of the afterglow [FIG. 25].

You have no idea how stunningly I am painting every part of it. Every part speaks of reality. I begin to feel now that I have got at what will always be in demand at good prices, and I feel my interest in this sort of thing gradually taking the place of landscape. They are

FIG. 25. George Inness, *The Old Veteran*, c. 1881, oil on canvas, 38 1/8 x 26 1/4", Montclair Art Museum, Montclair, New Jersey, Gift of Mrs. Daniel J. Schuyler, 1953.70.

certainly more satisfactory, although at present I have to apply myself very closely.

My next I shall no doubt do with much greater ease and certainty. We have had one or two rather warm days this week, but it is cool enough now; in fact, on the piazza it is almost cold. I hope, darling, that you are enjoying yourself and having a good time. I thought at one time that I might find some subjects at Alexandria Bay, but if I did, it would be difficult to get models and opportunities which I get here. Here I have everything just as I want and need at present, just such subjects as suit me, and every convenience of time.

The old man and his children, together with some little girls who are running about, make capital models, and I must not neglect this opportunity if I intend to paint these subjects. If I do not do it now I shall never do it, and if I can get these pictures in the style of the one I am painting finished this summer, I shall feel pretty sure of being able to get myself into smooth waters.

All the friends here send their kind regards and good wishes, and some of them will await your return with impatience as time lessens the distance between us.

I am never in a very good condition to write, as my work is pretty constant and uses up my powers pretty well, although otherwise I thrive under the work. To-day I got interested in a book, and have been reading all day, which rather upsets me for writing very brilliant letters. Give my love to all,

Your affectionate GEORGE.

Milton, July 6, 1881

My darling wife:

I received your very dear letter this evening, and with it the others from Mr. Smith, which did not, of course, make me feel very brilliant; so I went to work with some charcoal and made some sketches until I got myself in a more comfortable condition. I did not feel very much disturbed, however, as I always thought the sending pictures to London was nonsense. I thought that the small one might do something at a moderate price, but the works of an unknown artist are not worth anything until some known dealer works them up. Still, as they are there, perhaps Mr. Smith may find a dealer with whom he may make a bargain; but if he does, it will be for very little.

It is going to be a scorcher to-day. It is now half-past six, and the thermometer is at seventy-eight; so that we may expect to be among the big figures about noon. I am in excellent spirits, however, and only fear that my old man may find it too hot to stand for me. I got my canvas stretched and the figures drawn in charcoal from the sketch yesterday afternoon, but the old man did not feel very well, so I sketched in the background with some minor matters, and left the canvas, etc., at his house for this morning, when he promised to stand.

As I write I feel a breeze spring up from southwest, so that it may turn out cooler. I am much stronger in many ways than you think. It is not so much the body as it is the discouraging anxieties which I have had to endure, and which come over me at every landscape that I complete. It seems to say, what use am I? It is therefore desirable that I get myself firmly fixed in this painting of figure and overcome the tendency to an old sympathy.

If I had gone with you to Alexandria Bay the fresh scenery there would have at once put me off the track, and I consider it a good thing that this figure picture had got full possession of my mind. I begin to feel the increasing interest in them, and I find that the landscape which I introduce has a charm greater than when painted alone. There is a calf fastened to the side of the lane of which I can make great use in something; in fact, I begin to see how the interest of figure and landscape are to be combined better and better every day, and how the charm of the latter can be vastly increased thereby.

[unsigned]

Milton, Sunday, July, 1881

My darling wife:

It would be very pleasant for me to be with you to-day, but distance and expense stand between us as too great for a short visit; for I could not leave what I am doing permanently, and I am sure you would not desire it at the expense of neglecting my work.

The weather is at times pretty warm, but on the whole I get on very well, working easily and successfully. I have now had four days upon my figure picture, and it is very satisfactory. I am convinced now that I can paint these things without any lack of character or accuracy. Mr. Gurney says he would choose it sooner as it is than any of my landscapes, and as long as I can get a model, I can get on as easily with one as with another. You may feel assured that two or three such pictures as this is getting to be will get us out of trouble. If I do not sell a landscape, I feel that I am getting stunning characters, and I see several things to do which will be as good. I think it probable that I shall get through this week, but am not certain; in any case I do not think it advisable to leave a field where I am doing such successful work and enjoying good health at the same time. If I had money, I might feel differently; but if I do not hear something favorable from the pictures I sent to New York, I must go there and try to stir up something. It will never do for me to wait until I am almost out of money. It seems to me that until affairs are in better shape I must remain nearer my base of supplies.

I am glad to know, my dear, that you are enjoying yourself. Be happy and feel certain that our short separation will end in a great satisfaction to us both in the knowledge that my stay here has been pecuniary profit. I have obtained the box for Nell. It is from Mr. Duly, a very handsome mat of fox-skins, which I presume is for looks rather than use.

It was my intention to write you a good long letter to-day, but I find myself very dull, I presume from having got interested in one of those subjects which absorb the mind to a point of exhaustion; so you must not think I neglect you for my greatest happiness is to be where you are. All the friends here inquire of me as to how you are enjoying yourself, and send much love. Give my love to Nell and Scott, and remember me to all.

Your affectionate husband, // GEORGE INNESS.

["Nell" refers to their daughter Helen Hart Inness Hartley; "Scott" refers to Helen's husband, the sculptor Jonathan Scott Hartley.]

⬥•✦•⬥

Milton, July 13, 1881

My dear wife:

I do not think it wise for me to leave here at present. My work is going on well, and I am well. So you must not expect me for some time, and it may be that I shall stay here until you come back. I have already written you why I consider it necessary for me to stay. My picture is a great success and progresses rapidly. A few more days will finish it. C—— was here to-day on his way to Palenville. He seems to think it will create a sensation and will command ready sale. It is certainly a very striking picture, and as soon as it is finished I shall commence another, which I have composed from nature.

I think these things will bring money readily, and I am determined to get out of debt this winter, and the sale of landscapes is too uncertain.

I trust, my dear, that you will enjoy yourself just the same. The weather is rather warm, but nothing distressing. I do not mind it. Give my love to all. Does baby remember grandpa?

Your affectionate // GEORGE.

Milton, July 19, 1881

My dear wife:

I have just received yours of the 17th inst.

I still have our room, so that if you conclude to come on the first of August we can be accommodated as before. I feel very lonely sometimes without you, although I keep myself so thoroughly employed that I drive away anything like the blues. I hope that you will come, but I do not feel that I shall press you against what you think you should do. All the friends here are anxious that you should return soon. If Nell can get on without you, I do not see why you should stay.

I have commenced the new picture. It is a part of the lane near the old man's house, including him and several figures of children, a dog and so forth. I just write this in haste as a requested answer to your last. So you must excuse its shortness. I shall write again in a day or two.

Yours affectionately, // George.

[Milton,] July 22, 1881

My dear wife:

I have been so busy that I have not been able to write to you since Tuesday last, as I intended to. I have just been looking over my picture of the old man, which I have laid aside for a day or two. There is certainly something wonderful in this picture, as several persons have said. It is exceedingly elaborate, but sufficiently broad. I still have about a day's work upon it, which I shall do when I feel perfectly fresh. The picture is a warm, mellow russet-gray, and gives the feeling of the time very strangely, and whoever looks at it once will not get away from it very easily. My second picture progresses very rapidly, and is to be fresh and green, though not violent. I shall soon paint the figure with great power. I commenced another picture to-day, which I had made a small sketch of and have had in my mind for some time. The size is thirty-eight by twenty-four. Subject, "An Evening at the Pond." I have taken just a small bit by the water, with rushes very near and a dark wood on opposite bank against the reflection of this wood. I have a figure of a girl in light grays and white in shadow, and a boy, feet in water, throwing a stone at some large birds which are rising from the rushes. A brilliant evening sky at the right, seen over some lower forms of wood, is reflected in the foreground, and the back of a black cow is seen going out of the picture. This tells the story of the girl and boy without introducing more cattle. The girl is about twelve inches high. The effect is grand, and so is the color; in fact, the picture seems to me to express grandeur better than anything I have done. All these pictures are painted with very gray colors, which I find give me the truest tone of nature, so that, although they are very rich, they are full of air.

The picture of the lane is very real-looking. How is the little tot? I want to see her very much, as I do all of you, but I must carry out my program. I wonder sometimes at what I go through, but though I sometimes feel pretty well used up, I soon recuperate, and find it best not to give way to the notion of fatigue, as work agrees with me, and a little change of subject rests me better than to do nothing.

Good-by, darling, // Your affectionate husband, // George.

Milton, July 22, 1881

My dear wife:

I hardly know what to write to you to-night as I feel rather dull and in no condition to write. It is not that I am not well exactly, but a sort of depression which will not relieve itself in words. I presume it is the natural effect of hard work, and I presume the rest I have had to-day will bring me all right by morning. I am glad to hear that you have determined to return on the first of August. You may depend that I shall be very glad to see you again. I have found some beautiful walks, which we can take together as we did in the old times.

The pictures go on all right. This afternoon it has been rather warm, but nothing to speak of. On the whole, it has been very comfortable, and I do not think we shall have much warm weather this summer. Excuse this short letter, and give my love to all.

Your affectionate husband, // GEORGE.

[undated]

Dear wife:

Milton is where you left it, and all things are about the same. Work goes on as usual, and all is serene. My picture interests me more and more as it goes on, particularly now that it begins to have force and gets nearer and nearer to the tone of nature. I shall continue working on it as long as I can improve it, so that precisely when it will be finished I cannot say; however as long as I obtain what I want the time is not to be considered. I presume you are enjoying yourself; that is, if you can keep cool. It is pretty warm here to-day; about ninety, I think.

We expect you to bring lots of news upon your return. All hands seem to miss you, and none more than I. I shall look for you on Saturday. Give my love to Julia and George.

Your affectionate GEORGE.

["Julia" refers to Julia Goodrich Roswell Smith Inness, the wife of George Inness, Jr., and a daughter of Roswell Smith, founder of The Century Company.]

—•◦•◦•—

Sconset [Nantucket, Massachusetts], Aug. 2, 1883

My dear wife:

We are still having very fine weather, and I find myself in excellent condition. Everything goes on well, and my work is advancing with tolerable rapidity. I have advanced the picture, commenced while you were here, very considerably, and have a very good start on another which promises well. I am obliged to refuse to show my work, as the curiosity of people becomes a nuisance; so I told Nichols that when they are finished he can have them at his house, and put up a notice on the town pump that they are on exhibition. . . .

I find plenty of employment, so that the time passes easily, and if I improve as I have done the last two days, I have no doubt but that I shall gather considerable strength for the winter. I find new and interesting points continually, and I do not know but that the very grandeur of the scenery forces me to make telling combinations. At least I obtain something new and out of the usual run of subjects. I saw a very fine sunset last evening from Mr. Burbank's house which with figures could be made interesting and striking, and I do not know but that I may send for two larger boards and paint two more extensive scenes which have impressed me. This, however, is to be considered hereafter, as I wish to clean up pretty well as I go on. Give my love to Nellie and kiss the babies for me. Tell Rosie that I may find something for her when I come back.

Your affectionate husband, // GEORGE.

[The ellipses are in Inness, Jr.'s original transcription.]

—•◦•◦•—

Sconset, Aug. 4, 1883

My dear Lizzie:

I have just been out to see the setting of the sun, strolling up the road and study-ing the solemn tones of the passing daylight. There is something peculiarly impres-sive in the effects of the far-stretching distance, the weather-worn gray of the buildings, and the general sense of solitariness which quite suits my present mood. I find more and more to interest me, and shall no doubt find my stay here profitable. My first picture is very nearly complete, and has, I think, an exquisite tone without losing the sense of brightness. The second progresses very satisfactorily, and will take but a few days more to finish. The third picture is all arranged and ready for paint-ing in color, which I hope to do quickly as soon as I am ready to commence it.

I have had a great success with another painted out of doors back of Nichols' barn—some sheep coming through a gateway. For that I have used one of the large mill boards, so that although I stroll about and work at intervals only, there has been considerable work done.

I took a walk just before dinner, and was very much taken with the effects of a broad field, with its faded yellow grass, terminating against a blue sky with white clouds sailing along in the clear atmosphere, and if I have time I hope to paint it. If I can only get the sense of vastness with which it impresses me I think a picture of it will be very novel and very telling.

I called upon Mr. Flagg yesterday, who insisted upon my staying to supper. I had a very pleasant time and a bit of bluefish done to perfection. I thought I had never tasted anything so nice. He appears to be *au fait* in this sort of thing, and takes a great deal of pride in having everything for his table done in the best manner. I also called with Nichols upon Miss F—— this afternoon, so you can see I am getting to be quite a society man. I should not object, however, to the ladies having a little more beauty, for a homelier set of women than have taken possession of Sconset I think I never saw together in one place. I am afraid, my dear, that you have spoiled me. I always think—well, I wish I could see my Lizzie. But so much of the brown earth and blue water separate us now that my only satisfaction must be in asking you to kiss yourself for me.

Your loving GEORGE.

--◆◆◆--

Goochland Courthouse, Va., Sunday, April, 1884

My dear wife:

I have read your two letters, and you may be sure that I am much gratified at finding you greatly gratified at my success. I am glad, darling, that I am able to contribute to your pleasure in life. I am very busy now and have been since you left. I painted a twenty by thirty to-day from nature, and it is a great success. Wind clouds, a plowed field, with a sower and oxen in a road in the foreground. It looks very breezy and like out of doors. I have now thirteen pictures, studies, and sketches. I think, after all, the prisoner is going to prove a decided success. It has been very warm to-day, rather uncomfortable sitting in the sun. Then foliage is gradually coming out, and the grass does not make much headway.

I hardly know what to think of California, but have plenty of time to make up my mind. I shall start for home on Wednesday week. When do you expect to go to Milton? I want to get to New York before you go if I can, as I presume I will have to stay in the city a day or two. If I conclude to go to the Yosemite, however, your stay at Milton will be short. Let me know your plans in that event. I have a little work to do this evening, so I will write no more. Every instant is occupied till bedtime now, yet my health is better than usual, as I do a great deal of walking. I have walked about seven miles to-day. Give my love to all.

Yours affectionately, // GEORGE.

Goochland Courthouse, Va., Wednesday, May, 1884

My dear wife:

I received two of your welcome letters yesterday, and should have written last night, but was so busy through the day that I could not bring myself up to writing. The study I wrote you last about I consider the most desirable of all, as I have attained a certain thing which I had not as yet got thoroughly hold of. I feel sometimes provoked that the figure-picture has cost me so much time, but it is doing this that has enabled me to do the other quickly, and besides the figure-picture promises to be all that I aimed at and a remarkable piece of landscape and figure combination; yet what is curious, the modeling of the grass is the most difficult part of it. I want to make one other study, and then I think I shall begin my preparation for moving. I want you to send me a check for twenty-five dollars, as I leave sooner than Wednesday next. I may go to Richmond and make a sketch of a scene which impressed me very much, and then return by the Shenandoah road to Washington and spend a day there, and I may not have enough.

I shall be with you again in a week.

Yours affectionately, // GEORGE.

"The Sign of Promise" (1863)

[This unsigned and undated text was published on the occasion of Inness's exhibition of *The Sign of Promise* in January 1863 at Snedecor's Gallery, 768 Broadway, New York. It is likely that he authored the first essay and compiled the excerpts from the reviews.]

Now on exhibition at Snedicor's [*sic*] Gallery, 768 Broadway, New York.

The design of the Artist in painting this picture, and the peculiar title he has given it, seem to require a few words of explanation. "What is promised," and by what "sign" is the promise guaranteed?

The public taste in Art for some years past has been led to desire what *is called* the real in landscape, that is to say, the local and particular, and not the universal or the ideal. Such is unquestionably, at present, the prevailing tendency of American landscape painting. Mr. Inness, on the contrary, has long held the opinion that only the elements of the truly picturesque exist externally in any local scene, or in any aggregation of scenes, and that the highest beauty and truest value of the landscape painting are in the sentiment and feeling which flow from the mind and heart of the artist. He does not offer this picture as a perfect illustration of the epic in landscapes, but only as the visible expression of a strongly-felt emotion of Hope and Promise. How well that emotion is expressed, the public must judge for themselves. The feeling sought to be conveyed, the true meaning of the picture will not be found in hieroglyphics, for which those who seek them will seek in vain. If the picture presents not to the observer more than he sees, the picture is clearly a failure—at least to him. Besides the desire to express the feeling, of which an intimation is given by the title of "The Sign of Promise," it was the intention of the Artist to delineate certain combinations of scenery on the River Delaware, in which are to be found some of the most striking and beautiful features of American pastoral landscape.

The *N. Y. Evening Post,* speaking of the original study for "The Sign of Promise" says:

"It would be impossible to give one's impression of this work of exalted genius, because it suggests so much of those deepest emotions of the soul which we in rare instances feel in looking at nature herself. Inness's picture contains that subtle essence which merges the spiritual and the material. It may be in the vaporous clouds which float between you and the pure azure, or in the golden grain-fields where the sickle is at work; perhaps it is in the distant glades and forests where homes lie nestling, or in the mysterious shadow of the far-off mountains, or in the wondrous unity which pervades the whole scene. Wherever it may be, there is in this little bit of canvass [*sic*], an absorbing satisfaction which seldom comes to us from any mere work of art."

James Jackson Jarves, in a notice of "The Sign of Promise," contributed to the Boston *Transcript*, while the picture was on exhibition in that city, thus analyzes its design and qualities:

"This picture fulfills its title. It is a sign of promise to Art as well as to the artist's mind. The public owe much to it, not only in what it promises, but in what it fulfills. Not the least of its merits is, that it is a living protest against the popular materialism in American art, which, on account of the cleverness of mechanical execution in the best specimens of the school, threatens to mislead the public mind as to the higher purposes and meaning of art. Inness's example, therefore, is the more valuable, based as it is upon the higher principles of art. It develops the fact from the idea, giving the preference to subjective thought over the objective form of its fundamental *motive*. With him the inspiring idea is principal; form secondary, being the outgrowth of the idea. His picture illustrate[s] phases of mind and feelings. He uses nature's forms simply as language to express thought. The opposite school of painters are [*sic*] content with clever imitation. This calls for no loftier tribute than admiration of scientific knowledge or dexterous manipulation. As appeals to the soul these works are lifeless. Being of things that perish in the using, they can never become a "joy forever."

"The one school of which Inness is as much a type as is Church of the other, *believes;* the other *sees.*

"The "Sign of Promise" reveals the aspirations and sentiments of the artist. It is a visible confession of his theory, faith and aims. Outwardly, a beautiful composition of mingled stream, meadow, field, hillside and forest, with its rich associations of harvest and human labor, overcast by storm, through which gleams the rainbow, of hope; inwardly an eloquent symbol of a struggling soul. This double sense ranks it as inventive art, to be judged rather from that high aspect than from a merely material point of view.

"But its excellence in this respect is also striking. It renders broadly and vividly the qualities of air, earth, vegetation and water. We feel their genuineness, because they do not catch the eyes as a dexterous imitation of form and substance, but as it were suggest nature. The scientific truths of the French school, harmony of composition, breadth of treatment, unity of variety, well-disposed masses, distances, proportion and perspective, are combined with subdued coloring and that repose which is the attribute of real power. Throughout, slight means produce notable results. The painting is not faultless, for it has defects in what may be termed the grammar of art. But these defects are such as probably suggest themselves to the artist's own eye, in the present flight of the picture. There is too much of his rough smoky texture of storm-sky, ending in opacity; the light is not sufficiently warm or transparent in places; more care is requisite in gradations of hues effecting distances relatively, the figures in the foreground need strength and projection; and we should prefer an increase of warmth and tenderness as a whole. Time itself will soften and mellow this painting. Its deficiencies are superficial; its merits positive. As a whole it makes a decided advance in American landscape painting."

In reference to some passages in the above quoted notices, it may be well to state that since it was exhibited in Boston many alterations and improvements have been made in "The Sign of Promise."

"Inness's Allegorical Pictures" (11 May 1867)

[According to Inness's son, "a syndicate of gentlemen" gave Inness $10,000 in 1866 to use during the course of a year to paint a series of works on a Swedenborgian theme. (See Inness, Jr., *Life, Art, and Letters of George Inness*, op. cit., pp. 68–69.) The "syndicate" consisted of Fletcher Harper, a Methodist and one of the founders of the publishing house of Harper Brothers; Chauncey Depew, Chairman of the Board of Directors of the New York Central Railroad Company and a two-term United States Senator from New York (1899–1911); and Clark Bell, President of the Medico-Legal Society in New York. They were not members of the Swedenborgian church but demonstrated some interest in spiritualism.

Inness's primary source for his series was Swedenborg's *The Last Judgment (and Babylon Destroyed)* (1758), in which the author described the Last Judgment, as foretold in the Book of Revelation, as an historical event that he had already witnessed. It described the end of the "old" Christian church, the

Lord's Second Coming, and the establishment of a new church, or "New Jerusalem," in the spiritual world. He also used themes from John Bunyan's *The Pilgrim's Progress from This World to That Which Is to Come* (1672) and the Twenty-third Psalm ("Yea, though I walk through the valley of the shadow of death, I will fear no evil....").

The three paintings were *The Valley of the Shadow of Death* [FIG. 26], *The Vision of Faith*, and *The New Jerusalem*. The following text, probably written by Inness, is from a circular that accompanied the exhibition of the series at Snedecor's Gallery in May 1867. The series received extensive press attention

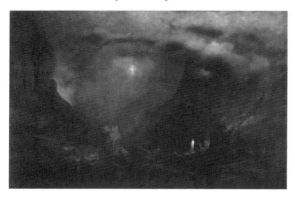

FIG. 26. George Inness, *The Valley of the Shadow of Death*, 1867, oil on canvas, 45⅝ x 72⅞", Frances Lehman Loeb Art Center, Vassar College, Poughkeepsie, New York, Gift of Charles M. Pratt, 1917.1.6.

both before and during its exhibition. Indeed, at the time, more people may have seen these paintings than any others by Inness to date.

The three paintings were separated shortly after their exhibition at Snedecor's, with one going to each of the three men who commissioned the series. *The Valley of the Shadow of Death* went to Fletcher Harper; it then passed into the collection of Charles M. Pratt, of Brooklyn, New York, who gave it to The Frances Lehman Loeb Art Center at Vassar College in 1917. *The Vision of Faith* went to Chauncey Depew. According to Inness's son, it burned in the Chicago Fire of 1871. *The New Jerusalem* (then known as "The Delectable City") went to Clark Bell, who lent it to an exhibition at the Madison Square Garden, New York, in April 1880. There, it was damaged when a ceiling in the exhibition space collapsed. (See Inness, Jr., *Life, Art, and Letters of George Inness*, op. cit., p. 69.) Although the painting was thought to have been destroyed, recent research by Michael Quick has shown otherwise. In the course of writing *George Inness: A Catalogue Raisonné* (New York and London: Rutgers University Press, 2006), Quick determined that three paintings compose the majority of *The New Jerusalem*. They are *The Valley of Olives* (Walters Art Museum, Baltimore, Maryland), *Visionary Landscape* (private collection, North Carolina), and *Evening Landscape*

(Krannert Art Museum, Champaign, Illinois). Having been informed of the original identity of *The Valley of Olives*, Eric Gordon, Head of Painting Conservation at the Walters Art Museum, conducted technical examinations of all three paintings that revealed striking similarities among them, such as identical types of paint and canvas weaves. (See the Press Release on his work and on the exhibition of the three paintings at the Walters in September 2004.) When reunited, the three paintings provide a sense of the tenor of *The New Jerusalem* and accord with Inness's description of a "landscape where no part is left uncultivated, but all is made subservient to the pleasure and happiness of its residents." They also reflect the hopeful, ecumenical view of salvation favored by Christian Romantics in the 1850s and early 1860s.]

"THE VALLEY OF THE SHADOW OF DEATH.—In this picture I have endeavored to convey to the mind of the beholder an impression of the state into which the soul comes when it begins to advance toward a spiritual life, or toward any more perfected state in its journey, until it arrives to its sabbath or rest. Here the pilgrim is leaving the natural light, whose warm rays still faintly illumine the foreground of the scene. Before him all is uncertainty. His light hereafter must be that of faith alone. This I have represented by the cross, giving it the place of the moon, which is the natural emblem of faith, reflecting light upon the sun, its source, assuring us, that although the origin of life is no longer visible, it still exists; but here, clouds may at any moment obscure even the light of faith, and the soul, left in ignorance of what may be its ultimate condition, can only lift its eyes in despair to Him who alone can save, and lead it out of disorder and confusion.

"THE VISION OF FAITH.—Here, the soul, lifted from out the Dark Valley, is ministered to by angels. To represent this idea I have taken the story from Bunyan's beautiful allegory, where Christian has arrived at the Delectable Mountains. Shepherds are pointing the way, and he, lifting the glass which they have given him, is striving to catch a glimpse of the Holy City, where his journey ends. I leave each beholder to look for it with his own perspective glass, giving my own feeling of what it is, so far as I am able to convey it, in the last picture of this series.

"THE NEW JERUSALEM.—This picture represents a state of peace and rest, after the states of depression and elevation to which the soul has been subjected since leaving the natural light. I have endeavored to convey this thought by a landscape, where no part is left uncultivated, but all is made subservient to the pleasure and happiness of its residents. Here the cross is no longer a burden to be borne, nor is faith any longer its emblematic character; but it has become the love of the purified heart, and the perfected understanding, now always acting from its true source of life, acknowledges nothing as the effect of human intelligence, but that all things come from God."

"Colors and Their Correspondences"
(13 November 1867)

[This rare published essay by Inness was first printed in the *New Jerusalem Messenger*, the leading Swedenborgian newspaper of its day. See my introductory essay, "George Inness: Artist, Writer, Philosopher," for commentary on this important text.]

In reading Dr. Bayley's sermon on the *Ribband of Blue*, I have been impressed with the thought that if the word "Techeleth" signifies warm blue, as Dr. Bayley intimates when he says "God commanded the ribband of warm blue to be worn, &c.," there has, probably from the want of a practical knowledge of colors, escaped his notice, a correspondence which, it seems to me, would make his argument much more perfect. Having given the study of color great attention during the larger portion of my life, I have been frequently impressed with numerous beautiful correspondences of the same, while reading the Word and the writings of Swedenborg, and the beauty of this one has struck me so forcibly that I have thought it my duty to put it on paper. It is generally known that there are three of what are called primitive colors, but it is not generally known that, of these three, one, namely, red, is positive, and apparently the parent of the two others, blue and yellow. Of these latter, blue presents an idea of what is spiritual and appears like something intangible. And yellow, presents an idea of something brilliant or external and can be shown to be an attenuation of red. The blue of the sky is produced by light over darkness, and white rubbed thinly over black has, when properly related to the other two colors, an appearance of blue that would astonish one who knew nothing of the art, and so even over red as in veins, particularly where the skin is delicate. The most intense transparent yellows are red in bulk, as gamboge, which is then hardly to be told from the lakes, but when spread out thinly or when mixed with white is bright yellow. But red is red and nothing else, be there little of it or much of it, it is always red, and no surrounding colors can do other than intensify it. Red corresponds to love. Blue corresponds to faith, and yellow corresponds to what is natural and external. In a work of art red in excess produces fineness, or what is artistically called hardness. Blue in excess produces coldness. Yellow in excess produces vulgarity, but the perfect combination of these three colors in their relative proportions produces harmony. This can only be done by what artists call *feeling*. Science may lay down rules but they cannot be of much service in any creative process. Blue when tinged with red loses its value as blue, without attaining any great degree of warmth, and becomes purplish, tending to the color which corresponds to royalty. Mingled with yellow it loses value as blue and becomes greenish, tending to the color of the natural, *par excellence*. But tinge blue with both and the greatest warmth is obtained without altering its value as blue at all, and not only so, but it will in this condition bear a greater amount of white, which corresponds to light and to wisdom, without loosing [*sic*] its value as pure blue, than even the purest blues that are known, as they always discover their parent red—tending to purple—when so mixed. But yellow is simply weakened by white without losing any value as yellow, and in this condition corresponds to science, which never discovers God. Faith which blue represents must be warmed by love to God and love to man. These are bound in one by love to the Lord, in whom is equally of heaven and earth. The blue ribband of Israel is then warmed with orange, the color of ripeness, the color of the most delicious fruits, the color of the pure, celestial flame that warms while it illumines. Seeking for God, the rational is developed; loving humanity, the scientific is built up. Faith in the Lord joins them in harmonious union and is a "blessing to both."

GEORGE INNESS.

[The following note was added by an editor of the *New Jerusalem Messenger*. "A. C." refers to Swedenborg's *Arcana Coelestia*.]

[In corroboration of the above we read in A.C., no. 1042, "For the production of natural color there must necessarily be a ground which either absorbs or reflects the rays of light from the sun or which is, in other words, either black or white. Now according to the various conditions of this ground as to absorbing or reflecting power, or as it is termed, as to blackness or whiteness, is that modification of the inflowing rays of light which gives rise to colors, some of which partake more or less of the obscure or black property and others more or less of the shining or white properity [*sic*], and hence arises their diversity." Again in the same work it is said that "there are two fundamental colors, from which the rest are derived, red color and white color; red color signifies the good which is of love; and white the truth which is of faith."]

"The Logic of the Real Æsthetically Considered" (12 April 1875)

[In this fascinating and complex lecture, Inness establishes his fundamental understanding of the spiritual source of all ideas, notably aesthetic ones. He maps out, in a pragmatic fashion, a variety of topics: the emotional nature of sight, the fact that we see general features and not specific details, the mathematical process by which one can see the landscape as a single unity, the idea that the horizon reflects the middle tone (the point between the brightest brights and the darkest darks), the spiritual significance of colors (an idea discussed earlier in "Colors and Their Correspondences," above), the spiritual significance of the spiral (a theme of Cartesian and Swedenborgian discourse), and his fascination with principles of optics, discussed here as they relate to the color spectrum.

This lecture was originally published in the *Boston Daily Advertiser* on 12 April 1875 and is reprinted here for the first time since then.]

Lecture Before the Boston Art Club by Mr. George Inness—Form and Color and Their Significance—Heat and Weight.

Mr. George Inness delivered a very interesting and remarkably instructive lecture, entitled "The Logic of the Real Æsthetically Considered," before the Boston Art club on Saturday evening [10 April]. A large audience assembled to hear his remarks, which proved eloquent and impressive. Mr. Inness, after a few introductory remarks relating to the division of his subject, spoke as follows: It is well known that the first effort toward the accomplishment of any artistic creation exists in the ideal faculty or power of conceiving. The circumstances of time in which are conditioned the facts or things whereby ideas are formed form also their limitation or power of being ultimated. The mediate principle lying between these extremes of idea and limitation is that which judges and weighs all possibilities; and within its compass exists everything spiritually as well as æsthetically real. This principle in which exists all honest judgment may be called the rational human principle, and its growth and development within the mind forms the true and eventual measure of every human spirit that breathes the experiences of this or any other earth. It condemns the falsities and lusts of material condition, and resolves the created into a relational dependent on the Creator; the perception and acceptation of this relational being is its reality. As spiritual truths relate to the interior good, a harmonious relation of man to his Creator, so æsthetic truth relates to the harmony of the sensorious perceptions; the growth of which in the mind forms that emotional, sensuous principle which we call taste. I shall endeavor, so far as I am able in the time allotted me this evening, to show the principles which govern this harmony of sensuous impressions in relation to my own art, and particularly to my own avocation in that art. The one condition limiting harmonious impressions received from natural objects reflected upon the retina is distance, it limiting impressions of form and color, the former of which characterizes as the latter qualifies objects. We have, then, first, form characterizing objects; second, color qualifying objects; and third, distance relating to objects as to character and quality or form and color. I will first endeavor to unfold to you the law of harmonious vision whereby we have true ideas as to distance or limitation. What is seen through a space at the distance of three times its diameter or diagonal, in other words at the distance of its own boundary, is seen in unity. For instance, cut a circular opening in a piece of cardboard six inches in diameter. I remove it from my eye eighteen inches. Through this space at that distance all objects are seen with equal distinctness. The distance at which the vision is seen being equal to the line which bounds it, we are to what we see as end is to cause, and cause is to effect, the true conditions of unity. There is no conscious movement of the eye, it being exteriorly controlled by the limitation of an emotion which will not be moved to gratify a puerile curiosity. The will becomes passive, the mind becomes receptive. It is thus genius sees. The external form in which it works may be given, it cannot create the image; that comes from within, what is without being only the creation of that power which made it visible to the mind within. While the mind is in this creative frame each object can be thoroughly weighed and the relative value of each can be equally felt. We have no curious ideas of perspective to confuse. Our point of sight is our whole horizontal line. While the eye is thus governed and flowers and grasses are before us we do not see the mountains, and if we look upon the mountains we do not see the grasses and flowers. While governed by this truth of emotional vision we do not find it necessary to paint an object an [*sic*] hundred feet from us as though it were close to our nose. The wool of a sheep's back gives way to the general form of the animal and the character of that form at the distance indicated by its surroundings, and our cabbage plants and dock leaves give way their general character of herbage. In fact, when emotion is allowed to have its full swing through eye and hand, we paint what we see and not what we remember of having seen. Whoever understands and learns to work by this rule will eventually be able to make all he sees obey this rule.

We are now within the law of limitation, and can consider the principle governing form, not form abstractly nor in itself, as that is not within the present thought, but form as to its visibility. Forms are made visible by light and shade. Chiaro-oscuro I take to mean, in its original form, simple relief. The chiaro-oscuro of a landscape simply understood is the relief of its infinity of forms as one or a whole, and this gives us what is called gradation. The simple law of chiaro-oscuro given in the example of a bunch of grapes has been sufficient for the painter of interiors, but the confusing light of out-of-door nature has thrown the landscape somewhat out of the compass of its simple truth; and a more subtle explanation has become necessary to form a barrier against what so frequently appears to be in opposition to it. The laws of optics teach us that the nearer a light is the brighter it appears. This being the case, we can conclude that—all things being equal, that is, objects equally hard and therefore equally reflective and equally illuminated—the nearest one will be the brighter. Then the vanishing will be halfway between light and dark, and must be the point farthest removed from us,—that is, as the horizon and the sky becomes [*sic*] the background against which each light and dark characterizes forms more or less distinctly, according to their nearness and elevation against it. Generally the landscape painter is apt to fix his eye upon the horizon at the expense of other points, and exaggerates the relation which it bears to other points in the scene before him. Not thoroughly understanding the law of gradation, he does not appreciate the power of a very slight variation from the middle tone to make a decided form or line. So little are the powers of the mind under the control of the will that without education it is impossible to perceive the truth of what we feel to be grand and beautiful. The tyro who would paint the head of a beauty defines where the master sees the undefined. Could he shut his eyes and paint from the pure feeling of his love, that harmonious relation between the defined and the undefined which he has felt would be transferred to the canvas. But the eye and the hand must first learn to be controlled by the understanding of what produces the appearance. When we look at external nature we are apt to paint a particular phase or effect according to our immediate perception of values as to dark against light, without reflecting that all truth of valuation in anything must be formed upon a standard more or less perfect. By violating this principle in painting natural effects a forced image is produced, which dazes the eye for a moment, but, not being based upon the truth of matured equalizing tone, fails in impressing us with the feeling that nature does. I will give as example the sea, which, when in cloud shadow, gives to the sky at the horizon the appearance of positive light; yet when through an opening in the clouds the sunlight dashes upon the water, the sky at the horizon appears decidedly dark, —yet the sky has not changed at that point; its tone is the same as it was before the light came.

The lecturer then gave two illustrations of his meaning on cardboard in half-tone, and continued: These illustrations serve to show, that paint in what key you will, the sky at the horizon must be your middle tone. For the purpose of showing the relation of color to light and shade, or black and white, I propose the idea of two principles; one the substance in which all things are formed and the other the action by which all things are formed. Those two principles, like light and heat, are never entirely separated. Red, the first of these principles corresponds to that in us which makes us say that it is warm. Blue, the shadow of light, represents the second and corresponds to that in us which makes us say it is cold. Almost everyone will see at a glance that fire and the colors of fire, yellow and red, correspond and represent each other; but with blue it is different. The term "true blue" is, however, very common, and we also have heard of the "true lover's knot," the color of which must be blue, a beautiful thing but a comparatively cold one. I will in answer try to give an idea of what I mean by the active and substantive principles. In doing so I will propose a mechanical theory of the evolution of the solar ray. From the rounded end of the spectrum we have fair reason to suppose that the solar ray is a tiny sphere. Let us suppose it such and make it more tangible to the mind; let us suppose it a little sun formed in the or [theory] by those principles of motion by which we may believe the universe of worlds to have been formed. As it descends from the great parent of light and heat, let us give ourselves to the idea of substantive power giving to itself substantive form. Now the simplest abstract idea we can have of power-forming is the idea of motion. The form of this generic motion, if I may so term it, is spiral, infinite, eternally the same, yet never repeating itself. The action of such a motion would produce a sphere, and wherever its point of conjunction that would be its centre.

It commences, enters, descends, producing friction and consequently heat; until arriving at its maximum of power it slowly retreats exhausted, yet, never entirely separating itself, it returns infinitely. When this conjunction by motion and substance are in equilibrium we have power, exhibiting itself in the form through the eye—to the intellect—of light, and through the nerves to the sensories of the will as heat. Present the prism motion is retarded, the form elongated and flattened, and the quality of its operation in marriage with substance shown up for analysis. Yet try as you will you can never entirely separate them. What do we find now? Greatest heat, red; less and less heat, orange, and then yellow. Again red ray least refrangible, orange more, yellow still more, green still more, until we come to violet, the least. In admitting that there is a substantial quality attaching to the heat rays which give us the warm colors, there is one fact of the spectrum, however, which would appear to falsify this theory; and this is it: If red, the least refrangible of colors, represents the substantive principle, how is it that violet, which might be called the bloom of red, is more refrangible than blue? For answer, I will first ask the question, How is it that in the prismatic spectrum we have no positive purple, yet the primaries form seven harmonious secondaries, and one of them is purple, the complement of green?

Let us return again to our mechanism. The active principle at the point where it is supposed to recede from the substantive does not entirely separate itself from it, but, as a moment's reflection will show, must draw with it a fine spray, as it were, which becomes the atmosphere of our corpuscle; this spiral alternation of substance is at its greatest or most attenuated state just before its conjunction with the maximum of substance, which it therefore overlaps; and we have violet the expression of the most attenuated state through which is seen the union of the two conditions of substance fixed by motion, as the darkness of opacity illustrated by the active principles which fixed it. The darkness of ignorance illustrated by intelligence, if you please, producing first heat—red, love; then the urging power of that heat—orange; then something done, a golden thing, yellow; then, by conjunction with faith in the power which conspired this good, green; a state of human rationality—elevated by faith, blue: we rise above the darkness of a beclouded understanding, indigo, to the purple of royal achievement, and revolving ever in the divine equilibrium we lighten the darkness of others and become a part of the great telegraph of God. I think enough had been said to lead us to the conclusion that red and its derivations touch the æsthetic sense as something of weight, and blue conveys to it the feeling of lightness. The mind sensitive to color receives warm tones through the sensories of the eyes as something of weight whereby is power, and cool color as something of activity or lightness. If you turn your eyes to the zenith you see that the deep, impalpable blue, with all the darkness of its appearance to the eye, fills the mind with such a feeling of lightness as, in high mountainous countries, to create almost a feeling of dizziness. Then turn your eye toward the horizon and a sense of something substantial or having weight comes to the mind, as the lightness induced by that something comes to the eye. Each color in its purity or completeness is a half tone, so that blue which appears dark to the eye is the exact equivalent of orange or red, which appears bright to the eye. So that if I show a spot of orange or red against a half-tone of gray, it looks bright by contrast, while a spot of blue against it has but little relief and that of dark; but if I warm my half tone or black and white with a little bright warm color the relief of a spot of blue against it is as strong in dark as the orange was against the black and white half tone in brightness, and *vice versa*. Yet everything on the paper is a half tone. In this balance of brightness—as to sight to lightness, as to sensation—exists the relation of color to light and dark. These principles varied form everything of positive power by which we oblige objectiv[e] realization, and governed by the limitation of distance produce that condition in which is the æsthetic as well as the speculative reality. That i[s] most real which is most true to these relations. Superficial nearness is not truth of condition. False relations force themselves upon the eye and do not leave the mind to feel. Nearness to natural quality does not so generally strike the eye as remarkable as false imagery. Imitative power limited by relational truth is a necessity of harmony in which is all true power.

The lecture occupied about [one] hour, and was illustrated at many points.

Letter to Nellie (13 February 1877)

[Taking as his theme transitional states of life, Inness wrote to his daughter Helen (nicknamed "Nell" and "Nellie") on the eve of her marriage to the sculptor Jonathan Scott Hartley. His advice is filled with metaphysical references to key Swedenborgian concepts, including that of "use," or the doing of good deeds from love by means of wisdom. According to Swedenborg, the power of influx causes love, wisdom, and use, together known as "the Divine essence," to "flow into the souls of man" from God. "Use" puts love and wisdom into practice; without it, they remain abstract ideas.]

New York, Feb. 13, 1877

My dear Nellie:

Although I have neglected to write to you as soon as you might have expected me to, the answer to your question will probably take so much paper that I will leave other matters and commence with that.

I perceive from your question that you are beginning to think, in fact that your spiritual faculties are beginning to unfold, and that you are now experiencing your first temptation, which is to leave the ideas in which you have been educated because you fear that they may disturb you in the enjoyment of your natural desires.

Every individual man or woman born into this world is an offshoot of that Infinite Mind or Spirit which we call God. God creates in us sensation, and through it we are made conscious of the world we live in. A world which we eventually find to be a continual changing state, but a state which forms the basis of all our knowledges. This state is continually changing because our spirits individualized here, or born, created as distinct from the Infinite, gradually recede from natural surroundings into what each one eventually becomes, viz., the embodiment of his or her own love or desires. Now, as your own love or desire eventually becomes the center from which all your activities must flow, it behooves you to see that your love or what you desire is rational and not the effect of a mere natural impulse, which may be one thing to-day and another thing to-morrow, thus disturbing the orderly centralizing of your spirit to a state of happiness. Now, the center of all life is the Lord himself, the mystery of whose existence is the mystery of our own, and which will gradually unfold itself to us as we learn to subject our natural impulses to ideas of use and make them eventually our delight and the consequent center of our spirit life, which then becomes one with the Lord Himself. This unfolding of intelligence in us takes place in varying degrees to eternity, and is a great source of happiness or of unhappiness, as we are obedient or disobedient to the truth which we know; for this truth becomes in us the voice of conscience, which cannot be disobeyed with impunity. Now, what the spirit sees is not the truth, but only an appearance of truth. For instance, we say the sun rises and the sun sets, but this is not true except as an appearance, and so it is with every fact of the natural world. The truth is the Lord Himself, Who creates and controls all which is thereby made to appear to us. This truth reveals itself as from mind to mind, and is from the beginning one God, whose children we all are. God first reveals Himself to the innocent mind as command which it is impossible to disobey and live. Next to the intellect as truth that it may become rational or act in the order of use which is the preservation of innocence. Third to the will as good or as a power conjoining or making one the innocence of pure affection and the operation of the intellect creating in His children an eternally increasing state of happiness. Now, we fall from innocence when we indulge the senses and accept their evidence as truth to guide us to happiness. When the truth is that the gratification of the senses becomes more difficult and eventually impossible as the body becomes aged, and that those spirits who indulge them and are led by their allurements become dull, miserable, and wretched for the want of life—God. Consequently the truth is, thou shalt love the Lord. This is the command which innocence accepts as its guide and its savior, and it becomes its protection against the allurements of the senses.

Now, the Bible is the word of God or the truth of life in its intellectual form, and by obedience to its commands we become recipients of life itself as an inflowing principle of goodness uniting all our thoughts to innocent desires, thereby creating in us a love of the highest and most beautiful uses, which is to extend the Lord's love, which is harmony itself, throughout the world we live in. Thus we become spheres of what we are of innocence, truth, and goodness, seen by angels as spheres of the love and wisdom of God. If you would have this life, read the Word and obey the commandments. If you find yourself at fault, look to the Lord Jesus Christ, Who is the only example of this sphere of innocence, and Who is therefore within it and forms it. He will communicate to you the power to deny the allurements of sense or your outer self and attain to the love of duty which is the road to heaven or the happiness of the inner life. This life is the eternal future ever present to all who love the Lord more than self. That is a life within the commandments rather than a life outside of or without them.

That you may be obedient to the law of life, and thereby enter into the enjoyment of it, is the sincere wish of your affectionate father.

———◦•✦•◦———

"A Plea for the Painters. Letter from the Artist Inness" (21 March 1878)

[On 20 March 1878, the New York *Evening Post* published a Letter to the Editor by the artist John La Farge. Responding to a previous editorial that had argued against defining printmakers as artists, La Farge defended the work of "wood-engravers," stating that, "if they are good in their calling," they are, indeed, considered artists by their colleagues. For La Farge, engraving required a painter's knowledge of nature, a draughtsman's rapidity of execution, and an artist's spontaneous investment of the self in his work. The following day, the *Evening Post* published Inness's reply to La Farge, reprinted here, in which he offered three reasons why the painter is *superior* to the engraver. The summary below is from the original publication.]

As a complement to Mr. La Farge the artist's able defense of the engravers, published in yesterday's EVENING POST, we print to-day a letter from Mr. George Inness, whose mastery of the mysteries of light and shadow, and the subtlest harmonies of color, has made his landscapes the delight and pride of his intelligent countrymen. It will be observed that Mr. Inness lays principal stress upon the greater degree of creative power required for the production of an artistic painting, and also upon the painter's distinctive and exacting vocation as a colorist:

To the Editors of the *Evening Post:*
I notice in the EVENING POST of yesterday a generous plea in behalf of the engravers, but it seems to me that the case is a little too strongly put. In one sense, indeed, all workmen are artists—a wood-chopper is an artist, a carpenter, and a tailor; but that the same artistic power is required in producing an engraving as in producing an oil painting I deny. There are at least three reasons why the best oil painters are artists in a higher sense than are the best engravers. In the first place, the painter does original work. The creative impulse is always urgent in him, leading him to choose the means that will enable him to convey his idea in the most rapid way. This power of producing rapidly is much greater in painting than in engraving; consequently a man naturally will not confine himself to engraving if he can paint equally well. In the second place, so far as the mere matter of representation is concerned, greater resources are necessary for the painter than for the engraver, the former being called upon to represent distances, spaces, etc., directly from nature, while the latter has this done for him, and produces an imitation, but not a translation, excepting so far as a reproduction in black and white from a picture in color is a translation. Even a knowledge of the laws of perspective is unnecessary for the engraver; by the simple device of fineness or openness of lines he can indicate aerial perspective.

In the third place, the painter must be a colorist—the most difficult thing in the world. Where are our colorists? Every painter tries to be one, but how many of us succeed? No artist feels that he perfectly succeeds with his color—with that which is the soul of his painting. The demands made upon a painter in this direction are so great that sometimes he feels that almost anybody can do work in black and white, but that nobody can adequately reproduce the harmonies of nature in color. For these reasons the painter has a right to be considered as an artist in a superior sense; although, as I have said, all engravers are, in a sense, more or less artists. Of course, where an engraver is also a designer he is in a higher sense an artist; if he is a designer in color he is in the highest sense an artist. It is evident to every one that the engraver as an engraver merely does not possess the creative power in the degree that the artist does. And the presence of the creative power is always acknowledged to be the quality essential to great art.

George Inness. // New York, March 21, 1878.

FIG. 27. Jonathan Scott Hartley, *The Whirlwind*, 1896 (cast), bronze, 30 3/8 x 10 x 13 1/4", Montclair Art Museum, Montclair, New Jersey, Gift of W. I. Lincoln Adams, 1914.1.

Debate with Clarence Cook
(9–13 April 1878)

[The *New-York Daily Tribune* published two Letters to the Editor by Inness on 11 and 13 April 1878 on the occasion of the National Academy of Design's Annual Exhibition. In them, Inness debated with the prolific and influential art critic Clarence Cook on the merits of one of his poems, "The Whirlwind," written to accompany a sculpture of the same name by his son-in-law Jonathan Scott Hartley (FIG. 27). Cook had ignited the debate on 9 April with a review in which he harshly critiqued Hartley's sculpture and Inness's poetry. He felt that there was "far too much literalness" in Hartley's work, too much of an effort to represent "a water-spout and a woman who has gone up the spout." He wished that Hartley could have conveyed and melded "the human nature" and the "elemental force" behind his subject more eloquently. He added the following remarks about Inness's poem: "The visitor, however, may easily think it [*The Whirlwind*] worse than it is, if, while looking at it, he read Mr. George Inness's 'poetry' appended to the title in the catalogue. This is a most comical production . . . and there is more of the same sort inscribed on the frames of Mr. Inness's own pictures in this exhibition, so that Mr. Hartley cannot complain that he is an exclusive victim." See C. C., "Fine Arts. National Academy of Design. Fifty-third Annual Exhibition. II," *New-York Daily Tribune* (9 April 1878): 2. The *Tribune* published Inness's response on 11 April.]

<hr />

George Inness, "A Poem and a Statue. Mr. Inness Explains his Poem"
(11 April 1878)

To the Editor of The Tribune.

SIR: When I wrote the few lines as a legend to Mr. Hartley's statue of the "Whirlwind," I had in mind just such a specimen of unintelligent wickedness as Mr. "C. C." is a small specimen of.

Fearing that "C. C." may not have perceived the significance of the above mentioned lines, I will, for his enlightenment, explain. The first part of the legend:

> Gnome of the ethereal sphere;
> I live at the behest of ever-changing
> Elements.
> Moved by the gentle moods of human love,
> I fan with Zephyr breath the fever'd brow.
> Raging with fiercest passions all unloosed,
> I rush with surging howls,
> And wild inhuman shrieks at fearful
> Speed; sweeping before me all that holds
> The timid soul in fancied rest,
> I thunder terror on devoted heads.—

represents what "C. C." would like to be. The second part:

> Arrested in my course I contemplate
> Myself; then, whirl in spiral gyres far

> Out beyond all human sympathies,
> Dragging as my train the earth
> And sea—

represents what "C. C." would like to do, were it possible for him wisely to contemplate his career of virulent criticism through many years. The last lines:

> Now; see ye me
> Ye mortal kind as but the
> Whirling wind—

represent, less the word whirling, just what "C. C." as a critic is.
> GEORGE INNESS.

Booth's Theatre, New-York, April 9, 1878.

[Cook responded to Inness the following day. He defended his criticism of both Hartley's *The Whirlwind* and Inness's poem. In an aside, he implied that Inness should have been grateful to him for *not* quoting his poem. "I spared him as much as lay in my power," he intoned. Cook added that although he disliked Inness's poetry he had always championed the artist's paintings. "Come what may," he concluded, "I will never believe that when I praised Mr. Inness's landscape I was either unintelligent or wicked." See C. C., "Artists and Art Criticism. A Rejoinder from 'C. C.' Why the 'Whirlwind' and 'Lot's Wife' Were Ascribed to the Same Sculptor—Mr. Inness's Poem and His Pictures—An Offer of Compromise," *New-York Daily Tribune* (12 April 1878): 2. When Inness replied the following day (see below), he only marginally acknowledged Cook's peace offering.]

George Inness, "Artists and Critics. George Inness Replies Again to 'C. C.'—Distinction Between Deserved Correction and Illogical Abuse"
(13 April 1878)

To the Editor of The Tribune.

SIR: Your Art Critic seems to have as little appreciation of my "poetry" as I have of his criticism. What is said complimentary of my work I suppose I must be duly thankful for, and to all judgmatic condemnation I submit as in duty bound. Nevertheless, I take the liberty to respectfully protest again the indiscriminate and generally unreasonable animadversions of the newspaper press upon the efforts of my profession. I do not object, and no one should, to any just censure of any defects in our efforts to portray nature or give expression to the artistic idea, and wherein we fail it is only just and proper that we should be criticized and the failure exposed; but such deserved correction is a very different thing from the illogical and absurd abuse so often indulged in, seemingly for the mere purpose of exhibiting "critical acumen" or eking out a reportorial occupation. We study, we think, we labor to accomplish a life-work, and are generally content and happy if at the same time we secure a life's subsistence, and proud withal if we achieve a modicum of credit or reputation among the benefactors of the race. Therefore you need not be surprised if we betray some sensitiveness at finding some capricious if not uninstructed and uncultured *soi disant* critic proceeding to pronounce the most sacred efforts of our minds and hearts failures, and even worse than that, without assigning any reason for the condemnation, or giving us any evidence of real judgmatic power. That may serve to fill up an employment, or serve a wage, but a respectable and influential press should reflect that it may thereby be working a grievous injury not only to a class, but to a community and a cause.

The same authority that says "man cannot live by bread alone," says "thou shalt not bear false witness." Try our works by any sound and established rules and principles of criticism, and thereby let them stand or fall. If you cannot praise, at least do not condemn unless it be for reasons given, and let it be done without insult. In times like these especially, the good and the beautiful that is offered for the elevation and enlightenment of "the image" of immortal mind, should be encouraged and promoted, rather than frowned down, reckless of reputations and regardless of consequences. The boasted "mission" of the press is absolutely defeated by the unreasonable, not to say disgraceful, censure against which this protest is entered.

Yours respectfully. // Geo. Inness.
Booth's Theatre, New-York, April 13, 1878.

[Following Inness's final letter, the Editor of the *Tribune* added this note:]
"Whether THE TRIBUNE's Art Critic is unreasonable or not, Mr. Inness certainly is. He knows a great deal better than to attribute to Mr. Clarence Cook either ignorance or mercenary motives; and he ought to be ashamed of himself for stooping to the insinuation.—He does not seem to see, either, how completely

he begs the question. He is perfectly willing, he says, to submit to reasonable criticism, but complains that Mr. Cook's is unreasonable. For this he assigns no particular reason save that Mr. Cook does not agree with him. Now, Mr. Inness should understand that when it comes to a question of judgment between himself and Mr. Clarence Cook, a fair proportion, at least, of art lovers in New-York will prefer Mr. Cook's judgment.—*Ed.*"

An "Extraordinary Incivility" (16 March 1881)

[On the evening of Thursday, 24 March 1881, a coalition of artists met at Sarony's Art Rooms in New York to pay tribute to one of their own, the National Academician Frederick Bridgman. Bridgman had spent many years studying art in Paris and was on the verge of returning; his friends planned to give him a proper send-off. Many artists signed a document testifying to their admiration for him. Not only was Inness absent from the event but he sent the following frosty letter, which had been published several days earlier in the New York *Evening Post*. It and the response it generated reveal that Inness's relationships with his fellow artists were not always harmonious.]

To the Editors of The Evening Post:
    The introduction of my name in connection with that of several others who are to make arrangements for some demonstration in the interest of Mr. B——n, is unauthorized. I think very highly of Mr. B——n's sketches and studies, but I do not feel called upon to do more than to acknowledge the fact to those with whom I associate.
    GEORGE INNESS. // New York, March 16, 1881.

[An editor from *The Art Exchange*, in which the letter was reprinted on 31 March 1881, added the following note under the heading "Extraordinary Incivility." In it, he refers to the six leaders of the committee in charge of Bridgeman's ceremony:]

"As an example of bad taste this could hardly be equalled. It is not certain where Mr. Inness's name was used; surely it was not with the sanction of Mssrs. Huntington, Nicoll, Gay, Smillie, Howland, and Hovenden. If Mr. Inness merely wishes to convince the public that he does not associate with these gentlemen, he has succeeded; if he intends to show that he has been damaged, he has chosen a particularly offensive way of doing so, and has failed."

⬦

Letter to Ripley Hitchcock (23 March 1884)

[This letter was evidently a reply to a request for information from James Ripley Wellman Hitchcock, art critic for the *New-York Daily Tribune*, for his essay "George Inness, N.A.," in *Special Exhibition of Oil Paintings, Works by Mr. George Inness* (New York: American Art Gallery, 1884). Inness refers to Ogden Haggerty, who was his first patron and financed his first trip to Europe—to Italy from 1851 to 1852. Haggerty was a New York entrepreneur and friend of such well known figures as the artist Asher B. Durand and the poet William Cullen Bryant. "Gignoux" was Régis-François Gignoux, an itinerant French landscape painter with whom Inness briefly studied in the summer of 1843.]

Goochland Court House // Goochland Co., Va.   March 23rd 1884

My dear Mr Hitchcock,

Your letter has just reached me the delay having occurred from my not having known in the beginning when I should land. My whole early life and much of the whole was bourn under the distress of a fearful nervous disease which very much impaired my ability to bear the painstaking in my studies which I would have wished

I began of course as most boys do but without any art surroundings whatever   A boy now would be able to commence almost anywhere under better auspices than I could then have had even in a city. I was in the bare-foot state and although my father was a well-to-do farmer, "the boys" dressed very much in Joseph's coat style as to colour, the different garments being sufficiently variegated[,] while schooling consisted of the three R's and a ruler with a rattan by the way of change   When about twenty I had a month with Gignoux, my health not permitting me to take advantage of study at the Academy in the evenings   This is all the instruction I ever recd. from <u>any</u> artist

At twenty-two I was looked upon as a promising youth and was able to sell to the Art Union as high as $250.00 and I believe in one instance $350.00   Some of my studies were very elabourate.

In 1850 I was married to my present wife   Mr. Ogden Haggerty [FIG. 28]

who had already greatly assisted me allowed me a certain sum for study in Europe I was then twenty-five. Spent about fifteen months in Italy returning through Paris and seeing the Salon   Rouseau [*sic*] was just beginning to make a noise[.] A great many people were crowding about a little picture of his which seemed to me rather metalic [*sic*]   Our traditions were English[,] and French art—particularly in landscape, had made but little impression upon us. Several years before I went to Europe however I had begun to see that elabouration in detail did not gain me Meaning   A part carefully finished, my forces were exhausted. I could not sustain it everywhere and produce the sense of spaces and distances and with them that subjective mystery of nature with which wherever I went I was filled

I dwelt upon what I saw, and dreamed, in disgust at my inability to interpret[.] I watched, thought and fought PreRaphaeliteism [*sic*]   I gave way to my impulses and produced sentiments the best I could, always finding myself in a hobble as I tried to make them look finished   Gradually year after year I discovered one truth after another until I had a scientific formula of the Subjective of Nature   My whole aim for twelve or fifteen years has been to apply this   Vast difficulties have lain in the way, a living to make involving the necessity of gratifying a false conception of nature and my own subjective being to answer induced a continuous internal turmoil   At times I come pretty near pleasing myself and some one else but I have never been satisfied. Long before I ever heard of impressionism, I had settled to my mind the underlying law of what may properly be called an impression of nature, and I felt satisfied that whatever is painted truly according to any idea of unity will as it is perfectly done possess both the Subjective Sentiment—the poetry of nature—and the objective fact sufficiently to give the commonest mind a feeling of satisfaction and through that satisfaction elevate to an idea higher—that is more interior than its own[.] Just as I have fought PreRaphaeliteism I fight what I consider the error of what is called impressionism   they both appear to me to be an attempt to reach the negation of mind which consists not of thought alone or of feeling alone but of both, the compound being will & understanding

FIG. 28. Ogden Haggerty, photograph, c. 1860-65, Courtesy Lenox Library Association, Lenox, Massachusetts.

These are the element[s] of mind and with out them more or less in unity we as human beings have no existence   And the use of Art, which in its whole meaning is the first great factor in social being, is as man rises from degree to degree to hold them in equilibrium

Whoever has been without sight and has sight given sees only surfaces   Shall we therefore ignore these experiences of vision which induce thought and try to paint as though we had never seen? Eden was, it will not be again. We must work our way to Paradise, the end of true culture   While Preraphaeliteism is like a measure worm trying to compass the infinite circumference Impressionism is the sloth enrapt in its own eternal dullness

Angularity, if involving Solidity, ~~Solidity~~ Rotundity. air & light involving transparency, Space & Colour involving distances, these constitute the appearances which the creative mind produces to the individualized eye and which the organized mind endorses as reality   A representation which ignores any one of these elements is weak in its subjective and lacking in its objective force and so far fails as giving a true impression of nature

I have changed from the time I commenced because I ~~was never finished~~ had never compleated my art and as I do not care about being a cake I shall remain dough subject to any impression which I am satisfied comes from the reageon [*sic*] of truth

Yours Truly // GEO. INNESS

I have been obliged to write this in great haste for the mail. I hope you will find something you can use

◆·•·●

Letter on Impressionism (late 1880s–early 1890s)

[Inness replies to an article published in a newspaper—it is not known which one—in which he was identified as an Impressionist. He soundly rejects the label. In "Mr. Inness on Art-Matters" (see above, pages 69–81), he criticized Impressionism because it arose, in his words, "from the same skeptical scientific tendency to ignore the reality of the unseen." Later, in his interview "His Art His Religion" (see above, pages 87–93), he would dismiss Impressionism as a "fad." Given the nature of his work, his criticism was understandable but excessive; moreover, it overlooked features his paintings shared with those of the Impressionists. Both Inness and the Impressionists presented alternatives to the academic traditions of mimetic, historical, literary, and mythological representation; both revealed a new, dynamic style of brushwork that led many critics to censure their works as "unfinished" or worse. However, Inness's allusion to the "reality of the unseen" is telling and resides at the heart of his objections. For the most part, Impressionists held an empirical attitude toward perception and were indifferent, even at times hostile, to religion and metaphysics. Although Inness believed that we perceive reality and form knowledge "through the eye," that is, through sensory perceptions, he also knew that we shape these impressions through innate ideas, or, as he put it, the ineffable feeling of satisfaction brought on by "the logical connection of parts to the whole." For him, this feeling was rooted in an artist's understanding of three-dimensional spaces and forms, an awareness, in his words, of "the invisible side of visible things." Inness disapproved of the Impressionist's desire to "divest painting of all mental attributes" and to paint on the basis of sensation alone. He addresses this subject further in his Letter to Ripley Hitchcock, which follows below. Finally, Inness's reference at the end of his Letter on Impressionism to the "little darky" who washed his brushes is highly offensive but had to be included for the sake of accurately reprinting the text.]

Tarpon Springs, Florida

Editor Ledger:

A copy of your letter has been handed to me in which I find your art editor has classified my work among the "Impressionists." The article is certainly all that I could ask in the way of compliment. I am sorry, however, that either of my works should have been so lacking in the necessary detail that from a legitimate landscape-painter I have come to be classed as a follower of the new fad "Impressionism." As, however, no evil extreme enters the world of mind except as an effort of life to restore the balance disturbed by some previous extreme, in this instance say Preraphaelism [*sic*]. Absurdities frequently prove to be the beginnings of uses ending in a clearer understanding of the legitimate as the rationale of the question involved.

We are all the subjects of impressions, and some of us legitimates seek to convey our impressions to others. In the art of communicating impressions lies the power of generalizing without losing that logical connection of parts to the whole which satisfies the mind.

The elements of this, therefore, are solidity of objects and transparency of shadows in a breathable atmosphere through which we are conscious of spaces and distances. By the rendering of these elements we suggest the invisible side of visible objects. These elements constitute the grammar of painting, and the want of that grammar gives to pictures either the flatness of the silhouette or the vulgarity of an over-strained objectivity or the puddling twaddle of Preraphaelism.

Every fad immediately becomes so involved in its application of its want of understanding of its mental origin and that the great desire of people to label men and things that one extreme is made to meet with the other in a muddle of unseen life application. And as no one is long what he labels himself, we see realists whose power is in a strong poetic sense as with Corbet [*sic*]. And Impressionists, who from a desire to give a little objective interest to their pancake of color, seek aid from the weakness of Preraphaelism, as with Monet. Monet made by the power of life through another kind of humbug. For when people tell me that the painter sees nature in the way the Impressionists paint it, I say, "Humbug"! from the lie of intent to the lie of ignorance.

Monet induces the humbug of the first form and the stupidity of the second. Through malformed eyes we see imperfectly and are subjects for the optician. Though the normally formed eye sees within degrees of distinctness and without blur we want for good art sound eyesight. It is well known that we through the eye realize the objective only through the experiences of life. All is flat, and the mind is in no realization of space except its powers are exercised through the sense of feeling. That is, what is objective to us is a response to the universal principle of truth.

Some things touch one more than another, and loving what touches us agreeably and disliking what touches us disagreeably, we look more at what we love than what we do not love; hence he learns to paint first what he loves best, but our love for certain forms, tones, or things cause[s] us gradually to tolerate other forms, and as connected with those we love through the alchemy of life in various ways, so that we tend eventually to ideas of harmonies in which parts are related by the mind to an idea of unity of thought. From that unity of thought mind controls the eye to its own intent within the units of that idea; consequently we learn to see in accord with ideas developed by the power of life, which also leads us through our own affections. Hence every one sees somewhat differently.

The art of painting is the development of the human mind, and to deny its traditions is the sign of an art fool; but to translate its traditions into new forms is the sign of a progressive art mind full and independent in his own concepts of nature, but bound to the past as the source of his inspiration. Originality outside of this truth is childishness, and its products absurd. The first great principle in art is unity representing directness of intent, the second is order representing cause, and the third is realization representing effect.

When the savage draws his hieroglyphics for the information of his companions, cause and effect are sufficiently considered in the intent; all his art is united to an end acknowledged to be legitimate, and any power which sufficiently renders the forms for recognition in that way would be good art to that end. When Raphael drew his Hampton cartoons his drawing, most of it great in the impression given of power to do, was amply sufficient to the end of the story, which impresses one directly—here is great art. When Leighton painted the walls at Kensington the excellent workmen so forgot the end in view that the story has to be hunted out,—here is a work with an intent outside of itself as a use, and that intent was to show his skill,—this is bad art, in which an impression is made upon the spectator involving an intent not in order with the one assured. The artist was not one with his subject; without inspiration he was in the sphere of twaddle. This is that very honest and highly respectable kind of humbug in the art world which we are apt to fall into more or less, against which the impression is a protest.

I have tones done on the boards of the loft which I occupy here by a little darky whom I employ to wash brushes and so forth which are very tony. In fact, give me the same impression that did the first Monet it was my luck to see. His had a little more white in it, but the style was about the same. Now, however, Monet decorated an impressionless plane with a dab of paint apparently in childlike imitation of trees, houses, and so forth without substance. Since the beginning "The Art of the Future," as it is called, has developed in a great variety of impressionists whose works I have not seen, as I am not interested in painters who find it necessary to label themselves. I admire the robust ideas of Corbet, but not his realism; that was his curse. It appears as though the Impressionists were imbued with the idea to divest painting of all mental attributes and, overleaping the traveled road which art has created by hard labor, by plastering over and presenting us with the original pancake of visual imbecility, the childlike naïveté of unexpressed vision.

***

Letter to the Editor of the *New York Herald*
(9 March 1889)

[In 1889, Inness's *Short Cut, Watchung Station, New Jersey* (FIG. 29), then owned by the American Art Association, had been included, without his permission, in the American section of the International Exposition in Paris. (It subsequently won a

FIG. 29. George Inness, *Short Cut, Watchung Station, New Jersey*, 1883, oil on canvas, 37⅝ x 29⅛", Philadelphia Museum of Art: Purchased with the W. P. Wilstach Fund, 1895. Photo: Graydon Wood.

gold medal.) Inness wrote to the Commission stating his strong objection to including the painting. He deemed it "an unimportant and non-representative work for the purpose of exhibition at that exposition." When pressed by an interviewer for the *New York Herald*, he explained, "I never promised to allow any pictures to be sent to Paris. I would have gladly exhibited could all the phases of my work have been represented at the same time. I felt that would have encroached on space to which my brother artists were entitled. Finding I could not have the requisite space and cheerfully conceding the justice of the situation, I positively refused to be represented by a single picture which is not fairly representative of my present work. I am indignant at the effort to represent me against my will and consent, in a manner to which I especially object." ("That Picture for Paris Row," *New York Herald*, 9 March 1889, p. 4). Meanwhile, Thomas B. Clarke, Inness's friend and agent, was blamed for failing to aid the jury and the artist and for failing to lend one of his many paintings by Inness to the exhibition. Clarke responded that he had kept his pictures ready for the jury until 12 February, the deadline for submissions, and had previously loaned many works by the artist to exhibitions in Washington, Chicago, and St. Louis. Inness came to Clarke's defense in a letter to the editor of the *New York Herald*, published on 10 March 1889. At the end of the letter, he refers to Roswell Smith, founder of The Century Company, who purchased his *Niagara Falls* (Museum of Fine Arts, Boston) in 1884 for the then princely sum of $5,000. The New York banker George I. Seney and Benjamin (B.) Altman, founder of the department store that bore his name, were both collectors of Inness's work.]

[Montclair, New Jersey // 9 March 1889]

Dear Sir:

In your paper of the 8th inst. certain remarks are made concerning Mr. T. B. Clarke in which my name is mentioned.

All I have to say is that as far as I am concerned Mr. Clarke has in no way influenced my action in this matter of exhibition. I have had friends urging me to exhibit to whose influence I did give way so far as to commence finishing several important works which had been lying for some time unfinished in my studio; but as I had really no heart in the matter, I could not find the requisite energy to do myself justice. Besides, money was before me to be earned, which I did not feel that I could afford to lose.

As for the charge of the want of patriotism, I care about as much as I do for the wind of the wood.

To the friends who have supported me am I alone responsible as an artist, and it is my proper business in this relation to make their interests one with my own, and I am satisfied that my interests are not to be served through the Art Commission.

I am free to confess that I am greatly indebted to Mr. Thomas B. Clarke for his determined faith in my art, and his persistent efforts to find purchasers for my works; and if art is of use and my reputation sound, then is T. B. Clarke deserving of gratitude from the public, and not of contumely.

What Mr. Clarke has done for me through the extent of my ability to win success he has done for many others through the extent of their ability to win success.

My art is not in its nature of a popular character, and had it not been for the generosity of Mr. Roswell Smith, Mr. George I. Seney, and Mr. B. Altman, together with the persistent efforts of Mr. Clarke, I should probably still be in the drag.

Yours respectfully, // GEORGE INNESS.

To the Editor of The New York "Herald."

Speech on Henry George (20 January 1890)

[Inness supported the ideas of the social reformer Henry George (FIG. 30), who advocated, among other things, a single tax (a tax on land) and free trade. The artist attended a "farewell dinner" for Henry George during a visit to New York in January 1890. It was held at the Metropolitan Hotel, located at Broadway and Prince Street. Inness probably belonged to a New York or New Jersey branch of the "single tax club," whose members hosted the dinner. Representatives from several branches of the club attended and gave speeches in Henry George's honor. Inness's speech is reproduced here. This text was discovered and first published by Leo Mazow. See his "George Inness, Henry George, the Single Tax, and the Future Poet" in the Selected Bibliography.]

It has been assumed, and is still assumed generally, that poverty is a natural evil, and under present circumstances I am willing to accept it as such; but I think in one who accepts the doctrine of the single tax, it must be a logical conclusion that when that doctrine comes to be applied, that poverty will become an unnecessary evil. (Applause.) For although I accept the great democratic ideal which involves that of absolute justice I see, being an idealist, that that proposed ideal can never be absolutely attained. But without that ideal no progress can be made. (Applause.)

FIG. 30. Henry George, photograph, n. d., The Henry George Foundation.

The ideal is ever the precursor of all that is done, and could we reach any condition which we assumed to be the ideal, the ideal would cease to exist. The evil of poverty will become unnecessary under the adoption of the single tax, because then we can trace the poverty to the individual as the author of his own difficulty. At present we can not help seeing it arises out of false social conditions. Under such a condition of things as we believe will come about with the adoption and practice of the single tax, the laborer will be no longer obliged to give the whole of his labor to the one who employs him. Again, he will not be obliged to beg of another work that he needs and bread to live upon.

Now I am a believer in spiritual trust because I believe that spiritual trust lies at the bottom of all voices of truth. I do not necessarily, therefore, believe in any story that may be presented to me; it may be true and it may not be true; it may be like the story of the cock and bull, but the substance involved in many that appear untrue frequently contains truths more profound than the political or financial prophets are capable of perceiving.

We hear a great deal of talk now about the goodness of the human heart; I deny it in toto. I do not believe a bit of it. I believe the heart is positively and distressingly weak. It is against sound logic, and a man who begins business or would commence to do anything on that theory is pretty sure to fail. (Applause.)

Some think there will be a great struggle in the single tax. Single tax is a straightforward, rational truth, and it will appear little by little to every individual mind until the majority will grow so large that the other side will be as nothing. It grows as the tree grows, naturally; it will develop to the ideal as I desire to have my picture developed, naturally, by attending not to my own desire, but in approaching an ideal.

There is much of statesmanship, there is much of false policy in the world at present; false thinking, false education, all this will disappear as soon as the man is free from that necessary want that exists under our present political condition. And your science, your literature will increase and the general intelligence of the whole community will increase the freer you make the individual, for society is made up by the individual, and if the individual is wrong society will be wrong.

At present there is one principle, a commercial principle, I mean a financial principle, that is universally accepted, that is that a thing that will not pay for itself must be discontinued. Society at this present day is not self-supporting: instead of being self-supporting it is supported by the individual. The individual has certain rights to that which he pays for. That which he does not create belongs to the community, and that is land.

Statement on *Sunset in the Woods* (23 July 1891)

[Inness almost never explained or described his paintings. This statement, recorded in a letter to Thomas B. Clarke in 1891, represents a rare exception. It refers to *Sunset in the Woods* (FIG. 31) and reveals an intriguing creative process, whereby the painting originated in a sketch made twenty years earlier and then developed over the course of several years. For Inness, sensory distance from the motif stimulated the artist's and the viewer's imagination.]

The Pines   Montclair N. J.
July 23d 1891

My Dear Mr. Clarke,

The motive for the picture was taken from a sketch made near Hastings Westchester Co. [New York] over twenty years ago. I commenced this picture several years since but until last winter I had not obtained any idea commensurate

FIG. 31. George Inness, *Sunset in the Woods*, 1891, oil on canvas, 48 x 70", The Corcoran Gallery of Art, Washington, D.C., Museum Purchase, Gallery Fund.

with the impression received on the spot. The rocks and general formation are like the place but the trees especially the beach [*sic*] are increased in size.

The idea is to represent an effect of light in the wood towards sundown but to allow the imagination to predominate.

[unsigned]

"Unite and Succeed" (August 1894)

[In 1894, the United States was in the second year of what would become a four-year economic depression, the worst in the history of the country to date. In April, the political activist Jacob Coxey led a group of unemployed workers on a protest march—the first significant popular march of its kind—on Washington, D.C., to demand the creation of new jobs in public works. *The American Federationist*, in which this article first appeared, was the official magazine of the American Federation of Labor (AFL). The article was published only four months after the march and remains an extraordinary statement of Inness's populist beliefs.]

All labor journals published throughout the land contain interesting facts and statements concerning the financial, political and industrial topics that should be read with interest by every intelligent worker from the Atlantic to the Pacific. But for instructive and entertaining literature, the FEDERATIONIST excels any labor paper I have ever had the pleasure of reading. It advocates the eight hour system. This fact alone should make it a welcome visitor in the home of every laborer. The time has come when eight hours should constitute a day's work. This fact is demonstrated by the idle men seen in every State of the Union. New and improved machinery is continually crowding the masses out of employment, consequently a reduction of the hours of labor is an imperative necessity. Were the eight hour system now in vogue, it would require five men to perform the labor done by four men under the present ten hour system. This would reduce the recruits of Coxey's army and the idle men in every community. There are many who state that ten hours are none too much for a day's labor, but they read little, if any, and are not posted on the necessities of the country. There are many who are contented to work ten hours, for the same reason that a slave in the Southern States was contented to be a slave fifty years ago, that is they know no better. There were excuses however for the slave. He was illiterate, was born and reared in slavery, had no opportunity for acquiring knowledge, and had no voice in the laws that subjected him to the tyranny of bondage; he was therefore a slave by compulsion. On the other hand, there is no excuse of the laborers of to-day (many of whom are a little better off than a well kept slave of fifty years ago), submitting to the tyranny of combining capitalists and corporations. As they unite to oppress you and keep you and your posterity in slavery and ignorance, unite ye also; for in unity is power. Remember the thirteen original colonies realized the power of unity in 1776; the residents of these colonies were no more than slaves to England then than you are to monopoly now. Therefore unite, use your power at the ballot box and educate yourselves, do not continue to vote yourselves slaves and forge the chains that bind you in bondage. There are no excuses for the voluntary slaves of to-day, as more than ninety per cent of the workers of the land can read, and it is a duty they owe themselves, their fellowmen, and their posterity, to read and discuss the industrial, political and financial questions of to-day. I am so happy to say that men who earn their bread by the sweat of their brow, are beginning to realize that neither the Republican or Democratic parties are doing or have ever done anything to better the condition of the toiling masses, and that their only hope is in uniting and sustaining each other and meeting capitalists and grasping monopolists in the battle for bread, and as an interested worker I would recommend the FEDERATIONIST to all laboring classes as an educator.

———◆•◆•◆———

Poems

[In writing poetry, Inness joins and augments the important tradition of the American artist-poet. His predecessors in this field included Washington Allston and Thomas Cole; his contemporaries and successors included Elihu Vedder, Albert Pinkham Ryder, and Marsden Hartley.

Inness's poem "The Whirlwind" is reprinted above, pages 124–25, in his Letter to the Editor of *New-York Daily Tribune* of 11 April 1878. Four additional poems, entitled "Address of the Clouds to the Earth," "Love," "Despair," and "The Pilgrim," are included in G. W. Sheldon, "George Inness," *Harper's Weekly Magazine* 26:1322 (22 April 1882): 244–46, which we have reprinted in full below, pages 174–79. Sheldon also reprinted the first part of "The Leaves and the Brook." See References for the sources of the transcriptions here.]

The Leaves and the Brook

Each, as we fall, that, gathered
By the tide, glides onward to the
Ocean waves tells it of brothers—
Little truths from off the trees of life
Earth-embosomed; while we, tossed
On the stormy wave, and moulded
By the deep, salting the waters of
Far-stretching memories, do there
Preserve the story of our brotherhood,
That truth may find her likeness
Here upon the sea and there upon the land.
Through that great power which pulsates
Nature into life (truth to its substance
Joined) we form an ever-flowing stream,

Which pours along that conscious shore
Where memory stands, the image of
The past—a present good.
Struggle on looking upward
Saint within and fool without.
Acts against thy conscience, moving
Sin to fear and truth to doubt.
But above, all overruling
In thy sin the saint is waiting.
Voice of God and voice of spirit
Truth and love are still creating.
Who is God and what is spirit?
Truth the one and love the other.
Father, mother of the mind
Both in thee, thy elder brother.
Gently through enclosing forest
Leading by his touch and word,
All he asks is but compunction
For the fault that has occurred.

Exaltation

Sing joyfully!
Earth-bound no more,
We rise.
Creation speaks anew
In brighter tones.
Life now enthrones
Its imaged forms,
Winged with a joy that
Ne'er from nature grew.

Sing joyfully!
The Lord has come.
We live.
Released, the spirit flies,

Robed with the light
Above earth's night,
A symphony.
We sweep along in song that never dies.

Sing joyfully!
Bright nature lives
In us.
Thought, sight, and sound,
Mind—all are one.
To gentle souls
We whisper thought echoes of loves profound.

Sing joyfully!
Life's sympathies
Speak truth.
Doubts but disease.
Resurrection is affection,
Spirit wakening,
From earth's tides to voyage o'er brighter seas.

Sing joyfully!
A real world we see.
Earth's meadows and its hills
Within thy heart
Their joys impart
To us as well as thee.
Sing joyfully!
God all space fills.

Destiny

O Being, wilt thou tell me what I am to thee and thou to me?
When all Nature bows beneath the load of world-enforced cares
　　My spirit weeps within the close circumference of a withered heart; and then necessity, a giant form, intrudes upon my sight.
　　Me, with his iron pressure baring, as in prison bound, from all those joys

which made this now so creeping time pass with the rapid stride with which the bounding blood of youth doth ever travel. While with a chill monotony his clammy breath falls on my ear in tones that shrivel all my thoughts to one fell word, which echoes through the empty chambers of my soul, nor leaves a cranny where my consciousness can hide itself from the dread sound of destiny.

Elect not whither thou shalt go, for thou art bound, forever prison bound, by me. I—I am destiny! And yet my quickened conscience tells me I am free.

Child of my love, son of that womb which is my other self, speak not against decree; for law is thy necessity, and as decree goes forth, so tireless mind builds it a home. That home is thee. Thou art thine own decree, yet see it not, for youth is blind to what is ever near us, thou the present heat or cold of life. And such is thy decree.

My footsteps sound along the shores of time, the measure of thy love. The note is low, nor is it in the power of sound to form a sweeter harmony than that which makes my step decree time's law to every occupant of nature's wide domain.

I am thy destiny; and I destine thee to be thine own decree. Yet never wilt thou touch the note that love decrees to thee till in thine own decree and, as with me, so is't with thee. All law is mine, and what is mine my love bestows, nor can withhold itself from being what it is to thee.

My law is thy necessity, yet what I give to thee is thine to use as best shall see thee fit. Necessity is not the giant of thy fears, but law compelling all, create to meet thy heart's desires.

I am thy life. To live is first necessity, and life I give. There is no absolute to thee but me. My movement is creation, and creation is that other self where I have formed my womb. There do I cease to be myself, and give to thee the touch that sets thee free, and brings thee to the knowledge of a world which I inhabit not, but where I do provide such imageries as shall convince thy being. Consciousness of the first truth which I create, reality—there I am nearer to thee than thyself, hidden within the consciousness of being, in what I am—life.

I cause all things to appear to thee. I move in thee. To touch, to know that law arrests desire, here to create in thee, nor does allow its energy to waste itself from thee, but so returns it all that in the consciousness of me thou 'rt conscious of thyself, thou 'rt free.

Did I who called thee into life impose the unit of my person on thy every sense? No image, then, could meet thy gaze, no sense of touch be thine. Thou 'dst cease to choose to be. But through the varied forms which I create by my infinity I offer thee the power of choice, and so from it, through nature, can redeem thy mortal thought to learn those truths within the bounds of which my all-creating will may lead thy spirit upward in eternal flight through worlds unknown to earthly eye or touch.

There where I rest in thee, as consciousness in all, I the substance of the world create, do thou gaze, and so excite desire, that thou of thine own life's necessity may 'st choose; for from the point where I conjoin in you of my full heart I give the will to thine own choice, which filled, my spirit moves to thine own joy, there to be free. Thus will is free, for unto every living thing my love goes forth, that they may take as theirs what yet is mine. This dual power of which I am the sole and only being I represent to thee, in that thou art the counterpart of yet another self with whom in union thou may 'st ever grow and never full the point attain where you are perfect one. So do I in all nature image forth myself that there may form a law which, as men multiply, shall serve to guide these yet unborn to endless time to that eternal destiny which love in them shall form. As unto life is she thine own desire counterpart, so is thyself to me. From thy desire is formed the image of thy choice, where housed in form as plays your nature love, quick memory builds the image of thy nature's self, the female of thy will. To worship here is then to love, and in the fond embrace, where light should dwell, and understanding form an Eden for the soul, thou givest life to fiery form, create of thought alone, who bind thee with a triple chain of fancied ills, and turn the Eden where I destined thee into a hell of fear, where trembling terrors mock my words of love and turn thy life to hate. The serpent tongue of lust beguiles with logic form thy selfhood's self to meet thee with the fruit of fate, to eat of which is death.

Thus is thy nature formed to be the subject of a choice in which no whit of evil is but good to grow in thee in varied forms when thou dost look to me and know that I am life, not thee. I to provide, I to fulfil what through thy conscious being thou shalt feel is thine, yet know is mine. Then shall my law as truth thine understanding fill with light, and in its glow my will in thee with bow and spear, the serpent of deceit shalt drive from out the precincts of the mind and every minion thought that fouls the aim of life thy lightening will, with loud resonant sound, shall clear away, and give me thee and paradise.

[Untitled]

A spirit came to me last night and said:
"I've seen the working of thy mind in thought.

As flowering trees within our worlds, they give out odor,
And when breezes from our Lord among
Their branches move their leaves to gentle rustling
They give out with its smell soft,
Zephyr sounds that yet are never sad,
But rise into a clearer tone at times
Like summer music.

"There is again a gloaming light
Which creeps along what seems the
Understructure of our home,
When questions agitate they [*sic*] mind and all
Thy brain is laboring with the hard and fearful
Logic of creation's mystery.
We see the laborer in the morning dawn
Delving with necessary toil the charitable globe.
And from the fullness of our souls let tear-drops fall,
Quickening the dews of love in tender sympathy at the
    masculine endeavor.
But yet we love the music most."

The spirit turned, and then revealed the features of an
    early day
When arm in arm we blessed the rising sun and cheered
    ourselves in one another's love as day declined.
One golden sunset found myself alone.
Since then she said the chord that bound us one, to outward
    eye unseen, has only finer spun,
And now within thy brain I see the heart
I loved in its reality.
Nor age to pale the fire, nor poverty, nor any ill
That earth can show to force itself between what thou art
    to me
And I to thee.
How good is God, and now with all these years of snow I, too,
    can say,
How good is God!

REFLECTIONS ON
INNESS'S LIFE AND WORK

George Inness, Jr., *Life, Art, and Letters of George Inness* (1917 / excerpts)

[The following excerpts from George Inness, Jr.'s biography feature Inness's identity as a painter and amateur philosopher. Written with the bias of filial admiration, they nevertheless provide a rich variety of kinds of information about Inness—"Pop," to his son (FIG. 32). Some parts are clear—such as the description of Inness's enthusiasm when seeing paintings by the old masters for the first time—and some rather obscure, such as the account of his belief that it would only be "through the awakening of perception of scientific genius firmly grounded in religious conviction" that a new "spiritual science" could arise. (On this subject, see Rachael Ziady DeLue, *George Inness and the Science of Landscape*, in the Selected Bibliography.) Many excerpts provide lighter fare: for example, descriptions of Inness skating in Medfield,

FIG. 32. George Inness, Jr., photograph, n. d., Local History Collection, Montclair Public Library, Montclair, New Jersey.

Massachusetts, where he and his family lived from 1860 to 1864. Through these texts, we also gain insight into Inness's proprietary relationship to his paintings, his relationships with clients and with other artists, and his constant need to improve his work. As a whole, they help us to construct a humanistic portrait of the artist.]

Inness's early inclinations toward painting:

Of delicate health, and endowed with a keenly sensitive nature, the boy was considered "different." He was a dreamer, an idealist from earliest childhood, and lived much in a world of his own imaginings. In speaking of his aims and ambitions, my father once told me that his desires first began to crystallize when, as a very little chap, he saw a man painting a picture out in a field. Immediately a responsive chord was struck, and his own nebulous groping for self-expression became at once a concrete idea. Then and there he made up his mind that when he grew up he would be a painter. He told me that he thought it the most wonderful thing in the world to make with paint the things that he saw around him, clouds, trees, sunsets, and storms, the very things that brought him fame in later years. He told me with what awe he viewed the difficulty of getting a piece of paper big enough, for he thought that to paint a landscape one had to have a paper as large as the scene itself—a thought as naïvely conceived as it was expressed, which showed even then the breadth and largeness of his nature as manifested in feeling and expression in his canvases.

Inness upon discovering the old masters and the works of Thomas Cole and Asher B. Durand:

"One afternoon," said Inness, "when I was completely dispirited and disgusted, I gave over work and went out for a walk. In a print-shop window I noticed an engraving after one of the old masters. I do not remember what picture it was. I could not then analyze that which attracted me in it, but it fascinated me. The print-seller showed me others, and they repeated the same sensation in me. There was a power of motive, a bigness of grasp, in them. They were nature, rendered grand instead of being belittled by trifling detail and puny execution. I began to take them out with me to compare them with nature as she really appeared, and the light began to dawn. I had no originals to study, but I found some of their qualities in Cole and Durand, to which I had access. There was a lofty striving in Cole, although he did not technically realize that for which he reached. There was in Durand a more intimate feeling of nature. 'If,' thought I, 'these two can only be combined! I will try!'"

The opening of Inness's first studio; Ogden Haggerty as his first patron:

He now opened his first studio, and began to paint according to the new ideas he had obtained from the study of the old prints. Not only friends, but fellow-artists, so called, tried to persuade him that he could never paint that way. Set rules were laid down for painting landscapes, and they must not be violated by a mere upstart boy who would not paint his foreground trees brown, and who persisted in leaving out the plant, the foreground plant, the key to the Hudson River school. In consequence his struggle for existence became more acute, until his brothers finally had to come to the rescue, and for several years kept his head above water by buying his pictures and reselling them when and where they could. His contempt for the commercial aspect of life was profound, and he made no attempt to conceal it. He has expressed himself many times in tones that left no room for contradiction that business was obligated to sustain art, and that merchants were created only to support artists.

Despite the opposition against which he battled there were a few progressive souls dominant enough and wise enough to recognize and proclaim genius. One day when Inness was out in the open square sketching a crowd gathered around him and gazed with awe. Such things as artists painting in the parks were unheard of in those days. The crowd, having satisfied its curiosity, melted away; but there remained one man whose interest was more than idle curiosity, for when the sketch was nearly complete he said to the young painter:

"If you will bring the picture to my house when you finish it, I will give you a hundred dollars for it."

That man was Ogden Haggerty, a prominent auctioneer in New York. He was the first to recognize my father's possibilities, and later became so convinced of his genius that he sent him abroad to study, and was one of the main factors in his development as a painter.

Inness's activities and studio in Medfield, Massachusetts, where the family lived from June 1860 until 1864:
[In this excerpt, Inness, Jr., refers to a passage at the beginning of his biography in which he describes his earliest memory: watching his father paint washtubs (p. 3).]

A sport that my father loved was skating and we had many parties on the Charles River in winter. When Pop skated he wore a shawl—in fact, nearly all men wore shawls in those days—and with his long, black hair and plaid shawl floating in the breeze, he cut a figure that in my young eyes was the quintessence of grace.

On our place in Medfield there was an old barn which was converted into a studio. My father's studios were nearly always old barns; there was none of the poseur or dilettante about him. He was perfectly content with one chair, an easel, and his tubes of paint. He never had such things as attractive rugs or broken plates or bits of rags and silk about his place. He never could do clever tricks with his pencil to amuse, and never was attracted by the so-called artistic room with Oriental hangings, and used to ridicule old plates and cups and saucers and canopied divans and Japanese umbrellas. There was nothing luxurious about his studio; it was his workroom, and was simplicity almost to bareness.

In this old Medfield barn some of father's most representative pictures were painted; there he painted many of the magnificent sunsets and elms and those dramatic storms which characterize George Inness. The original sketch of one of the finest examples of his work was done there. It was called "Medfield Meadows," and later was a wedding present from him to my wife and me.

Those were wonderful years for me. I used to sit there in his studio for hours at a time watching him paint, pictures now, not wash-tubs, while I, with a white canvas before me, a large brush, and a pail of water, imitated his movements.

When he painted he put all the force of his nature into it. Full of vim and vigor, he was like a dynamo. It was a punch here and dab there. He was indefatigable. He was a totally different man in his studio from what he was out of doors. Out of doors he was quiet, rational, absorbed. I have seen him sit in the same spot every day for a week or more studying carefully and minutely the contours of trees and the composition of the clouds and grass, drawing very carefully with painstaking exactness. But in his studio he was like a madman. He seldom painted direct from nature. He would study for days, then with a sudden inspiration would go at a canvas with the most dynamic energy, creating the composition from his own brain, but with so thorough an underlying knowledge of nature that the key-note of his landscapes was always truth and sincerity and absolute fidelity to nature. It was his honesty and simplicity that made him great.

"Never put anything on your canvas that isn't of use," he would say; "never use a detail unless it means something." He would start a marine or shipwreck, and with a gesture of impatience would say, "Oh, confound it! that doesn't look like water," and with a few swift strokes would put in some grass and trees, and more than likely, before he got through, it would be a snow-scene.

On Inness's friendship with William Page and their discussions on art and Swedenborgian doctrine; Inness and his love of "talking theory":
[Inness almost certainly had known the portraitist and Swedenborgian William Page since August 1851, when the two artists rented studio space in the same building on the Via Sant'Apollonia in Florence. Inness, Jr., refers to Eagleswood, the social reform community in Perth Amboy, New Jersey, where Inness was a resident artist from 1864 to 1867, and to Sir William Cornelius Van Horne, the Canadian railroad builder and art collector.]

Fortunately for my father, William Page, the portrait-painter, a one-time president of the [National] Academy of Design, was living at Eagleswood when we moved there. They became warm friends, and Page brought to my father the teachings of Emanuel Swedenborg. This philosophy came at the time of his life when he most needed something to lift him out of himself and the limited doctrines of orthodox creeds. He threw himself into its teachings with all the fire and enthusiasm of his nature, and although he did not adhere strictly to its tenets, it led to other metaphysical research, and he at last truly found that form of expression for which he had searched throughout his life—the consciousness of God in his soul manifested in every experience of his life.

During the latter part of his life he wrote constantly on these subjects, though few things were published. He was full of theories of art, religion and ethics, and would talk theory and preach theory to all who would listen to him. It made no difference whether they agreed with him or even understood; he kept right on talking theory. I have seen him pin a man to a chair and pound his ideas into him for hours at a time until he and his listener were both exhausted. One summer when my father and mother were visiting me at St. Andrews, New Brunswick, they met Sir William Van Horne, a most charming and cultivated Canadian gentleman. One evening after dinner my father cornered Sir William, and for hours poured into him his theories of Swedenborg, Henry George, the single tax, and paint, pounding each word in with a jab of his forefinger, until the poor fellow, in utter desperation, tore himself away and retired. The next morning when Sir William went out on the piazza he found father in the same chair and in the same attitude as when he had left him. Catching sight of Van Horne, father picked up the thread of discourse where he had left off the night before, and went on with his lecture. Sir William confided to me that he wondered if my father had kept it up all night, not knowing that he had gone to bed.

The single tax was a theme that interested my father very much. It was one of his pet theories. In telling me the foregoing story, Sir William was reminded of another, à propos of this topic.

"I entertained at dinner a number of distinguished Australians," he said, "among them an eminent publicist. The single tax excites much ridicule and discussion in Australia, and your father, as you know, had become an ardent Georgite. The talk at dinner turned upon the tax, and the Australian view was expounded at length by the distinguished publicist. Inness sat silent, his burning, black eyes under his black and shaggy fell of hair, fixed upon the orator, who talked the more complacently in the consciousness of so appreciative a listener. When his arguments were exhausted and the speaker paused, Inness shot from his seat, and thrust his forefinger into the speaker's face with, 'Did you mean what you said?' Then followed the most amazing exhibition of reasoning and

logic I have ever witnessed. With a display of memory and a grasp of understanding that was marvelous to see, Inness brought up every statement the great
publicist had made, showing his utter clumsiness of reasoning, putting his logic
to confusion, and exposing his falsity of statement.

"After propounding his theories with a conviction that made the audience
speechless, your father rounded up those giant Australians like so many sheep,
and literally drove them into the drawing-room. I have never seen anything like
it," said Sir William. "It was amazing the way he silenced that speaker with facts.
It was too good to be true."

**Inness's ruminations, in one of his unpublished manuscripts, on the need for
a new kind of science, a "spiritual science":**

"No man can possibly know what is good for another; he can only enjoy and
give of what he enjoys through the connected ministrations of the human race.
Error is in giving voice to the states that are not enjoyed. This science is bound
to be correct. For the word of Good (God) cannot be perverted without punish-
ment. 'As ye think, so are ye.'

"It can be only through the awakening of perception of scientific genius
firmly grounded in religious conviction that such a science—for a science it
must be, though unlimited—can become a possibility. Much has been said
about a scientific religion, and many appear to have hoped for it; but a new system of faith can be formed only upon what has preceded it, and to be a religious
faith it must be in accord with the universal bond of human sentiment. Science,
even unlimited, cannot make a faith any more than it can make a soul. Its truths
serve only to confirm. A spiritual science must be an inspiration from or through
the religious mind into the scientific mind."

**On the manifestation of the divine in human life through consciousness,
from an unpublished manuscript:**

[In this excerpt, from the same or a different manuscript, Inness refers to the
new form of expression that the "spiritual science" will take. The bracketed text
is from his son's transcription.]

"Its forms [of expression] may be various, but from its center comes the true
light which lighteth every man that cometh into the world.

"If we accept the philosophy that man was made in the image and likeness
of God, our hope of attaining an idea of God or the infinite cause for which

science is searching is not only by investigating or classifying material forms, but by subjecting such classification to laws or principles inherent as the properties or attributes of the reasoning mind. Let us endeavor, then, to clothe or illustrate an idea of the mind or thought in a form fitted to material comprehension by considering such idea as a point or center from which are intellectual radiations, in fact, as the reality or truth of a center of motion.

"Such a point can be considered only as the creation of being itself, which being is in us the affection or touch of life, felt as the consciousness of something existing as a substantial entity, which I appreciate as an idea from myself as an active center of thought, yet my idea proceeds from my peculiar affection of form of life, hidden from my understanding, partaking of its quality or substance, and from it radiates my thought, propelled by the extension of my life, creating in my ultimate act ideas of sensation or conviction of that which is not me, but which confirms me as an individual center, or the idea of selfhood."

George Inness and William Page debate the identity (and even existence) of "the middle tone":

There was only one subject that I know of that Page and my father disagreed upon; that subject was what they called "the middle tone." Now, the middle tone was Page's idea. He claimed that the horizon should be a middle tone: that is, it should be half-way between the lightest light and the greatest dark in the picture. Father agreed with him on that point, but what they could not agree upon was just what a middle tone really was. So Page, to explain more fully, took a strip of tin and painted it white at one end and black at the other, and then graded in stripes from both ends until it reached a gray tone in the middle. This he showed to my father and said triumphantly, "There's the true middle tone!" The next day father went to Page's studio with a similar strip of tin and declared that he had the true middle tone. When they compared the two hues, there was no resemblance between them. Then the fight was on, and these two gentlemen, after yelling themselves hoarse and saying some very uncomplimentary things to each other, would break away, and not speak to each other for days. Then they would come together again and resume the argument with renewed vigor. These hostilities were kept up, off and on for two years, when Page built himself a house on Staten Island and painted it white, then glazed it down to a middle tone. In a few months the sun had faded out the middle tone; at which my father declared that there was no such thing as a middle tone, anyhow, and that Page was a fool.

**On Inness's friendship with the painter Jack Monks, from an article origi-
nally published in the Boston *Transcript* and reprinted by Inness, Jr.:**

[Inness, Jr., refers to the American painter and etcher John ("Jack") Austin Sands
Monks, who shared studio space with his father in Boston during the late 1870s,
and to the American landscape painter George Nelson Cass. See below, pages
221–22, for C. S. Pietro's account of Monk's experiences with Inness.]

Mr. Monks' acquaintance with the master began in a way that he is naturally
and honestly proud to recall. Inness had dropped into the studio of George N.
Cass and his eye had fallen upon the realistic study of a willow tree.

"Who painted that?" he demanded in his brusk manner.

"A pupil of mine, a young beginner named Monks," replied Cass.

"Tell him to come over and see me."

A few days later young Monks presented himself at the new studio of Inness.
His first reception at interrupting the eccentric painter at his work was somewhat disconcerting, but as soon as it was explained that he was the painter of the
willow tree at Cass's, the great man's manner instantly changed; he begged the
young man to move in at once and bring over all of his things, and when this
was done requested him to place his easel in the same room, to help himself to
materials, overhaul the sketches, and in all ways to treat the premises as his own.
This intimate companionship lasted throughout Inness's residence in Boston,
including a painting campaign in the White Mountains, and was renewed later
when both artists were in New York City.

Mr. Monks' affectionate reverence for his great master is unbounded, but he
admits that his advice and teaching were not seldom bewildering. It was as difficult for the younger man to follow the elder's instructions as to model any particular methods upon so erratic and many-sided a style. One day Inness would
insist that the foundation or keynote of every landscape should be black;
another day it would be red that he believed to be the true basis. Having had
the advantage of no technical or academic instruction he was continually
sounding about and feeling his way for himself through intense ratiocination on
art and ceaseless studies of nature. He often lamented this lack of early experience in the school work of art, and acknowledged that it would have been a
shorter cut to his tardy success and have saved him an incalculable amount of
labor and discouragement while he was thus finding out the limitations and
possibilities of painting. But it may well be questioned whether quite the same
results of his powerful inventiveness and originality would have been developed

had he been spared the struggles which finally matured his Titanic strength.

Inness painted very rapidly, and if his pictures could have been taken away from him at the proper moment, Mr. Monks says, he would have completed a painting a day. But he would follow a sunset through its successive phases, until it became a maze of contradictions. He would sometimes change a broad sunlight effect of one day into a moonlight or "gray day" the next. He would paint from a sketch two years old with the same fervor, or more, than he would paint before nature; and yet he was a most faithful and ardent student of nature, and would dwell with tremendous force and effect upon the minutest details when he felt them to be essential to an effect or when making studies for future use. On the other hand he would revel in the "interpretation," as he called it, of the merest pencil sketch of another artist, or in painting from a few wild scratches of his own made at random to see what he could evolve from them. Per contra, he once studied with enormous care an oak tree against a brilliant sunset, painting the leaves so that they almost seemed to rustle. He could get more varieties of foliage into a picture, so as to be distinguished even in the distance, than any painter of our day. He had a touch for each kind of tree that expressed it instantly and perfectly. In painting a large picture before a great subject, as for instance Mount Washington, he would change it every day, so sensitive and receptive was he to every impression and eager to include every phrase, and leave it at the last a mass of "mud." At a safe distance, however, both of space and time, and with only his notes to rely upon he would complete a masterpiece upon the same subject.

"I well remember," said Mr. Monks, "the day we went out to make our first sketch together. He gave minute instructions about drawing in the lines and frotting in the masses and we went to work. After an hour of diligent silence, Mr. Inness came around to my picture and exclaimed, 'By Jove, you've got it better than I.' Then he added, 'Now paint in the mountain solid for background,' and when this instruction, diametrically opposed to what had preceded, had been executed, with the dire result to be foreseen under any ordinary methods of painting, the hilarity of the great man at the tyro's discomfiture was like that of a mischievous boy." Another characteristic incident was the scene in the Boston studio at the execution of the great Inness canvas intended for the Philadelphia exhibition—which, by the way, was not sent. He had brought home from Italy the study for the picture—which represented the grounds of a palace or villa overlooking the Mediterranean with an imposing procession of straight stone pines, which was always a favorite effect of his. He wanted a new sky painted into the picture, and Monks and his son George were given a large quantity of the blue color selected, and, mounting stepladders, worked carefully the whole sky over, while Inness busied himself below on the foreground. Towards night the result of this triplicate effort was viewed through a looking-glass, and through the legs of the painters, according to the custom of artists, and the atmospheric effect pronounced simply immense. The next morning Inness rose at an early hour and before either of his collaborators had arrived, the entire sky had been changed to a gray and with it the whole color scheme of the picture.

Inness was not, Mr. Monks says, as might be supposed from the fluency of his utterance and the vigor of his thinking on many subjects, an incessant talker at his work. When he talked it was always on some question of the principles of art or some phase of nature; it was never about himself or anybody else. He had no personal gossip or small talk about his contemporaries, no envy, jealousy or grudges, although at times his criticism was severe, and even savage upon popular favorites; entirely on general grounds, however, and from serious conviction, not spite. He was nobody's fool in business matters, but was generous to a remarkable degree towards any cause or person interesting him. His consideration and painstaking in the teaching he gave Mr. Monks (he never took pupils as a regular thing, he would never have a customer even in his studio that he did not like) are looked back to now as something beautiful and extraordinary by its recipient. He once came to his studio when business was blue with the young painter, and within two hours a dealer had been sent who cheered things up; but Inness absented himself for a fortnight in order not to be thanked.

Inness's working habits in New York, c. 1870s:
[Although this excerpt is rather long, indeed nearly all of Chapter VIII of Inness, Jr.'s biography, it presents Inness as a working artist. We see how he so relished the *process* of painting that he even lost interest in a work after he had completed it. Yet what was completion? His struggle to define this elusive condition often meant that he would destroy a painting in the process of reworking it. His somewhat virulent side emerged in his painful reaction to his son's modest criticism. Having studied art in Paris, the son was, by the 1870s, a working artist in his own right. The excerpt also highlights Inness's disdain for images that aspired to imitate reality, notably trompe l'oeil paintings. They were, in his view, simply a "lie" and gave no "sensation of truth." "Lizzie" is his nickname for his wife, Elizabeth Abigail Hart Inness.]

For a while during the New York period my father and I had a studio together in the old Booth Theater at Broadway and Sixth Avenue. Pop was growing richer and broader in expression with his maturer years and accumulated knowledge.

When he painted he painted at a white heat. Passionate, dynamic in his force, I have seen him sometimes like a madman, stripped to the waist, perspiration rolling like a mill-race from his face, with some tremendous idea struggling for expression. After a picture was complete it lost all value for him. He had no more interest in it. What was his masterpiece one day would be "dishwater" and "twaddle" the next. He would take a canvas before the paint was really dry, and, being seized with another inspiration, would paint over it. I have known him to paint as many as half a dozen or more pictures on one canvas, in fact, as many as the canvas would hold. One day he called my mother and me into the studio and showed us a picture that he had just completed.

"There, Lizzie," he said, "I've at last done the thing that I have been trying for all my life. I've done it this time. I've got it at last. Ah, that's it, and it's so easy. See the effect? I can do it every time now. It's just the easiest thing in the world. Can do it just as easy as eat. Well, Georgie, what do you think of it?"

"Why, Pop," I said, "it's beautiful. You have got it; your color and light couldn't be improved upon. It's beautiful. It's a masterpiece."

Several days after that I came into the studio and found father pacing up and down the floor in a nervous, excitable sort of way, saying:

"There, I have got it this time. Thought I had it before. Light and color weren't right; but I've got it this time all right. Just the thing I want."

I went over to the easel and looked at the canvas. My heart sank. It was ruined! I didn't say a word. I couldn't. I wanted to cry. The beautiful composition of the week before had been entirely painted over. For a while neither of us spoke; then my father, who was by that time highly nervous, growled out:

"Well?" I didn't answer. "Well?" he snapped. "What have you got to say about it?"

"Oh, nothing, Pop. Only what did you do it for?"

"Now, there you go!" he snapped, and began to stamp up and down the floor. "What do you know about it, anyhow?" He slammed the palette down on the table. "Can't you see I've improved it? Can't you see what I've done? Look how much better it is now. Why, before it was dish-water, pea-soup. It had no character. Now it means something. What did I send you over to Paris to study for? Come here telling me what to do! You don't know anything about it. Get out of here! Get out! I don't want you around."

[Inness, Jr., describes how, "hurt and disappointed," he retuned to his parents' home for dinner. A glum mood prevailed; not much was eaten. Later that evening, the son returned to the studio where he and his father worked and where he generally spent the night. He discovered that his father had already returned the painting to its former state. "I stared in my astonishment," he recalled. "It was the beautiful picture of the week before in all the spontaneous beauty that mother and I had admired." However, even that experience failed to "cure" his father of "that fatal habit" of repainting. One day, he visited his father in his studio and saw him standing in front of his easel. He recounts the rest of the story as follows.]

"Hello, Pop," I said. "Thought I would just run over and see what you were about. Got anything new?"

"Yes, I have a canvas here I've been fussing over. How does it look?"

"Fine, Pop," I answered enthusiastically; "all right, beautiful. Fine tone."

"Yes, it has things in it, but it's stupid. Confound it! it's too good; it's all tone. That's what's the matter with it. I've got too much detail in the foreground. That's a thing we are always running up against to tickle the buyer—to make a few dollars. Those weeds don't mean anything. Let's take them out; they are not the picture. This picture is very good, but it's all tone."

"Yes, Pop, but that's what I like about it; it's beautiful in tone."

"Perhaps; but that's what makes it stupid. Why in thunder can't we put something in that's out of tone? You see, there's no interest in this picture. It's well drawn, yes, well constructed, well painted, and perfectly tonal; but there's no passion in it. A picture without passion has no meaning, and it would be far better had it never been painted. Imitation is worthless. Photography does it much better than you or I could. In a bar-room in New York is a painting of a barn-door with hinges on it and a key-hole. It is painted so well that you would swear the hinges were real, and you could put your finger in the keyhole; but it is not real! It is not what it represents. It is a lie. Clever, yes, but it gives you no sensation of truth, because before you look at it you are told that it is a lie. The only charm in this picture is in deceiving you into the belief that it is a real barn-door. Now, in art, true art, we are not seeking to deceive. We do not pretend that this is a real tree, a real river; but we use the tree or the river as a means to give you the feeling or impression that under a certain effect is produced upon us." He had forgotten the picture in question for the time being, and had begun to pound away at me with his theories.

"Now let us assume that an artist, through a divine power, has been endowed with a keen sense to see the beautiful in nature that the ordinary layman who is chained to his desk cannot see. If we can give that man a canvas that will take him away from his desk and lead him into the field and make him feel what we feel when we hear the birds sing and see the grain wave, we have done something good. In our art this is what we should strive for. But unfortunately the poor devil who is chained to his desk generally has no interest in the canvas other than the fact that it may have a greater money value after our death. I tell you, George, if we could only create a public who would appreciate art for art's sake, buy pictures because they love them, and not be led by the nose by the dealer who knows less about art than the most ignorant farmer whose corn-patch you are painting. And why does the picture-dealer know nothing about the art he is selling? Because his judgment is warped by the money he may make. In the dealer's eyes the greatest work of art is the one he can make the most money on. It has been proved hundreds of times. How about Millet, Corot? And I might mention a lot of others whose works were worthless until they were proclaimed great by their brother artists. Take myself, for instance. What has your 'high-class painting' dealer done for me? Nothing was good without a foreign name on it. Why, when one of our biggest dealers on Fifth Avenue, was asked to procure for a gentleman two American pictures for one thousand dollars each, he said he could not take the order because there was not a picture produced in America worth one thousand dollars. Why? Because they can go to Europe, buy a picture for twenty-five or fifty francs, with a foreign name on it, and sell it at a large profit."

"But the dealers are handling your pictures, Pop."

"Yes, I know the dealers are taking up my pictures, but simply because the public wants them. No, George, it's all wrong, the whole system. There is no art in this country; we have no 'amateur.' If a man is going in for collecting, why does he not make enough of a study of it to be able to buy what he likes? In all my acquaintances of art buyers I do not know three who would dare buy a picture before he saw the name of the painter in the corner. Many a picture I have sold for fifty dollars. I wonder if it will be worth more after my death. If it is, I am quite sure it will not be a better work of art just because I am dead."

It is interesting to note here that many of these pictures for which he received so small a sum are now bringing in the Fifth Avenue shops ten, fifteen, and twenty thousand dollars each.

"Oh, well," he continued, "forget it. Maybe I have said too much. The dealer has his place, and perhaps we poor devils would starve to death without him; but when I see a dealer shed tears over a canvas that he expects to make five hundred per cent. on, I—well, let's get back to the picture."

Nothing warmed him up to a pitch of inspiration quite so much as to expound his theories. His eyes were beginning to flash; he was becoming tense, and as he turned, with a swift, intense movement toward the easel, I knew that that exquisite tonal picture was doomed. He seized his palette, squeezed out a great quantity of ivory black, and pounced on the canvas with the alertness of a lion. He dashed at the tree in the corner with a glaze of black, which he carried through the foreground.

"There you see, George, the value of the gray color underneath glazing. The transparency of it comes out in tone. The shadows are full of color. Not pigment; all light and air. Wipe out a little more of it. Never was anything as nice as transparent color." He sprang back several paces, held his hand over his eyes, and looked at the canvas through half-closed lids.

"Confound it, George! It's got too much tone! We don't know just what it's going to be, but it's coming. We don't care what it is so it expresses beauty." With a wild rush he swiftly painted out two of the sheep in the foreground. "Too much detail, I tell you." His hair was disheveled, his eyes burned with the fire of creative intensity, and the tail of his shirt, responding to the emotional stress of its owner, had been jerked from its usual abiding-place. "Now," he continued, waving his palette in the air, "we are getting some kind of effect. Don't know what the deuce it's going to be, but we are getting a start. Now we will suggest that tree in the middle distance with a little yellow." He stood off again, held his palette up to his eyes, and with another dash obliterated the tops of the trees with a dash of blue sky. The atmosphere was electrified. Pop was quivering with emotion, and I, too, caught the tenseness of the situation. He dabbed and smeared, and for a quarter of an hour the silence was broken only by his quick breathing and the jabs of his brush on the canvas. He was bringing a composition out of chaos.

"That old gnarled tree might make something; we'll use that. Take advantage of anything you can on your canvas, George. Confound it! now your mother will give me the devil for using my shirt as a paint-rag. I think that's asking too much. Can't have any peace. She won't let me do what I want. Now we'll put a dab of dark here and light over there. Just like music, George—the harmony of tone. We thump, thump, thump the keys to the distance, but don't forget to put in the harsh note, the accidental. It makes the contrast that gives interest and beauty to the whole, the gradation of light and shade which corresponds to music. What is art, anyway? Nothing but temperament, expression of your feelings. Some days you feel one way, some days another; all temperament. There, you see it's opening up. Tickle the eye, George, tickle the ear. Art is like music.

Music sounds good to the ear, makes your feet go—want to dance. Art is art; paint, mud, music, words, anything. Art takes hold of you—sentiment, life, expression. Take the poet. He does the same thing we are trying to do. Poe in 'The Bells,' for instance,—all the same thing,—it rolls, tolls, swells, dwells—all poetry, all the same thing. He uses words; we use paint; the other fellow uses a fiddle. You can't go any further than that. Oh, to paint a picture, a sunset, without paint! To create without paint! I'll tell you, George, if a man paints one picture in a lifetime that's good, he should be satisfied. When I've painted one picture that's a true expression, I'll be ready to go." Under the volley of words and strokes the composition was rapidly taking form.

"Never paint with the idea of selling. Lose everything first, George. You can put in a little dog, maybe, and it will buy you an overcoat. Be honest; somebody's going to find it out. You'll get the credit for it in the long run. Gad! the struggles I've had in my life to be true! Dealers come in and offer me money to put in this or that, and I have to do it because I have to live. There, see it grow—only a tone; but it makes you feel good." With a few deft touches he had suggested several sheep in the foreground. The whole picture was dark and tonal. But the dull-red house of the original composition still stood out incongruously in the new. He stepped back several paces and looked at it; then with a dash he slapped in a mass of yellow ocher over the house, and with two or three sweeps of the brush had transformed the old red structure into a vibrant twilight sky. All the rest was dark and in perfect tone. With that supreme stroke he struck the accidental, and pushed the harmony almost to discord, and the finished canvas stood before us a masterpiece.

On Inness's rather surprising habit of repainting the works of *other* artists:
[In describing his father's penchant for repainting, even works by other artists, Inness, Jr., refers to the landscape painter Alexander Helwig Wyant and the Realist painter John George Brown. He also recounts the story of how he realized that his father had painted over one of his own compositions, ultimately creating *The Coming Storm* (see above figs. 9–10)].

The tremendous desire to paint over a canvas did not limit itself to his own pictures. He was no respecter of persons or pictures, and it made no difference who painted the original, who was the owner, or what was sacrificed in the doing. Many of his contemporaries have fallen victims to this insatiate weakness. I believe he would far rather have painted on a picture than on a clean canvas. The composition, no matter how good, always suggested something that he could improve upon. It became so bad that Mrs. A. H. Wyant, wife of the artist, finally had to forbid him her husband's studio.

I remember on one occasion the artist J. G. Brown told me of my father coming into his studio in the Tenth Street Building, which is still one of New York's prominent studios, and after looking at a nice little bootblack who was making his black and tan dog beg for a piece of cake said:

"That's a good story, Brown, but your boy's too clean, and your dog's too black and tan. You've got too much in the picture; in fact, it's all cracker-box and dog and boy. What you want is breadth. Take out some of those details and tell the story more simply. Here, give me your brush; I'll show you."

"And," said Brown, "I wish you could have seen the way he went at that ten-by-fourteen canvas. With one sweep of the brush he had changed my beautiful brick wall into a twilight sky, and made a pool of water out of the cracker-box, wiped all the buttons off the boy's clothes, and changed boy and dog into a couple of dull-colored tramps. But I have that canvas yet, and nothing would induce me to part with it."

Such things happened often to me. About forty years ago I painted a picture of a team of oxen—a picture of which my father was as proud as I. In fact, he thought so much of it that he bought a handsome gold frame, and had it exhibited in the art rooms of Williams & Everett in Boston. Then the picture disappeared, and I wondered many times what had happened to it. I was sure that I had never sold it, and I had almost deluded myself into the belief and hope that some art lover had yielded to a great temptation and stolen it. But "what a check to proud ambition!" One day recently, while visiting my sister, Mrs. Hartley, I was looking at a very wonderful canvas of my father's that is hanging in her house, a powerful storm effect, and catching it in a cross light, I saw under the clouds and landscape the outline of my team of oxen. The mystery was solved. My oxen had come to light, or, rather, I should say, had been revealed in darkness. All these years they had been plodding through this glorious storm. Dear old Pop, in dire need of a canvas, had painted over my picture and immortalized it thus.

On Inness's belief that a painting remained his possession even after he had sold it; the repercussions of that belief:

My father had the idea firmly established in his mind that a work of art from his brush always remained his property, and that he had the right to paint it over or change it at will, no matter where he found it or who had bought it, or what money he may have received for it. Wherever he found his pictures after they had left his studio he criticized, and would in most violent language declare the thing was "rot," that the sky was false or the distance out of key, and in a very matter of fact way would say "Just send it around to the studio to-morrow and I'll put it into shape."

"But I like it as it is," the purchaser would reply.

"It makes no difference what you like; I say the thing is false. Here, let me take it with me, and I will make a picture of it. I see a fine idea in it, and I will have it done to-morrow."

In response to the owner's entirely legitimate objections he would continue:

"Nonsense! What right have you to like it when I find it false and discordant? Don't you think I know what I am talking about? And I want you to understand, sir, that I claim the right to go into any house and change a work of mine when I am not satisfied with it, and see where I can improve it. Do you think, because you have paid money for a picture of mine, that it belongs to *you?* If you had any knowledge of art, you would see that it is false and be glad to have me work upon it and improve it."

He was perfectly sincere in such convictions and honestly tried to carry them out.

A gentleman once bought from my father a large and important canvas. He was very proud of possessing it, and asked Inness to send it to the exhibition of the Academy of Design, which was to be held the next week, explaining that it would give him much pleasure to show his friends the picture he had bought, and to have it hung in the academy rooms. My father agreed readily, as he believed this particular picture to be the finest thing he had ever done. The last was always the best, the old story of the new baby. So he assured his patron that the canvas would be sent.

The next day Inness looked at the canvas.

"This has been sold," he thought; "it is finished and going to be taken away. I wonder if I can improve it. The foreground wants some lifting up; it lacks interest. These rocks are too small, and the sea that is beating against them looks hard, it has no motion."

On the impulse of the moment he seized his palette and dashed at the canvas. The quiet waves were turned into a ranging sea of foam, the sky was darkened to lower the tone, and over the whole picture an angry thunder-storm was cast. He stood off from the easel and looked at it.

"Confound the thing! I've ruined it. The sea is mud, and the sky has turned to lead. I cannot rub it off because the paint underneath is wet. It's getting dark, and I must catch the train. Curse the luck! I'll never do such a thing again.

When I get a picture finished, and any damn fool wants to buy it, I will leave it alone whether I like it or not."

When Pop reached home that evening it was quite evident to mother that something had gone wrong with his work. She always knew, and although he was very glum and wanted to be let alone, she, with an art of her own, drew the whole story out bit by bit, and when he had finished she sent him to bed convinced by her wise arguments that he had improved the picture, and with a few deft strokes could bring it back to perfection in the morning.

The next day, upon reaching the studio, he was still of the opinion that it had been for the best that he had blotted out "that stupid sea picture," giving him a real opportunity to make a beautiful thing. The big rock he changed into an apple-tree. With the aid of a palette-knife he scraped off the ranging sea, and in its place painted in a rich grass meadow. In the middle distance he placed a clump of elm-trees in shadow. He was happy once again, and as he sang and whistled the picture grew. Here was a new problem to solve, a new idea to bring into being, to create.

The postman dropped a letter in the slot, but Inness was in no mood for letters. He scarcely noticed it. When under the fire of inspiration he heard nothing, saw nothing, cared for nothing but the thing which he was creating. The picture was growing at his touch. A big bright cloud rolled up behind the elms, a heavy pall hung down from the zenith of the sky, and here and there little clouds floated in a soft, gray sky, and down upon the horizon settled a veil of deeper blue, throwing in relief a sunlit barn. Far beyond a puff of smoke rose from a rushing train. The darkened pall of cloud cast a shadow on the ground in front, leaving the rest bathed in amber light.

Exhausted, but happy, Pop filled his pipe, picked up the letter from the floor, and dropping into a chair opened the letter, which inclosed a check for the picture on the easel before him, the one he had just completed.

"The gentleman will be pleased," he said aloud. "The subject is nothing. It is the art he wants, and this is the greatest thing I have ever done."

The following week the academy exhibition opened, and according to my father's promise the picture was hung. The gentleman who had purchased it was there on the first day, eager to show the great masterpiece to his friends. He searched the galleries through, and great was his chagrin at not finding it; but when he caught sight of the new Inness he exclaimed to his friends that this one was finer than the one he had brought, and expressed his regret at not having seen it first. A crowd had gathered around the canvas, artists and laymen, and were looking with unconcealed admiration at the work of the master when my father and I entered. Catching sight of Inness, his patron rushed up to him and exclaimed:

"Mr. Inness, how could you disappoint me so? You promised to send my picture here, and you have sent this one."

"Why, this is your new picture," said Pop, "a little changed, perhaps; but then, you see, I had not finished it."

On valuing the opinion of others; the influence of Thomas B. Clarke:

Because of my father's intolerant attitude of other people's opinions where his own work was concerned, he was continually getting into trouble, and but for Mr. Clarke's diplomatic handling of these rather awkward situations many of his patrons would have become totally estranged. One instance of this remains vividly in my mind. A New York gentleman bought a picture from my father that he admired greatly, saying that he would send for it the next day. He had hardly left the studio before Pop began to "tickle it up" a little to carry out a thought. He kept on "tickling it up" until the canvas was an entirely different picture, and one that, I regret to say, had lost rather than gained in the process of tickling.

The next day the gentleman came to the studio to see his picture, and, finding it unrecognizable, insisted that this canvas was not his.

"Yes, it is," replied Inness. "I have changed it just a little to give it snap."

"Why, the picture's ruined," said the purchaser, "and I refuse to take it."

"Very well," answered my father; "you couldn't have it now at any price. Your money cannot buy my art. I give you what I choose, and whether you like it or not is a matter of indifference to me. What right have you to tell me what you like or what you do not like? I am the only one capable of judging my own work. The picture is finer than it was; it had no strength before."

For all his blustering manner, dear old Pop knew that his patron was right and that the picture was ruined, and he knew that he had been a fool to touch it. But he had to do something to cover up his embarrassment and chagrin, so he continued to throw all the blame on his innocent patron, who, he declared, would cut a better figure before a stock-broker's ticker than sitting there telling him how and when to paint. Justly indignant, the gentleman walked out of the studio and to his friend Clarke, who had originally introduced him to Inness, and to whom he told the whole story, declaring that he would never give to "that ranting fool" another chance to insult him. But Mr. Clarke, who understood and loved them both and would not see a break between them, said:

"Never mind, old man. You know Inness well enough to know that he would not intentionally insult you for the world. He is in a high-strung, nervous condition, and is no doubt suffering at this moment to think that he lost his temper and acted like a brute. I will just run around and see him."

Upon entering the studio Clarke noticed immediately the nervous state my father was in, and was wise enough to sit quite still and not refer in any way to the episode which had occurred that morning. Father, ignoring his presence, kept right on painting. It happened to be the canvas in dispute. He was never disturbed by an audience; in fact, he rather liked one, because it gave him an opportunity to talk and to expound his theories. So after painting in silence for a while, he turned to Clarke and said:

"I got in quite a muddle over this in trying to fix the sky. It lacked sparkle and interest. Sometimes, Clarke, it is hard to find just where the thing is wrong; it doesn't seem to hitch. It may be in the sky or in the patch of light across the foreground; and then you will find that it isn't that at all, but the fault lies in the composition, and those trees in the right are out of place and mar the breadth and grandeur of the picture. But then the misery of the thing is that you can never get back the thing you had before you touched it. Clarke, if I could only learn to leave a thing alone after I feel that I have what I want! It has been the curse of my life, this changing and trying to carry a thing nearer to perfection. After all, we are limited to paint. Maybe, after we get to heaven, we shall find some other medium with which to express our thoughts on canvas. I had this picture very fine, and then I knocked it all to pot. It's the one our friend bought. He was in here this morning, and we had some words because I changed it. I tell you, Clarke, I shall have to keep these fellows out of here. You had better take the pictures to your rooms and let them see them there, for if you don't, I'm afraid the canvases never will be done. Sometimes I almost wish I had another trade. But I'm getting it now; this is going to be the greatest thing I have ever done. Don't you see how brilliant it is? The thing is real. I would rather starve to death than give up art."

Mr. Clarke, who had come into the studio at a later stage of the evolution of the picture than had his friend, had been spared the shock of seeing it in the discouraging stage of transition in which, unfortunately, the gentleman had seen it, and had been justly disappointed. Through that marvelous ability which the master possessed the canvas had been brought back from utter failure to a composition even more beautiful than the original, and it was this that Clarke saw and pronounced good.

"It is a wonderful picture, Inness," he said, "and that fellow is mighty lucky to own it."

"Own it!" snapped my father, flaring up again at the thought of the disagreeable episode with his patron. "He does not own it, and he cannot own it now at any price. I'm through with him, and I don't want him to come here and bother me with my work."

Clarke did not press the point, but a few days later succeeded in persuading his friend to forget the little unpleasantness that had occurred, and go with him to Inness's studio. When they arrived my father greeted them coldly. The picture was turned face to the wall, and nothing was said regarding it. Inness knew that the picture was good and was so pleased with it that he wanted above everything else to have them ask to see it, only his pride keeping him from bringing it out and saying, "There, that is the greatest thing I ever did." An abstract subject was introduced, however, on art in general which struck a responsive chord, and after a few moments of enthusiasm in explaining some theory Inness forgot about his grievance and became himself again. Whereupon Clarke suggested that he show them the picture that their friend had purchased.

"He has purchased no picture," said my father, coldly, "and he might just as well understand now that I claim the right to paint my pictures as I choose, and the fact that a man has purchased one does not deprive me of the right to make any changes in it for the better that I like."

A little smoothing down from Clarke, however, had the effect of oil on troubled waters, and Inness[,] inwardly delighted, brought out the picture. When the patron saw it he was amazed at its beauty, and exclaimed:

"Mr. Inness, if you will let me have this canvas I will accede to your demands and allow you the right to change your pictures whenever you wish."

"All right," laughed my father. "Since you see it in its proper light, I will deliver the canvas to you whenever you want it."

The purchaser said he would send for it and left the room, to return in about five minutes with a man he had picked up on the street, and together they carried the canvas off in triumph.

Inness, Jr., on his father's painting practices:
[Although Inness, Jr., does not indicate precisely when his father employed this pictorial technique—it is likely that he used at least some of the procedures throughout his life—it provides a useful primer for understanding the artist's basic painting practices.]

His method was generally to stain a canvas with a light-brown tint, say of raw umber, and when dry, take it out to the place he had selected, where he would draw in most carefully with charcoal or pencil the forms of the things he saw and wished to have in the picture. He would often leave out a tree or other object that interfered with his composition. After the whole was drawn in, and every little crook in the limb of the tree that would give character, and every little sway of the roof of the barn, the twisting and rising and falling of the road, every clump of golden-rod or a straggling daisy that found itself out so late, would be put in with care, if it lent vigor to the composition. If not, it was as though it did not exist. Then with raw umber and some strong drier he would go over all the outlines, correcting here and there a bit of drawing. Then he would paint on the lights or opaque parts of his picture as near the local color of the object as he could, and the sky a rather neutral tone of yellow ocher, black and white. That constituted the first day's work; that was all.

The next day, due to the vehicle he had used, the canvas would be dry, and he would rub in the shadows, always keeping them transparent, and imitating as he went the texture of the rocks, the trees, and the grass. I have known him to keep at one study for a week or more at a time, using a quick-drying medium which enabled him to glaze his picture every day if he found it necessary. Glazing is done by passing a transparent color such as umber, black, sienna, or cobalt over the canvas or parts of it, thinned down with oil or some such medium to make it flow. This lowers the tone of the canvas, but brings the whole in harmony, and enriches the color of the opaque parts of the picture. On this glaze the artist generally paints again with opaque color to bring up the light and add to the texture. This sometimes has the effect of darkening a picture too much. In such an event the whole canvas has to be scumbled again to bring it back to a lighter tone, although this is rarely done.

Scumbling is done by passing an opaque color over the picture, say white, yellow ocher, or cadmium. A scumble always has to be worked in, and if the shadows are to be kept transparent, it is necessary to wait another day for the scumble to dry that it may be glazed again. Any transparent color will form a glaze.

Thus, according to this method, my father would drive along, glazing down and painting up the lights, rubbing and scrubbing, but *always keeping the color pure* until the picture was finished to his satisfaction or until he wearied of the subject.

These canvases rarely got to the public in their original condition, but would be worked over in the studio and often to such an extent that there was nothing left to suggest the subject first painted.

Inness's effort to create "a perfect harmony of vision":

His pictures are always beautifully composed, and with a thorough balance and completeness. As I have said before, one can always look into an Inness picture. It is complete in every part, so that the eye travels from one object to another without effort, and everything is enveloped and held within the vision. Many paintings [by other artists] are so faulty in perspective and drawing that it is impossible to see both ends of the canvas at the same time, no matter how small it may be. This fault is never found in Inness. He paints only what the eye can take in in one vision.

Cut a hole in a piece of paper, say two by three inches, then measure diagonally across it from corner to corner, the distance being about three and a half inches. Multiply this by three, and the result is ten and a half inches. Now hold the paper ten and a half inches from the eye, and whatever can be seen through the opening can be grasped in one vision. Hold it closer to the eye, and it will be necessary to shift the eye to see all that is contained within the opening. My father held invariably to this mathematical exactness which gives a perfect harmony of vision.

◆━◆◈◆━◆

G. W. [George William] Sheldon, "George Inness" (22 April 1882)

[Born in South Carolina, George William Sheldon graduated from Princeton University and tended to soldiers in Grant's army during the Civil War. During the 1870s and 1880s, he was a critic in New York for the *Evening Post* and the *Commercial Advertiser*, and later wrote several art books, including *American Painters* (1879) and *Hours with Art and Artists* (1882). In this profile of Inness, published in *Harper's Weekly Magazine*, he presented several of Inness's poems and portions of two of his manuscripts, the originals of which have almost certainly been lost. "Suggestions by an Artist" contained some of Inness's most metaphysical, mystical statements. "The Mathematics of Psychology" offered long discourses on the writings of the English philosopher and political economist John Stuart Mill and the English political economist and theologian Richard Whately.]

I.

It was just sunset as we were leaving the University Building on Washington

Square, and the lingering rays lent a mournfully evanescent beauty to the naked trees and the reviving sod. "See the tone of that grass," exclaimed Mr. INNESS— "its local color as affected by the conditions of the moment. See those trees, how sharply defined are their outlines, and how dark, without being black, are their surfaces. Many artists who should try to put them on canvas would be apt to make them black. But they certainly are not black. It is so hard to paint this tone. Look at those two trees, one of them ten feet in front of the other; it is so hard to get their exact relation to themselves and to their surroundings. Few painters attempt it. To keep the local color of that grass and those trees, and yet preserve their tone, is the greatest of pictorial problems, and ROUSSEAU is about the only man I know who solved it. Yet the public does not appreciate ROUSSEAU. The public craves exaggeration. People can't see a wart on a man's nose unless it is twice as big as it really is." Mr. INNESS is a famous talker on art matters, as everybody knows who has read the report of his conversations in a paper entitled "A Painter on Painting," in the number of HARPER'S MAGAZINE for February, 1878. I do not propose to quote from that paper here. But there lies before me an unpublished manuscript essay of his, headed "Suggestions by an Artist," from which, by his courtesy, I am able to give a few selections:

"The master should exercise his control over the pupil by restraining the latter's tendency to imitation, and by leading him to the perception of those principles through which facts are represented according to their relative significance."

"The footstep of Love is necessarily law. Love moves to find its mate, Wisdom."

"The artist reproduces nature not as the brute sees it, but as an idea partaking more or less of the creative source from which it flows."

"Beauty and goodness are the substance of real truth, and the tests of purity and simplicity both of life and of art."

"The overlove of knowing is a chronic trouble with artists, and produces in their works the appearance of effort and labor, instead of that freedom which is the life of truth."

"The light that comes to the mind is from what is above the mind. Its reflected ray presents an image of the invisible."

"Knowledge must bow to spirit."

"The wisdom of love guides a man into the consciousness of the truth of that which he loves."

"If your genius necessitates your living in a small hut, be content; the hut will stand you in more than a great mansion."

"Facts are the straws of sense."

"The memory is the daguerreotype shop of the soul, which treasures all that God creates to consciousness through eye and touch. What we painters have to learn is to keep this shop closed in the presence of nature: to see, and not think we see. When we do this, our eyes are lighted from within, and the face of nature is transformed; and we teach the world to see reality in a new light. Such is the mission of art."

"Our intelligence is occupied with the contemplation of effects. It should be occupied with the contemplation of cause. In this case art would cease to be mere imitation. Through the representation of forms its purpose would be to communicate intelligence."

"A bit of old-fashioned inspiration says, 'Give me understanding, and I will keep Thy law.' Understanding is a spiritual foothold, fixed upon and mastering the senses."

"Judgment is the power of holding the balance between the restraints of thought and the impulses of feeling."

"The emotional life is the substantial pabulum of æsthetic power."

"The divine life in man is in the harmony of the interior forces of the soul; the æsthetic life is in the harmony of the exterior forces of the soul."

"The paramount difficulty with the artist is to bring his intellect to submit to the fact that there is such a thing as the undefinable—that which hides itself that we may feel after it. The intellect desires to define everything; it is a pre-Raphaelite *par excellence*; its cravings are for what it can see, lay hold of, measure, weigh, examine. But God is always hidden, and beauty depends upon the unseen—the visible upon the invisible."

"This abominable tendency to believe only in what can be defined, this desire to realize all things of life sensuously, is the cause of human misery. It is the life of the beast-mind. How sweetly, when the animal-mind has been subdued, is the chastened spirit charmed with the hidden story of the real!"

"Let us believe in art, not as something to gratify curiosity or suit commercial ends, but as something to be loved and cherished because it is the handmaid of the spiritual life of the age."

"We can not be impressed by that which does not touch us."

This maxim is excellent, is it not? And how useful might be the consideration of it to some of our advanced young painters—clever fellows they are—whose single fallacy is that they strive to impress by that which does not touch!

II.

It is not generally known that Mr. INNESS writes lyric poetry, although everybody knows that he paints it. Embodiments of the beautiful he is felicitous in creating with both pen and brush, and in each instance his art fulfills the loftier function of depicting not his own subjective emotions alone, but those of the human race. His Muse has not yet expressed herself in love ditties or drinking songs; she is as grave as MICHAEL ANGELO'S, and as chaste as MILTON'S. And she does not care a fig for rhyme or for metrical structure; in fact, she disbelieves in both. What Mr. INNESS has written was written *currente calamo* [lit. "with running pen"] at intervals of painting. The thoughts came to him, and were recorded while the inspiration lasted. The verses that follow are the first of his to appear in a public journal, although last year he prepared to break the ice by printing a few stanzas in the catalogue of the New York Academy of Design's annual exhibition of paintings. A few months ago he was represented in the gallery of the Union League Club by a picture called "Breaking Up," in which clouds were breaking over mountains, the landscape marked by brilliant lights and strong shadows, and the whole executed with great dash in about four hours. Somebody told him that another somebody had said that a third somebody did not understand it. He sat down soon afterward, and wrote the following lines, and sent them with his compliments to the lady who had bought the picture:

Address of the Clouds to the Earth.

We have wept our burden,
We have filled thy streams;
Thy fields are vital with the
Greenness of a freshened
Life, O Earth, our brother;
And now we court the
Winds. Hilarious
In our wedded joy,
O'er thy high-reaching hills
We break in varied forms,
And make thy groves and meadows
Ring in joyous laugh
At our black shadows as we

Pass. Soon will we join ourselves
In softened forms, and, far
Extended on thy horizon,
Lie stretched along in sweet repose,
As pearly pendants to thy distant
Mountain-peaks. Thy hills
Revealed, and all thy body
Bathed in shining light, we
Throw our kisses at thee
As a vapor's breath.

The special interest of these beautiful lines is not that they are true poetry—other poets have written true poetry—but that they are GEORGE INNESS'S description of one of GEORGE INNESS'S landscapes; that they contain his philosophy of painting; that they reveal what to him is the true significance of landscape art. His clouds call the earth their brother; they court the winds, and wed them; they elicit laughter from the groves and meadows; they rest as pearly pendants to the mountain-peaks, and they disappear in kisses. They are not SHELLEY'S clouds, which are literary; they are the painter's clouds, which are pictorial.

The next poem, "Love," was intended to accompany a picture representing a primeval man in the act of carrying his dead wife in his arms to a cavern, where he was to bury her. His sweetest self he is to lay in the earth, separating himself from himself; yet will her body germinate within the dark chaotic wastes, and live again, a new creation, its mystery and delight infinitely greater than before. This new-begotten seed is himself too, which yet is not himself; it is his other self, his sweetest self, whom he is about to place "in thy cavernous jaws, O Earth":

Love.

Bone of my bone, flesh of my flesh,
My sweetest self, into thy cavernous
Jaws, O Earth, I place. What though
I separate me from myself, and in
Thy bosom place this so sweet body
Of my love! A fiery life I so

Inspire within thy dark, chaotic
Wastes, and rouse thee from thy
Vacant death to bear me forth a
New creation from myself, which
Yet is not myself. Then shall I dwell
In an eternal new-begotten seed—
The mystery, the delight, increased
From one to numbers infinite.

I once suggested to Mr. INNESS that occasionally a verse of his might be considered a little obscure. He replied, quietly, "I don't expect everybody to understand these things"—a poet's answer. The story of this poem is the poet's doctrine of the resurrection of the body.

III.

The first poem that Mr. INNESS ever wrote is called "The Leaves and the Brook," and was suggested by one of his simplest landscape sketches in pencil. The leaves drop into the brook, and are borne to the ocean. They tell the ocean of other leaves left behind on the ground—other little truths, their brothers. They salt the waters, and thus preserve the memory of their brotherhood. They represent the truth, which, like salt, has a preservative force. The leaves left behind represent the good, which loves. The two classes of leaves unite, and keep on uniting:

[Here, Sheldon quotes the first seventeen lines of "The Leaves and the Brook." The entire poem is reprinted on pages 140–41 of this volume.]

"Despair" was written in connection with a picture of a figure in a cell, expressive of hopeless grief. On one side of a sheet of paper is INNESS'S sketch for the picture; on the other, the poem, hastily and rudely recorded. It is a mighty man's despair: "I feel within me all creation turning back to chaos." The speaker is no longer conscious of nature; his vital currents congeal; the thoughts that peopled his soul become withered fancies. Unless God assures this despairing mortal that He (God) is a man too, unless man can find sympathy and help in a God-man, he is but the personality of naught. It is a variation of the old Hebrew melody, "I am poor and sorrowful: let Thy salvation, O God, set me up on high." INNESS, inspirationally, is Semitic rather than Aryan. The sources of his prophesying are not Greek, but Hebraic:

Despair.

I feel within me all creation turning
Back to chaos: no other self to whom
To give myself; myself unmakes
Myself, and Nature dies away
From memory's consciousness.
The sappy greenness of my heart
Turns to a solid death, and my
Unpeopled soul sinks 'mid a
Vacant life of withered fancies—all
Unreal to sight, to sound, to touch.
Without a God to signature himself
A man to me, I am the
Personality of naught, the scattered
Ashes of a burnt-out sympathy.

"The Pilgrim" was meant to be a part of a longer poem describing man's progress from superstition and darkness into reasonableness and light. But it is complete in itself, and, like all Mr. INNESS'S poems, seems quite different from anything ever written by anybody else:

The Pilgrim.

A pilgrim, passing through
    The gates of Rome,
Transfixed in gaze, stood
    On Campagna's heights,
And thus to me he spoke
    At my approach
As from his dream he woke:

"Far have I travelled, guided as
    In sacred trust,
To bow my knee beneath
    St. Peter's dome.
There willful nature's debt to

Superstition paid,
My soul expands as now I gaze,
Returned from faithless error's
          Step, upon this rising sun,
To me henceforth the emblem
          Of eternal good.
Proceeding from that lamb-like love
Which shines, as truth, its light,
Within the mind of man;
          Nor yet my spirit bears me ill
          That through St. Peter's gates I
          Came or went."

The eagle eye denied to mortal man,
His baser passions rise before his ken,
And color reason's ray in bloody tones;
Yet do those mists but serve
          To obscure the light
And make weak vision safe
          To catch the useful form.
The bird of Jove with faultless eye
          That sweeps horizon's line
Is but the fiend that swoops
          Upon the dove, the lamb,
Until, trained to the voice of Ganymede,
It bears the love it serves,
          Burdened with truth
Pressed out from earth to heaven.

See now how as those vapors
          Rise in grotesque form,
Imagination fills them one by one
          With imageries
Of things that be, from bird to beast,
From castled towers to ships and fish
          That sail or swim the sea;
Waves, lines and angles, confused

Crags and peopled towns,
Serve us with gorgeous color concerts,
Vapors though they be.

The blazing light obscured,
The vision drowned, life still
Reveals the Unknown as an
Inspiring love,
An endless voice that gives a
Conscious language to the soul,
Numbering its hopes and fears
In colors gay or sad,
As spirits, moving forms of things,
To be to memory as man's
Weak man's, reality—

Weak unformed image of divinity,
In whom imagination rules the sight,
And from projections of his own
Desire, creates a lower form
To be the fetich of his will,
Till contrast with the round reality
Shall tell his soul the story of an
Ever-flowing, all-pervading good,
Eternal, real, yet to the mind
That seeks to see,
Forever the unknown; for
What is seen is not reality.

The pilgrim looks at the sun, that is, at the infinite, after his experience of religious superstition has failed him. The forms made by the clouds represent the fetiches of man's own desire, that is, his fancies. As these clear away, the round sun, the reality, appears. If the reader will refresh his memory with some of MICHAEL ANGELO's sonnets, he will see not only that the spirit of INNESS's productions is not less serious and noble, but that there exist some very interesting correspondences between the former's sonnet on the death of his friend VITTORIA COLONNA, and the latter's verses entitled "Love," although in some respects INNESS'S sentiments are larger and choicer than those of the great sculptor. But if the reader will contrast INNESS'S lines with some of the frivolous jingling which TURNER committed to paper, he will perhaps smile to see how much more frivolous this jingling appears by reason of the juxtaposition.

IV.

The distance between a man's poetry and his religious sentiments is not so great as to need a bridge or boat. It is only a step between them. "I do not see," said Mr. INNESS, in answer to a question, "that what I believe can be of any particular importance to anybody else, nor do I think well of giving it a definite shape. In such a form it would be at best a scientific formula of my present state of mind, and such scientific formulas change as our states change. The real truth must always be a cropping out of a man's experience; it then need disturb no other man's faith, but may meet their needs in accordance with their desires. No man has a right to assume that that is a material fact—even though it may be a fact—which is contrary to the whole tenor of his experience, and consequently of his reason. This always makes bad work, and is a sin against God, because it rejects the burden of thought, which if borne patiently would soon cause to disappear our hereditary stupidities. Yet it seems to me that that man is but a comparative clod—whatever may be his scientific attainments—who has not perceived that no good thing, no true thing, no beautiful thing, comes from himself, but that he rather stands in the way of all these."

"The Bible is a book of inspiration. It is the story of the progress of the human soul. Every man's experience is there."

"The potency of being in you is body, soul, and spirit; in matter, it is length, breadth, and thickness; in God, it is love, operation, and use; they always act in one form, and always must be in one form."

"The tendency is to look upon God as something abstract, and not as a being who gives life and bestows the consciousness of personality. God is the only real personality. When we are conscious of personality, we are conscious of God, who acts in and through what He has created."

"The evidence of immortality is that man believes in immortality. I can conceive of creation only as something produced in every moment of time from its first cause, God, of whose act I am conscious. As I am a point conscious of this movement of the Infinite Being, I can not cease to exist; for my consciousness forms a point of that infinite movement. Therefore my consciousness must be infinitely continuous, as the movement of the Infinite is infinitely continuous. This is the argument intellectual, though to me it is of small importance. The consciousness of immortality is wrapped up in all the experiences of my life, and this to me is the end of the argument. The other is simply a piece of ratiocination that has occurred to my mind at times—a sort of sky-rocket."

"When we know how imperfect the human eye is when compared with the eyes of some insects, although it is so wonderful, why should we undertake to say that states do not exist of which we have no physical perception, and can have none? Why could not we exist in a subtle condition imperceptible to sense?"

"'God is a spirit, and they that worship Him must worship Him in spirit and in truth.' That is my creed, and it covers the whole ground."

"Jesus is the Divine love and wisdom represented in human form."

"To be afraid of truth is to be a fool. To deny common sense is to assume an ass's burden—though many persons do so in the hope of reward here or hereafter."

V.

From theology to metaphysics, also, the passage is easy; and INNESS is a metaphysician too. I have seen pounds of manuscript in his handwriting, which one of these days may be known to book-buyers as *The Mathematics of Psychology*—a contribution to the philosophy of numbers, which, as INNESS treats it, is a veritable *scientia scientiarum* [fig. "warehouse of knowledge"]. "Before my first trip to Europe," he said, one afternoon, "I became impressed with an idea of the significance of numbers, and worked at it for two years, till I reached number six. Then I got blocked. In Rome I picked it up again, and went on." In this treatise he demonstrates that number one stands for or represents the infinite; that number two represents conjunction; that number three represents potency; that number four represents substance; that number five represents germination; that number six represents material condition, etc. The treatise is necessarily fragmentary. Its principles could be carried into the hundred thousands were human life long enough. Each successive step involves a distinct and laborious demonstration. The two passages about to be quoted are simply comparatively unimportant side issues, in refutation of the doctrine of evolution, and of a dogma of JOHN STUART MILL'S:

"No class or function can merge into another class or function. We find no cow which is at the same time a horse, no beast which is at the same time a rational being; for although men may become so degraded as almost to lose the semblance of humanity, man and beast are still distinct ideas fixed in the mind

as differences of function. Consequently, scientists have been unable to distin-
guish precisely the boundary between animal and vegetable life, having
changed their opinions many times, and this because animal and vegetable are
fixed ideas of function, and can not be measured by ideas of things. We may
extend our ideas of function indefinitely, but it remains function still; all that
we can do is to classify the various functions themselves. One person may call
a certain animal a sheep; another may call it a kind of goat. Still it remains to
each person what it appears to each. In one person's mind the idea of sheep
may be contracted; in another person's mind the idea of goat may be extended;
but no argument can prove a sheep to be a goat, nor can any science show the
point where one species becomes another. Manhood is the true standard of life
and of its functions, yet nothing has manhood but man; and what differenti-
ates him from every other species is his capacity to receive life in an intellectual form, as truth, by which he can rise from the closest semblance of the
brute to the highest realm of reason. The brute, on the contrary, must remain
a brute from generation to generation. An ape could be endowed with this
capacity to receive truth only by a distinct act of creative power. He could
never get it from another ape."

"WHATELY says that reasoning from generals to particulars is not a special
mode of reasoning, but the mode in which all men reason, and must reason if
they reason at all. MILL, on the other hand, denies this position, and asserts
that not only may we reason from particulars, but that we are perpetually doing
so. The child, he says, who, having burned his fingers, refrains from thrusting
them into the fire again, has reasoned or inferred, though he has never thought
of the general maxim, 'Fire burns.' He knows from memory that he has been
burned, and on this evidence believes when he sees a candle that if he puts his
finger into its flame he will be burned. In this process, continues MILL, he is
not generalizing, however; he is simply inferring a particular from particulars.
In the same way brutes reason, says MILL. Now it is evident that WHATELY
and MILL are using the term 'reason' in different senses, WHATELY meaning
by it the power of ratiocination, or arguing from cause to effect—a power possible only where there is conscious thought concerning effects—but MILL
including in it the instinct of self-protection, which man possesses in common
with the brute. It is unfortunate for Mr. MILL'S position that the word
'instinct' has been used to explain such acts of self-preservation. If instinct and
reason are one, whence arose the necessity for two distinct words? Do these
not stand for distinct conceptions? If a man supposes, with MILL, that he can

reason from a particular to a particular, let him try it. Let him try to reason from a horse to a lamp-post. The case is simple. The two words are necessary, because they denote two different modes in which life manifests itself as a discretive power, that is, a power producing distinct states. One of these modes is animal instinct, which is the basis of all affectional or emotional life; the other is a spiritual principle, or the rational faculty. Now the power of acting contrary to the animal instinct is the prerogative of man alone. It is not found in the brute, nor in man's own animal nature. It comes from the human will; and the intellectual or passive exercise of the will we call reason, by the use of which we make the passage from cause to effect. But the brute has only an active exercise of desire and its instinctive perceptions. To call this reason is to confound terms. No instance can be found where a brute, however much it may have seemed to exercise powers of reasoning, ever really acted contrary to the dictates of its affectional instincts."

A late writer, after showing that TURNER wrote ambitiously very miserable poetry, and talked—outside of professional topics—very shallowly, concludes that the artistic faculty is, so to speak, an exclusive faculty, existing unaccompanied by any extraordinary manifestations of other great faculties. He seems to think that TURNER'S case proves the proposition. But LEONARDO DA VINCI was a great inventor, architect, sculptor, engineer, and scientist, as well as a great painter; and MICHAEL ANGELO was a great anatomist, mechanician, architect, painter, and poet, as well as a great sculptor. I was not surprised, therefore, one Sunday afternoon, after INNESS had been trying to arrange some of the scattered, confused, disordered sheets of his *Mathematics of Psychology*, so that he might read aloud a passage or two, to observe his enthusiasm on the subject, and to hear him exclaim: "Years ago, if I had only had money, and hadn't had to paint, I should have got into a lot of all this kind of thing." Passionate as is his fondness for painting, he is most passionately of all a metaphysician. If the *Mathematics of Psychology* ever see the light, the folios of the schoolmen will seem more trivial than ever.

VI.

Here is a short, swift biography which Mr. INNESS gave of himself one evening: "Born at Newburgh, New York, May 1, 1825; brought to New York city in a basket when a baby; lived in Greene Street and Centre Street till six or seven years old; went to Newark, and staid there till fifteenth year; returned to New York city; art-life began at almost any time; always drew a little bit, and fiddled along from one thing to another; studied engraving with SHERMAN & SMITH, of New York, off and on for two years; gradually began to paint; sick during the whole of early life; couldn't stand the pressure of being stuck fast; three trips to Europe; admired ROUSSEAU more than any other landscape painter, though saw few of his works"—a narrative recited by jerks, and impatiently, as if not worth the telling. INNESS'S landscapes, varied though they be in motive and technique, are always the faithful records of pictorial impressions received from nature by a mind of unusual endowment, cultivation, and sensitiveness. They tell what the artist feels rather than what he sees; and in victory over sunlight and local tone, in translucency and splendor of aerial lights, in breadth and grouping of cloud masses, in subordination of the subject to the expression of the sentiment in fullness and glory of color, in eloquence serene or impassioned that is nourished only by noble thought, in simplicity and suggestiveness, many of them belong to the category of supreme achievements of landscape art. Certainly his landscape in the Northwest Room leads all the other landscapes of the present Academy Exhibition.

Edgar Spier Cameron, "The Cusp of Gemini"
(c. 9 October 1882 / excerpt)

[Born in Ottowa, Illinois, Edgar Spier Cameron was a student at the Chicago Academy of Design and, later, at the Chicago Academy of Fine Arts. In 1882, he entered the Art Students League in New York to study with William Merritt Chase and Thomas Wilmer Dewing. In "The Cusp of Gemini," his unpublished autobiography, he recalls hearing a guest lecture at the league by George Inness. The "Webb" to whom he refers may be Dr. William Seward Webb, who married Eliza (Lila) Vanderbilt. Cameron mentions the lecture again in an undated letter, of which only a fragment remains: "we had a lecture from Geo Inness Saturday evening and the compostitions [sic] were not criticized" (Edgar Spier Cameron papers, Archives of American Art, Smithsonian Institution, Washington, D.C., reel 4290, frame 68).]

Sometimes on Saturday night, artists or other people of note came to talk to our composition class on subjects related to art. On one such occasion, George Inness Sr. had addressed us on the subject of color, and when he had finished the students were crowded about him, listening to more informal talk when a former student, a relative of the Vanderbilt family by the name of Webb, came in with Oscar Wilde who had come to this country to lecture on that aestheticism which was an outgrowth of the Pre-Raphaelite movement in British Art. After introductions, Inness who was a wirey, nervous little man intensely imbued with a conviction of the soundness of his theories of art, continued to expound them as if he were still talking to the students. When there was a slight pause, Wilde broke in with "There are facts in Art", but Inness galloped ahead with his discourse, until at another pause Wilde interjected "There are facts in Art", but we never learned what these facts were, as Inness never gave him an opportunity to tell us before he was drawn away by Mr. Webb to meet people of greater social importance than a group of students. I wrote to my parents of this occasion, "We had a 'singularly deep' lecture from George Inness last night on the principles of gradation and the relation of color to light and shade. He is extremely scientific in all his art, but he only told us the philosophy of things which we would do naturally from feeling. After Inness had finished, a friend of the League by the name of Webb came in with Oscar Wilde, whose ideas on art we have heard so much about. He did not talk to the class."

"Homage to George Inness: Memorial Services in the National Academy of Design" (24 August 1894)

[From this text, Inness's obituary in *The New-York Times*, we learn that he was eulogized by the Reverend Dr. John Curtis Ager. A Swedenborgian minister and translator, Ager had baptized Inness and his wife in the Swedenborgian Church of the New Jerusalem in Brooklyn, New York, on 4 October 1868. See Sally M. Promey, "The Ribband of Faith . . . ," in the Selected Bibliography, for documentation on this important moment in Inness's life.]

Attended by Many Artists and Kindred Minds Who Had Known the Man and Recognized His Genius—Eloquent Tribute of the Rev. Dr. Ager of Brooklyn, a Close Personal Friend—Mrs. Inness Prostrated and Unable to be Present.

Inness, to whom a Hellenic people would have raised statues, received yesterday the most delicately impressive homage that the modern world may pay.

He had been great enough to deserve the name of artist, which is grander than everything, and the members of the National Academy of Design, their friends, and the representatives of the larger class who, hopeless of emulating him, at least tried to understand his work, were united in the services held in the rooms where his personality had, for a quarter of a century, expressed its admirable distinction in imperishable paintings.

Strength and implacable serenity had been easily read in life in the expression of his face, vigorously modeled, and the eyes of which were profound and mystic, while the forehead, pure as the entablature of a Greek temple, was radiant with interior light.

Yet he had known the envy of rivals, the hatred of fools, cold indifference, the sufferings of those he loved, atrociously mingled with fever of creative fervor, and all the misfortunes, accidents, ridiculous annoyances and crimes of fate allied in perpetual vexation against the genius of man.

In the artistic circle of which his mortal envelope was the centre yesterday, Inness's long baptism of labor and pain could not be realized. There were impulsive thoughts only of the morning landscapes, tender, vaporous, ideal, where leaves imperceptibly tremble in a soft, undecided light, and enchanting visions in the foliage furtively glance at dark fountains faintly whitening; of evening landscapes, inflamed from skies, where walls and citadels crumble into melting gold; of heights that seraphita climbed, and of all the rhapsodies of epic poems which Inness impressed for Americans in accurate records of their country's widely magnificent natural scenery.

Phidias himself, who knew the secrets of his art, could not have sculptured the figure of an imitator, and to make a camp follower none could think of the immortal Indra on his chariot, drawn by horses of azure, or of Zeus, Clarios of Tegeus, at once god of ether and god of light. None could think yesterday of Inness at any period of his career vanquished or feeble, since he is splendidly triumphant in his art, and, doubtless, already perceives with new senses, as he expected in his Swedenborgian confidence, the peaceful glory of beauty and the silent music of the stars. He was the very reverse of an imitator, and his long years of suffering in the most hideous of mundane circles, the one where great works are received in mute unconcern, were his penalty for being one of the world's greatest artists. None could think yesterday that there was humiliation for the public in the fact that wealth had not flown into Inness's studio at once, as he deserved, like metal in the streets after the burning of Corinth. But the reflection comes inevitably now and makes more dreadful than chance of error in overappreciation, the fault of not recognizing genius at its first appearance.

The ceremony at the National Academy of Design was simpler than any impression which its relation may convey. Inness disdained glory even more than money. He has obtained glory more solid, more durable, and more universal than many great men of his time. But he never courted it or made the slightest sacrifice in its favor. Without hoping for success, he tried to satisfy his refined instinct for the beautiful. He asked of color to express the soul, the thought, the mysterious attitude of the intimate being which is in nature, and he succeeded by force of passionate endeavor. Pompousness did not illuminate his life, and would not have fitted his obsequy.

The casket of silver and velvet was covered with palm leaves and wreathes [*sic*] of white roses, ivy, and lilies of the valley. The ribbons were violet. On a pedestal the fine bronze bust of Inness by Hartley, stood at the foot of the casket, and its eyes had a life-like glance. The paintings shone in their usual places on the walls, in all their gayety. Only the balustrade at the stairs was draped in black. The flaging was at half mast. The air in the rooms had the perfume of flowers, not of incense, and the minister, solemn but not grave, spoke in pleasantly-modulated tones of irrepressible conviction. He stood in the arch separating the council room from the long reception room, in front of the casket that tall palmetto leaves colored. Without a gesture, his head a little inclined, he told the interpretations of the Arcana Coelestia, the state of death which is changed to a higher life, the eternal humanity of the Father, the necessity of works for salvation that faith alone may not procure, and the state of the spiritual world which has the same relation to the natural world as the soul to the body. Those who knew Inness know how impatient of contradiction he was in his religious faith. He talked for hours of the Swedish philosopher.

Neither by geometrical nor physical nor metaphysical principles had Swedenborg succeeded in reaching and grasping the infinite and the spiritual or in elucidating their relation to man and man's organism, though he had caught glimpses of facts and methods which he thought only lacked confirmation and development. He was a man who won respect, confidence, and love of all who came in contact with him. Though people might disbelieve in his visions, they feared to ridicule them in his presence.

His theosophic system was founded on the point of view that God must be regarded as the Divine man. His essence is infinite love. His manifestation, form or body is infinite wisdom. "Divine love is the self-subsisting life of the universe," Inness quoted. "From God emanates a divine sphere which appears in the spiritual world as a sun, and from the spiritual sun again proceeds the sun of the natural world. . . . In God there are three infinite and uncreated degrees of being, and in man and all things corresponding three degrees, finite and created. They are love, wisdom, use; or, end, cause, and effect. The final ends of all things are in the Divine mind, the causes of all things in the spiritual world, and their effects in the natural world. . . . "

The minister's eloquence had tenderness, not enthusiasm, and it came to an end in a prayer and benediction of gentle, crystal clearness.

There was an artistic inclination in his well-made phrases when he spoke of Inness's conception of nature as all symbolical, and of his art to reproduce this, not in the crude forms of outward expression that the common mind may easily grasp, but in spiritual suggestions.

An artist might not have expressed better a sense of the aristocracy of art, the exaltation of the best in everything which it signifies and the religious inspiration which it demands, since genius is not logical, has only perception, and attains its highest flights in pure ecstasy. The sentiment sent a thrill of appreciation in the audience of artists that nothing more sensually expressive might have produced.

They sat on sofas, chairs, and benches of the reception room and formed a compact crowd, prolonged into a tall, black mass, in the vestibule. They sat around members of the family in the council room, bright as the cool sacristies of the ancient monasteries.

The light that came through the small colored window panes made the scene resplendent with an undefinable grace. There was not an unimpressioned person among the painters, poets, and sculptors there, to whom art itself is a religion intolerant and jealous. There were only thoughts, minds, and conceptions heartily united in Inness's vision of the ladder of men and angels, the highest line of which disappears in pure sideral light, and in their own vision of long lines of artists in the front rank of which stands Inness.

The sermon and eulogy of the Rev. Dr. J. C. Ager were listened to with the deepest attention. The minister is the pastor of the Brooklyn Society of the New Jerusalem, the Swedenborgian Church at Monroe Place and Clark Street on Brooklyn Heights. He was for many years the personal, close, and intimate friend of George Inness, and stood closer to him than any other man. A man of artistic instincts, there was always a mind of the closest sympathy and interest between Pastor Ager and Painter Inness. This much the audience, especially the artists, knew, and the eulogy, coming from such a source, possessed a peculiar significance and interest for the hearers.

The Rev. Dr. Ager prefaced his personal remarks by a series of running quotations from the Bible to point and enforce the Swedenborgian doctrine of the hereafter.

"This that we call death," he said, "is not death. It is but the entrance to another state. Here in this life, on this world, we develop only the primary faculties of life. This is our initial stage. Here we begin to open our faculties. Here, on this earth, we have the opportunity to make a complete choice between good and evil.

"Death sets us free from the conditions of this life, and sends us into the future life, which lies alongside of this. There we will be no more subject to the laws of space and time."

The minister closed his Bible.

"This was, in substance," he continued, looking upward with folded arms, "the religious faith of this brother who has passed on into the higher life. If his voice could be now heard, he would emphasize the doctrines which I have stated.

"It is hardly possible for me to deal with the professional character and position of George Inness. I believe, with many artists, that his fame will be a lasting one, and has not yet, by any means, reached its limit.

"It was my lot to know him at the somewhat critical point in his life when he was drifting away from every definite belief and had just begun to find in the writings of Swedenborg a solution of his difficulties.

"Those of you who knew George Inness know how intense a man he was. That word 'intense' perhaps better describes him than any other in the language. He was an intense man. He was a genuine man.

"He was a true genius. He had little sympathy with those who did not share his beliefs. Perhaps I should not say sympathy but certainly no sense of companionship. To many, I know, he seemed ungenial, cold. But those who knew him well understand the reason for this opinion of him.

"His opinions, beliefs, convictions, were everything to him. If he had a conviction, that conviction was the truth, simply because he saw it, and not because he arrived at a conviction by any cold and formal process of reasoning or logic. This intuitive perception of truth is the characteristic of genius. That is the way George Inness reached his conclusions.

"In Swedenborg George Inness found the basis for his theories of art. He found there the true solution for all the problems of expression. To him all nature was symbolic—full of spiritual meaning. He prized nothing in nature that did not stand for something.

"That was the secret of his theory of art. He cared for no picture that did not tell a story; not necessarily to common minds by this kind of symbolism, but telling a story to the feelings which it suggested, and to the thought to which it gave expression.

"This philosophy of art, as some of you know, was immeasurably dear to George Inness. Out of it all his pictures sprang. He was as genuine in his own life as in anything else. In religion he was as intense as he was in art, and as dogmatic. But with all of his intensity of feeling and purpose, he had the gentleness of a woman.

"We do not know what the rest of the world will think of George Inness, now that he is gone, but we who knew him know that that other life into which he has gone will not be to him one of inactivity. All his powers will find there a more active development. You who knew him know that he was sometimes impatient of his own limitations. Often he was lost in fits of despondency because of what he considered to be his lack of success. In the life to which he has gone there will be no limitations of his genius."

[The obituary concludes with a list of family members, friends, Academicians and other dignitaries that attended the funeral service.]

———◆·◆·◆———

Stanwood Cobb, "Reminiscences of George Inness by Darius Cobb" (c. 1894)

[After serving in the 44th Massachusetts Regiment of the Union army during the Civil War, Darius Cobb returned home to become an artist and writer. He befriended Inness when Inness returned to Boston after a five-year visit to Europe (1870–75). His son, Stanwood Cobb, taught philosophy and religion at Harvard University and published on a wide range of topics, including early child education, mysticism, and jade. Darius's recollections of Inness, probably recorded shortly after Inness's death in 1894, were published for the first time in the *Art Quarterly* in 1963.]

My introduction to George Inness was unique. When he returned from Europe a score of years ago (1875), I wrote for the *Boston Traveller* a critical paper in which I endeavored to analyze him, and follow the course of his mind from his early period to the time of his return from abroad. He had been charged with departure from the breadth of his early manner to an undue attention to detail and ornateness in his European work. I followed his impulsive mind from one period to another, and described its operation in Italy, where he curbed his impulse and pursued a course of thorough study, with nature for his master.

Some days after the publication of this paper I entered my studio, which I had left for a few moments on an errand to a brother artist, and was accosted by a stranger who rose from a chair to greet me. He was of medium height, and spare in build. I would not describe his movements as nervous or quick, but rapid. He seemed charged with electricity; and as his expressive face confronted me, with the dark eyes throwing their intense light through his glasses into mine, I was drawn to him at once. He warmly clasped my hand and said, "This is Mr. Cobb?" On my responding to his greeting he said, "I have come to thank you for your analysis of me in the *Traveller*. It is gratifying to find a man who understands me. I do not thank you for your compliments, but for presenting me as I am."

He told me of his purposes in art, and commented on my studio work. He was vivacious in his speech, crisp and comprehensive. His words were like bullets. Not one was wasted. He was very magnetic, and I felt like listening and saying nothing.

During the preceding summer I had made a number of studies from nature, and on these he commented in language that evinced his rare knowledge of landscape art, giving me most valuable suggestions.

Mr. Inness soon afterwards went to the White Mountains; and on his return to Boston in the Fall he called at my studio. We had another talk on art, in which I got more ideas from him than any school could furnish. During the conversation he surprised me by saying, as he pointed to my sketches, that they had haunted him while he was among the mountains. He spoke in flattering terms of their color and effect, admonishing me to keep the sky at the horizon sufficiently deep to give value to the entire picture. He urged me to devote myself exclusively to landscape, prophesying results in language so emphatic that had not my purpose in art been decided on, I should have been inclined to heed his request.

I told him that my landscape work was to be subsidiary to the historical painting, which I was to enter on in the near future. He then said with enthusiasm, "That's it! Paint a big picture and *sell* it, and the little ones will follow! I'm painting my *Barberini Pines* (a picture ten feet long) [FIG. 33] to get some bigness into my work."

He desired that we should interchange visits and that I should see him paint in his studio, especially on his large picture. The studio was on the floor with Thomas Robinson and Frank Hill Smith, over the Boylston Bank, corner of Washington and Essex Streets.

FIG. 33. George Inness, *Pine Grove of the Barberini Villa*, 1876, oil on canvas, 78 ¾ x 118 ½", The Metropolitan Museum of Art, New York, Gift of Lyman G. Bloomingdale, 1898 (98.16).

His studio being temporary, there was no furniture except a stand. An easel was opposite the door and there was a pile of sketches thrown carelessly on the floor against the wall at the left. Most of these were his recent studies among the mountains. He was painting like one mad, dashing out a light and sweeping in a modulating tone with an impulsive stroke that would have seemed reckless, had not the effect produced been marvelous in strengthening the picture.

When I entered the studio Mr. Inness was grappling with a large treetrunk in an Italian scene. It was lunch time, and instead of a plate of beans or a porterhouse steak, he was dining on a piece of mince pie which he held in his left hand while he gripped his brush with his right, the palette lying on the stand. He paced rapidly up to the landscape and then as rapidly backed from it, paying no attention to his pie except to automatically devour it.

At last he hurried to the stand, and having disposed of his lunch he seized his palette; then clutching the brush close to the bristles he filled it with gray, and striding to the tree he swept the brush down the entire trunk, which was a high one, giving it a sinuous motion with the descent. The effect was wonderful. Here was a tree which some landscape painters would have puttered over for hours; and yet with an instantaneous stroke this magician gave the trunk a relief, a roundness, a completeness of modelling which no amount of hard labor could have produced.

"Good!" I exclaimed—"Let it be!"

"I will!" he responded. And satisfied at last he stood contemplating the picture. The only thing he had been indifferent to was the delicious pie. I learned much from this remarkable artist, by seeing him paint.

He took just pride in the work of his son George, which gave the promise that has been fulfilled. And here let me say, that the wife and mother must have been an inspiration to both husband and son. With my brother I spent an evening with the family at the Continental Hotel. We passed a most happy evening with that brilliant trio. I remember Mrs. Inness as a picture. If her husband had been a historical painter her face would have been an inspiring study for him.

In posting me on his methods of keying his landscapes Mr. Inness said that he first put his sky tones in at the horizon, which was always deep, and his highest light—usually some white object—in the foreground. He thus secured room for wide range of color.

When I was painting on the portrait of a lady he said, "That's right; paint light on light. That's Rubens." He warned me not to rely on black shadows for force, but to keep the shadows transparent. He never advised the laying on of thick paint in the shadows merely for the sake of saying that the canvas had plenty of pigment piled on to it.

I was painting a bank in a copy of a sea-shore study, and was working out some of the stones with much affection for the prismatic effects.

"Paint! paint!" exclaimed Inness. He seized my brush, and with the sort of stroke he gave his Italian tree he swept over my darling details, and gave the bank one broad mass of warm gray. The effect was magical.

Another time he was looking at a sketch of Pulpit Rock, at Nahant, that I had made after a shower when a rainbow appeared over the sea. I had faintly suggested the rainbow; but in my haste to catch a train I had failed to secure the golden light that the storm-freed sun cast over it. As the cliff was set against a white-cap cloud I left it dark, rather liking the effect. No artist had detected the lie till Inness saw it.

"Tell the truth!" said he. And taking my brush he dipped it into the red, blue and yellow, and with toning colors emphasized the rainbow. Then catching up a lump of raw sienna he splashed it over the cliff, breaking it with white and umber. "There, now you've got what the sun gave you!" With these words he handed back the brush.

The violin teacher of my youth used to take my instrument from my hand, place it under his chin, and then resting the bow on the strings prepare to draw out a tone to exemplify some suggestion, with the words, "Will you allow me?" and then produce his tone without further ado. Inness never deigned the "Will you allow me," but took my brush and "went in" without a word, his work speaking louder than words.

Once he was nonplused. He had often praised the color in my pictures with such unction that I began to see more color in them than I ever saw before. On this day he took my palette to strike off a sketch from one of my recent studies. He looked over the palette in bewilderment. To him the colors seemed mixed in confusion. "How am I to get any color from here?" he queried. "It must take brains to get color out of this!"—On seeing me smile he resumed, "Well, you ought—" Then he hesitated. "You know you always liked my color," I interposed. "Yes—I see—" He pondered a moment, and then with the words, "Each man for his palette," he sprang into his sketch with a success that led me to say to him that he never did a better thing. He glanced at my study, then at my palette and said, "Good reason."

A certain critic referred in an over-caustic manner to a couple of well-dressed figures which Inness had painted in the foreground of a White Mountain scene. This criticism was so unfair to the artist's motive that Inness felt compelled to answer it in the columns of the same paper, and he brought his manuscript to me for my opinion. It was a strong paper, filled with indignant rebuke in which he had underlined several emphatic words. I suggested the elimination of those italicized words, that the full strength of his paper might appear; relating to him the incident of the learned professor who told a student that with all the brilliant points cut out he would have a good discourse. Mr. Inness was struck aback for a moment; then he laughed and admitted the point. His answer appeared in the next morning's edition and he was never troubled again.

The painting of my *Back Bay View* in connection with Mr. Inness has been so graphically described by Mr. Baxter in the *Sunday Herald* that I must apologize for presenting this theme again, in a more personal way.

From the roof of Studio Building I had made a sketch of Back Bay, with the Common and a section of Park Street Church in the foreground, Covey and neighboring hills in the distance and "Holy Land," with Public Garden in the middle-distance. The church spires and towers formed a picturesque relief against a mass of illuminated cloud, and the Autumnal foliage of the Common and Public Garden presented a rich body of color, with broad lights and shadows. I embodied the idea which Mr. Inness had imparted to me. On seeing it he urged me to carry it out on a large canvas, promising to give me during its progress all the knowledge he had gained on both continents.

I procured a fifty-inch canvas and went to work. Our enthusiasm was evenly balanced. Mr. Inness called nearly every day; and while watching my work he gave me the knowledge he had gathered for years. "Put blue into the shadows of distant objects," he would say: "and you can paint the lights with warm colors." "Pile light on light." "Drive shadows into points." While he was painting a sea-storm from one of my sketches he said: "They don't appreciate the value of black as a color."

I painted over two months on the picture—I may well say in conjunction with Mr. Inness. I called on him repeatedly, by his invitation, to see him develop his own pictures. He being happy in the expression of his thoughts, I derived great benefit from these visits as well as from his visits to my studio. And all this was telling favorably on the *Back Bay*.

When I had got well along on the painting he suggested a broad light on the foliage, stating that there should be a geometric relation between the form of light in the clouds and that on the earth. He waved his hand vigorously over the sky and then brought the motion at an acute angle across the foliage in the Public Garden and that portion of the Common which adjoined it. He accompanied this movement with the remark that the foliage he had indicated should be lit by luminous color.

Mr. Inness was impelled to seize my brush as usual to carry out his thought, but he refrained because he deemed my foliage too good to spoil.

Suddenly an expedient came to his mind. "Have you pastelle?" he asked. I had none, so I went to Schirmer's studio and borrowed some of him [*sic*; his]. Mr. Inness no sooner got the pastelles into his hand than he began the work of illumination. The paint was hard, so there was no risk in this performance, as the pastelle could be wiped off if the experiment should prove unsatisfactory. He worked with such zeal that the effect was soon secured. The light produced was so gorgeous that we passed a unanimous vote to secure it in oil. He said that the idea of experimenting on a painting with pastelle had never occurred to him before, and he should buy a set of pastelles and give his *Barberini Pines* a try.

I secured this effect in oil. The artists who had called frequently to see the picture in its progress (the knowledge of George Inness' vital interest in this painting had become widely circulated) greatly admired this flood of light, and begged me to let the picture be, and touch it no more.

But Mr. Inness was now thoroughly aroused. It seemed as if he gave his mind more to *Back Bay* than to *Barberini Pines*. A few days after the pastelle experiment he took a long look at my sky, which had been well complimented, and then pointing to the sky on the sketch he exclaimed, "You haven't got that yet. Let me show you!" I, of course, assented. Thereupon he painted over my sky; and with a poet's inspiration making my sketch the basis, which he declared sufficient study for the grandest sky—he produced one which was the peer of any sky that either he or any other artist had ever produced. I affirmed this to him, and he pointed significantly to my sketch. "It may well be," he responded.

I shall never forget the inspired and inspiring motion of the brush as he worked hour after hour, throwing in a light here, a shadow there, and combining all with exquisite mezzo-tints, black, umber, sienna, yellow, white—about all the colors of the palette being called into requisition. "They don't put color enough in their skies!" he said as he dashed in a golden tone. "Clouds will stand rich color."

Well, the sky was finished at last. And then I had a problem to solve. "What am I to do about exhibition of this picture, George?" I queried. "There is my lower half and your upper half of the painting. How is it to be exhibited as mine?"

"I'll stand it if you will," was his laughing reply, as he opened the door.

I was left alone to enjoy the wonderful sky, and ponder over the situation. The next morning I stood before the painting and thought and thought. It was about ten o'clock when I reached a decision. The brush work on my part of the picture did not satisfy me. I had packed away into my brain all the ideas Mr. Inness had given me while painting on it for the past two months, but the work didn't express the knowledge and confidence which should appear from what I had gathered from. It must be repainted with an instrument by which no style could hamper me—the palette-knife.

I loaded my palette with color, and then in a sort of fury I plastered the colors over sky and all—leaving no portions untouched in the upper left-hand corner of the sky and the lower part at the extreme right, near Corey Hill, that I might have the touch and color of George Inness ever on the picture. I repainted all the towers and spires with the palette-knife, except the Arlington Street Church, which is left as I painted it with the brush, and which lacks the crispness or "bake" that the knife has given to the others. I put the knife-work over the distance, all the objects in the middle distance, the buildings, trees and the light that the palette had suggested, and the section of Park Street Church. In fact, the entire picture was repainted with the palette-knife except the two portions of the sky I have mentioned, and Arlington Street Church.

At three o'clock I had it finished. At four o'clock Mr. Inness called, expecting to see the picture as he left it. I had placed it off in another part of the studio, and he stood in silence looking upon it, the color rising in his cheek as he contemplated my "departure." At last he broke into a low laugh, and said "Let it alone!" and I did. William Hunt bade me to let it be and so did other prominent artists. I never touched it again, save to paint Trinity in with the knife as that massive tower was not finished when I made the sketch.

I must not omit to add that one more sign of George Inness appears on the shadow sides of the swelling houses on the Back Bay. I had these shadows dark throughout. Mr. Inness took a brush and quickly passed a gray tone over the shadows, leaving my dark tones in the corners, saying as he did so, "Don't forget to drive the shadows into points."

The following was the expression of my opinion of George Inness' works twenty years ago, in the *Boston Traveller*; it is the writer's opinion today:

"The highest and boldest features of the French schools are found here, with the addition of qualities which no French artist that we have seen has attained to. In the vastness of space, the infinitude of skies, the relations of sky, foreground and distance, the development of truths by facts, and the elevating of facts by truths, the power, in short, of imparting to landscape painting a character corresponding to the greatness of the historical, and of portraying the full grandeur of nature's poetry—in all this Inness now stands preeminent. Broad and suggestive he omits no detail that is necessary to the full expression of his idea; and nature seems a living reality before you, while the poetic element mellows and strengthens all with its subtle power. As American painter Inness ranks with our standard poets; for his works are poems on canvas—poems that impress one as do the thoughts of our greatest heads."

◆━◆◆◆━◆

Elliott Daingerfield, "A Reminiscence of George Inness" (March 1895)

[Born in Harpers Ferry, Virginia, Elliott Daingerfield was the son of a Confederate general. He moved to New York in 1880 and studied at the National Academy of Design and the Art Students League. He soon discovered Barbizon painting, which would influence his work for the rest of his life.

Around this time, he met and befriended Inness, about whom he would ultimately write eight articles and essays. We have reproduced two of the most
informative of these in the present volume.]

To a young man in any of the professions it is an event of no little importance
when he is brought into close contact with one who has already achieved fame,
and the loftiest position his profession offers. It was with a certain exaltation, a
quickened hopefulness, that I met George Inness in the early days of '85, when
his own power was reaching its summit, and his works were glowing with that
unusual lustre which makes them the most dignified efforts in American Art.

When, for the first few weeks of my acquaintance, he failed to remember
me—even the very name was lost to him—there was in my mind no sense of
resentment. One with quick perception could readily see that Inness had no
interest in the external man—he was often unconscious of himself; the real *ego*
was that great striving quantity unseen with eyes, the soul, the heart, the brain
of a man, and through the expressions of these, only, could he discover himself
or recognize the individuality in another. Day after day, I went into his studio,
only two doors removed from my own, and there, watching the progress of
numerous canvases in silence, and with the sort of reverence one must feel in the
presence of genius, grew up a knowledge of the man and the mighty engine of
his mind, its purposes and achievements, which will ever remain a heritage of
strength in the struggles of my own life.

Invincible, is perhaps the one word which defines George Inness's character.
Arrogant, he has been called, but falsely; egotistical, selfish, and all the other
phrases that unsuccessful jealous minds usually apply to those who are intolerant
of false effort, and falser success, in the fields where alone Truth is the aim and
Truth the goal. Never once, in all my long acquaintance with him, have I known
Inness satisfied with a work of his own. Times without number I have seen a new
light flash in his eye; a quick eager toss of the head and thrusting back of the hair,
when some problem with which he had been struggling for days or months—perhaps years—was yielding under the sway of his fierce energy; then it was he gave
vent to those expressions of satisfaction which have been called conceit; but, mark
you, when the morning came, or the new mood, be that canvas never so fine if one
thing there jarred on the man's artistic sensibility he attacked it with all the old
enthusiasm, with a dogged determination to bring it to his own high standard.

This spirit absolves him forever from all charges of vanity. The pleading of
friends, artists, or buyers availed nothing. His creed was ever to make his work

more perfect; and it is a truth well attested, that, however beautiful the first attempt might have been, the completed work was almost always the finer. It was in such struggles that Inness conquered his limitations and grew into the powerful, virile, and poetic painter we now see him.

His moods were so well known to me that I could readily tell from his very knock at my door whether I was to be taken off across the hall to his studio, to view some great advance in his picture, or whether he was to drop into a chair in silence for a while, worn, tired, and with that depression of spirit which only the artistic nature can understand. At such a time, one word upon some abstract theme, no matter what, if really serious, would stir him into life and intense speech. It would not be argument, as between two; for, when Inness talked, the flame needed no draught. It blazed and flared until his own conclusions were reached, and then faded, even as the glow on some of his own forest trees seems to fade in the twilight time, until the deep silence left no room for speech. Nor were his arguments always carried to logical sequence: what mattered it? Does the storm forever sweep across the exact field you or I have chosen for its path? The rush and go of it were all there and the interest. If there were sympathy, which means understanding, in the listener's soul, these monologues of his yielded many great truths to him.

He came into my studio one day, with all the unrest and nervous eagerness which characterized him when thinking intensely; threw out several sentences about his picture, his purpose in it, etc., when with a sort of mad rush he said:

"What's it all about? What does it mean—this striving—this everlasting painting, painting, painting away one's life? What is Art? That's the question I've been asking myself, and I've answered it this way:" (I drew a writing pad to me, and jotted down his words; they are worth thinking about oftener than once.) "Art is the endeavor on the part of Mind (Mind being the creative faculty), to express, through the senses, ideas of the great principles of unity."

Perhaps no more characteristic sentence has ever been recorded of him. It satisfied him. He had made his conclusion and expressed it. He did not propose to supply us with brains to understand what the "principles of unity" may be. We might struggle as we pleased with that problem, as perhaps he had struggled with the other, although to a tyro the last seems exactly the same as the first. Art, Religion, and the Single Tax Theory were his chief themes, and, by a curiously interesting weaving, his logic could make all three one and the same thing.

Oblivious to externals, both of persons and things, he often said and did much that evoked harsh criticism, but at heart, it may be truthfully said, he was as gentle as a child, even tender, and swiftly sympathetic. What a delight it was to watch him paint when in one of those impetuous moods which so often possessed him. The colors were almost never mixed;—he had his blue theories, black, umber, and in earlier days bitumen: he even had an orange-chrome phase. With a great mass of color he attacked the canvas, spreading it with incredible swiftness, marking in the great masses with a skill and method all his own, and impossible to imitate; here, there, all over the canvas, rub, rub, dig, scratch, until the very brushes seemed to rebel, spreading their bristles as fiercely as they did in the days of yore along the spine of their porcine possessor.

But stand here, fifteen feet away. What a marvelous change is there! A great rolling billowy cloud sweeping across the blue expanse, graded with such subtle skill over the undertone. Vast trees with sunlight flecking their trunks, meadows, ponds—mere suggestions, but beautiful; foregrounds filled with detail, where there had been no apparent effort to produce it, delicate flowers scratched in with the thumb-nail or handle of the brush. One's imagination was so quickened that it supplied all the finish needed.

Inness used to say that his forms were at the tips of his fingers, just as the alphabet was at the end of the tongue. Surely it was true, and when he "struck a snag," as he called it, and he almost always did (I used to think sometimes, for the fun of the struggle that was to follow), 'twas in the *construction* of his picture, not in any mere matter of painting. He would find out where the "hitch" was and then go on.

Under excitement of this kind he could do most astounding things. One morning a frame came in which had been mismeasured; he sent for a canvas to fit it, rapidly sketched in a composition, and produced one of the most limpid, lovely pieces of pure sunlight I have ever seen him paint. But, alas! he said there was a "hitch," and subsequent labor transformed it—one of the rare cases when I wish "well enough" had been let alone.

I once had the good fortune to paint a little picture that pleased him; he caught sight of it lying on the floor against the wall and exclaimed:

"Hello, who did that?"

I told him. Stooping down he caught it up, pushed his glasses far back on his head, and examined it, with many expressions that I remember with deep satisfaction, put it down and walked out of the room. The next morning he came in again, and, taking up the picture, asked: "What do you expect to get for that?" I mentioned a price, thinking he meant to advise some one to buy it, but he answered at once, "I'll take it," and walked to the desk, and made out a check.

Then, as if he meant to aid me still farther up the hill, he caught up my palette and brushes, and for an hour painted at a figure picture, which I had thought finished, to show me "how" it ought to be done. I have never touched that picture. It remains a souvenir of the day I had my biggest lesson in art, and I value and feel the importance of every word he then said.

It was not always, however, that he was so interested, or so complimentary. Years after I undertook a picture which had a line of rail fence running down to the foreground; he saw it and objected somewhat to the arrangement. I undertook to argue the point, and said, "Why can't I have it that way, if it pleases me?" "So you can," was his answer, "if you want to be a d——'d idiot." I changed the fence.

So incident upon incident might be multiplied of this strange, erratic, always artistic nature, that forever lived at white heat, unveiling in vast waves his visions of color, tone, and grandeur of line, until we were drawn nearer to the nature he loved, and in his art perceived the earnest seeker after Truth.

With the works of all the great painters he had a profound acquaintance, and an analytical as well as synthetic knowledge. His admiration for the really great results was sincere and often enthusiastic. For the evanescent, soap-bubble successes in art, he had no toleration, and with a force quite irresistible he pointed out the fallacy in efforts which were the result of mere skill, or a certain jugglery in color, brush-work, or what not. "Limitation there must be in art," he would say; "how hopeless it all seems when we look at nature."

For Titian, Angelo, Raphael, Rembrandt and many others of the great men, he was unstinting in praise. To make a landscape as perfect in its unity as a portrait by Rembrandt was an ever-present ideal. Rousseau, Millet, Corot, Constable, Turner and Claude, he quoted often as being at the head of the list, and, perceiving their faults, as he often did, their merits never escaped him. Of the great Englishman he said hard things for his brutality and "stupidity," although to certain works, such as the "Pier at Calais," he gave unlimited praise. As his own ideals were high, so was his condemnation of all failure or frivolity of intention severe, often bitter, but not unjust.

No reminiscence of Inness would be complete without some mention of his great power as a colorist, for all his philosophy, all his many-sided nature, seemed to express itself in the fulness and beauty of color. We are not to make comparisons with the work of others—that were needless, Inness's color was his own. The early morning, with its silver, tender tones, offered him as great opportunity for the expression of what he called "fulness of color" as did the open glare of the noonday, or the fiery bursts of sunset. Mention has been made of his different color-moods, and one fairly held the breath to see him spread with unrelenting fury a broad scumble of orange-chrome over the most delicate, subtle, gray effect, in order to get more "fulness;" and still more strange was it to see, by a mysterious technical use of black or blue, the same tender silver morning unfold itself, but stronger, firmer, fuller in its tone quality. "One must use pure color," he would say: "the picture must be so constructed that the 'local' of every color can be secured, whether in the shadow or the light." Many of his canvases are criticised because of an over-greenness, or an intensity of the blues, but deeper study shows the man's principle, for which he strove with the whole force of his nature. A perfect balance of color quality everywhere in the picture. The mass of offending green will be found to balance perfectly with the mass of gray or blue of the sky. So that the whole canvas, viewed with that perceptive power without which there is no justice in either the criticism or the critic, becomes an harmonious balance, with all the intensity of his powerful palette. Inness maintained that the "middle tone" was the secret of all success in color—he strove for it until the end, and so great was his effort that the latest works are but waves of wonderful color, marvellous and mysterious—the very essence of the beauty of nature. When he chose to put aside his theories and produce a "tone study," following the habit of those masters who have glorified modern French art, he was as subtle as any of them, and far less labored; but it is in his very intensity that he has preserved his individuality, and if we are to understand him aright, we must study him from his own standpoint. In his earlier life his drawing was precise, and accurate to a wonderful degree, being elaborated to the very verge of the horizon.

In the beginning Inness strove for knowledge with most untiring effort. His early pictures are full of intricate, elaborate detail; 'twas thus he gained that knowledge of forms which put them at his finger-tips. Always, however, there was the largeness of perception which enabled him to understand masses, and divide his compositions into just proportions of light and shade; and under all, one saw the poet and the philosopher. Painfully objective as were those early efforts, they were tasks along the great highway which at last led him to those heights whence he saw and understood the *subjective* in nature, and expressed it in his art.

Analytical, profoundly so, when he chose to be, with increasing years his art grew more and more synthetic, and the very latest works are most so of all, and strangely beautiful in the total elimination of needless detail, and sure grasp of *idea*. His art became at that time a sort of soul-language, which, if you have not the speech, you may not understand, but it is none the less beautiful. To-day we are at too near a view. Let us await the coming years, he will then need no defence.

Reginald Cleveland Coxe, "George Inness" (1908)

[A native of Baltimore, Reginald Cleveland Coxe moved to New York City in 1879 and studied at the National Academy. Like Elliott Daingerfield, he kept a studio in the Holbein Studio Building in New York. In regular contact with Inness, he provided an invaluable primary account of the artist at work.]

I feel it almost a duty toward those who come after to write down now, ere I, too, go to my separate star, what I remember of George Inness. However great our future may become in art, he will hold his own place, if not as a master, yet as the American painter especially called to interpret American nature according to the great principle first recognized by Constable, and spread through his influence in France. Already he is a master to some of us, and a future age may unanimously account him one. If he is not, then several other painters to-day regarded as such will disappear with him. Every personal reminiscence of a great man is interesting, grown the more valuable as memory fades, and as he comes to be known only through books.

A New York morning newspaper of wide circulation and weighty influence in affairs artistic, as well as in other directions, has recently published a leading article in which George Inness, Homer Martin, and Wyant are treated with scant respect and less admiration for their work. In that article George Inness is held up as a painter of very modest ability, who has been bolstered into an exaggerated fame as a great painter and who will straightway sink out of any lasting esteem.

I see evidence to-day of promise that, given twenty, yes, ten years more, we shall have a school of landscape painters not only of independent character in their work, but who will influence, by its strength, every other country where painters are developed. Yet do there live, and with minds capable of judging, people who believe in Inness as a very master. Time alone can show his correct standing beside *les Maîtres d'autrefois;* but these people, too, believe that he will hold an important place in the history of American art, and that his influence will only grow with years.

I shall write here, only of what I knew of him during several years near the close of his life. Our studios were adjoining, separated only by double doors. I saw him almost daily, and friendship resulted which in some ways was intimate. I never stood in the relation of being his pupil; he never talked down to me, but always with me: he himself making my position, so I was not afraid to disagree with him. When he did not like it, he would almost shriek at me and tell me very plainly what he thought my opinions were worth. He was not always wrong, either, for I was tempted often to say something that would draw him out, and what is the use of being young if one cannot lessen callow ignorance even at the expense of making an old gentleman angry?

His studio was bare of any comforts, or ornamentation, and he himself generally looked like many old painters I have seen, who labored away with well-meant, but sad endeavor—until you saw him at his work—his head, his eyes; for then he had the vigor and enthusiasm of a League student—or, rather, of the whole body of them compressed into one frail self. Then I felt the influence of his strength; and still to-day, he and Constable and Millet live with me, walk with me and criticise me when I dare to paint. In my mind they are his only equals in a broad understanding of all nature.

It was in the winter of 1885, I think, that Inness first showed his finished "Niagara" in his studio, and later, at the American Art Association's galleries, together with a large collection of his work. I did not then have a personal acquaintance with him, but I accompanied more favored friends, saw his paintings and heard him talk in that high-pitched and rather raucous tone that was natural to him. If his heart spoke through his mouth, it seemed a very queer organ. His personality did not invite a closer acquaintance; I was not particularly impressed with the "Niagara"; it was too wide-spread and panoramic, but its beautiful color and atmosphere were admirable. His enthusiasm, as he talked to those around him, was amusing; he was so naïvely egotistic; and it was evident that for him there was but one landscape painter in the world. I had just returned from having spent several years as an art student in Paris, and to me the Fontainebleau School of nature painters represented everything that was great. Only they who had learnt their trade in France, knew anything. The old Hudson River School was to us simply a collection of ignorant artistic fossils, and so on. Inness might be a strong painter if he only had known how to paint—understood the cool grays of Corot, and how to draw a tree as could Rousseau. Yes, it would be our own fresh, imported ability that would make our country famous, our art great. We were the chosen ones, the coming men of future years. Those of the past were—oh, pooh!—and would be but a hideous memory before long.

It was with such feelings that I mounted the stairs of the American Art Association's galleries to look condescendingly at Mr. Inness's paintings. I knew the color would be harsh and raw, the drawings execrable, and the atmosphere not such as we had known in France. I felt that I was showing a broad and generous feeling in gracing Mr. Inness' exhibition; I knew that others felt that way, too, and I really would try hard to find something of which I could conscientiously utter words of well-guarded praise.

It was a very humble man that, after several hours, walked down that same stairway. It was no longer "Mr." Inness, but "Inness the Master," and I was thankful that I had not to await his death and future years to learn the fact of his mastership. That year showed me a new Spring season which I had never known before; a golden Autumn I had never understood, and that most heavenly of all seasons in any land, our Indian Summer; and Inness, the American painter, had interpreted all these for me and had revealed to me the glory of our own American possibilities.

Once I was walking in New England with a fair maiden and a superfluous young man. The time was sunset, and the brilliancy of the sky was subdued by a pleasant haze. It was very beautiful, and we gazed at it enrapt and silent. Finally, the other young man said: "What a splendid sunset!" "Yes," said the maiden, after a pause, "it is really quite artistic." Our companion looked at her in amused amazement, but I understood her. She, likewise, was an art student and only meant that it was not like our usual strong and violent American sunsets, but was cool and delicate, such as it would be possible to paint, and such as Daubigny understood, but, to the average American painter on that day, a sealed book. Inness would not be "artistic." I went one day in later years, to see a collection of Corots in a Fifth Avenue gallery. It was a bright Spring morning; the trees were fresh with the young green, the sky bright and the whole world laughed, and I in tune with it. The gallery had a subdued light, in harmony with the delicate tones of Corot's color; all a delicate gray, with here and there a suspicion of blue sky, with trees that seemed ashen rather than green. But somehow I felt that one picture talked to another, they seemed highly respectable and decidedly well-bred. So I got out again where I wanted to be, and saw our own Spring and the character of our own nature. I knew that Corot had interpreted the cultivated beauty of France, but that a greater master had shown a greater country, to inspire me. I know in this thought I am a foolish heretic to many— very many,—but history shows that many a heretic of former days is now venerated as an accepted apostle of truth.

Inness, when I knew him, cared not at all for any other man's painting. Nature was seen solely through his own eyes; but that is the rule with all great painters— as they grow old they become self-centered, and their own work sufficient unto them. I never heard him express enthusiastic admiration for the work of other men, except, perhaps, for the great Englishman, Constable. The men of the Fontainebleau School were too nearly his contemporaries for him to admire them unreservedly, although, naturally, they influenced him. He paid them the greater compliment of showing what he would praise by engrafting it into his own painting. And he felt the entirely worthy jealousy of their fame and influence amongst his own people as compared with his own modest recognition. When he spoke of the high prices their works brought at public sales, I reminded him that they were dead, did not themselves benefit by the money they brought, and that in times to come his own work might be as sought after and as highly treasured as theirs. It is, indeed, very doubtful whether any of them received nearly so great sums for their work as Inness did in the last half of his painter's life.

Inness painted on impulse, and the weather often directed his painting moods. One foggy, wet and altogether disagreeable Spring day, when the whistles were playing calliope fantasias on the rivers, he arrived from Montclair, full of something he had seen from the car windows. He selected an old canvas on which there were some prominent trees that furnished him a ground and composition. He told me, with a young student's enthusiasm, of his *motif;* that he would paint it straight through and finish it really *au premier coup,* that day. He began gloriously; I watched, with his own enthusiasm, the growing wet landscape. One felt the fog dropping from the branches on to the soggy ground, and it was beautiful, a true "symphony in green and gray." But, by noon the day began to clear; so did his picture, with a patch of sky showing through the fog. At three o'clock a strong west wind came up, with an entirely blue sky and brilliant white clouds, which bothered him when they drove across and hid the sun; the same conditions struck his picture. It was a grand sunset that ended that day—and finished the canvas. I believe he hardly remembered the fog at all.

I never saw him begin on a clean canvas and work on it more than a couple of days, after which he would lay it aside to be taken up at some future time when the right mood came along. In front of the double doors connecting our studios, racks for holding canvases were built, extending from floor to ceiling. These were filled with early paintings, sketches, half-finished canvases and pictures which did not satisfy him. He would pick out one of a morning, using the ready-made *motif* and transform it into a finished work by night. Or he would potter over it for a week, sometimes perhaps ten days, during which it sang all kinds of beautiful songs, only in the end to be returned in disgust to its former resting place. Often I appealed to him to stop; or if he were in good humor with me, threatened to "take it away," but his picture was always "going to be far better." Sometimes it was and sometimes it wasn't.

In his later years, at least, he worked without much regard to the subject of his pictures. Once, after completing a sale in his studio, his purchaser asked: "Now, Mr. Inness, where is that taken from; what part of the country?"

"Nowhere in particular; do you suppose I illustrate guide-books? That's a picture."

I think I had heard this story once, but Mr. Inness himself told it to me, adding: "Whoever cares what scene a Corot represents?" I do not believe what he said was true; his memory was such a store-house of places and things which he had studied in early days that he drew on it and painted a truth laid away in his memory—and an actual scene. I saw him once paint a bridge in a picture, not an ideal bridge or one painted from "chic," but so constructed as to bear a loaded cart and carry it safely over, and which he had at some time or other studied, though, probably he might not be able to say exactly where. He was a thorough impressionist; I do not mean in the sense the word is used to-day, which has nothing to do with its real meaning, but in its truest definition. A gentleman once asked him of a certain picture in which there was a barn: "Mr. Inness, what is that spot there alongside the barn?"

"What do you think it looks like?"

"Well, I should say it was a wheelbarrow."

"Good," said Inness; "that's just what I thought it was, too."

That sounds very like him. I regret that I cannot put down his exact words and expressions, for they were characteristic of the man, but a memory only of the substance of what he said remains; his nervous manner, the fire of his excited eye when interested, and the skeletons of what he said remain as perfectly with me to-day. I never saw him use a sketch to paint from, nor memoranda in any form, nor did I ever see him use a pencil. His early work, like that of Corot, had much of the detail of the Hudson River School, where every leaf and fern was carefully painted. But the results of those early days were but a means to an end, not the aim of his effort. Such a painter—every original one—goes through three stages in his life: First, the minute study of forms and local color, when the storing up of material for future use goes on; next comes the full-grown and mature use of his brush and paint, the accomplished workman; last, the mellow poetic art that approaches more nearly the divine idea, from which all material influence seems withdrawn. So it was with Inness.

His peculiar disposition and rather eccentric character kept him separated from his fellows, because he thought they underrated his power. It was shyness rather than pride that put a false mask before his face. He was fond of Wyant and often spoke of him and his work with, what was for him, enthusiasm. Wyant, when a youth, had made a pilgrimage to know him and his work better; and that he had done so, in preference to seeking Church and Bierstadt, the then famous men, was a bit of homage he enjoyed looking back upon. It was evidence of real appreciation on the part of a painter of promise that gave great comfort to a very sensitive heart.

My own admiration for his genius opened the way for me to know him. The group of young painters to which I belonged, influenced and taught altogether by France, did not appreciate the genius of the old painter of Montclair, and his sensitive nature felt this deeply. We did not know—we seldom even thought— that his eclectic mind had absorbed the lessons worth absorbing, from our dear Fontainebleau masters, long before we ever began to draw in the schools; nor did we understand that he had already then learnt good from the moods of Constable, the grays of Corot, the peace and color of Daubigny and the draw-ings of Rousseau. Inness was one of them, only he had a country, an atmosphere and a sky to interpret, unknown to them and very different from theirs.

It was almost a revelation to him that a lover of Corot, Rousseau and the mod-ern French methods could see anything great in him. When he found that I rated Constable as greater than the other Frenchmen, indeed, but Millet as greater than all, and that I abominated the work—but never the gentle character—of Diaz, he thought me a rather sensible fellow and found that we had something in common.

His crabbedness was often, but wrongly, laid to jealousy, and once he unwisely gave color to that idea in print, on the occasion of a reception given by the painters to one of their number who had won distinction in France. It was no mean paltry breaking of the Tenth Commandment, but it was a painful sense that the gewgaws won in another country carried greater weight with his fellows than the patient original search after what was greater than mere technical excel-lence. "I like Puvis de Chavannes," he once said: "he dares to draw badly at times; he isn't all Bouguereau." He feared a striving after technical excellence and cor-rectness was overshadowing the "better thing in art."

———◆·◆·◆———

Elliott Daingerfield, "Inness: Genius of American Art" (September 1913)

[In this article, Daingerfield gives us a lively, first-hand account of Inness at work in the Holbein Building in New York, where he and Inness rented studio space during the 1880s. In a rare and much-deserved tribute, he also acknowledges the importance of Inness's wife.]

The fact that an American citizen has waked to the value of American art to the extent that he will invest a large sum of money in the works of a single painter, is a matter no longer of slight importance, but is a national event, because it speaks not only of public spirited citizenship, but calls attention to the much more significant point that American art has produced works of permanent and splendid value.

That he should give such a group of pictures to a public museum in a great city, where the humblest street gamin, equal in privilege to the millionaire, may see and study them and receive their message, each in his due degree, gives the matter a national educational significance, and such an action on the part of Mr. Edward B. Butler, of Chicago, in recognizing and giving to the Chicago Art Institute the group of pictures by George Inness, is a move that is truly patriotic.

In order that these works, and their great influence may be properly known and felt, and that those who see them may know the great American painter of landscape better and more intimately, it is well that as great publicity as possible be given to the characteristics of a man who had the power to create such distinguished works of art.

In the old Holbein Studios on West Fifty-fifth Street, New York City, Mr. Inness maintained for many years a studio. It adjoined and connected with that of the distinguished sculptor, his son-in-law, Jonathan Scott Hartley, and when I went into the building, in 1884, I began an acquaintance with Mr. Hartley and with Mr. Inness, which later became one of the most forceful and valued factors in whatever art development I may possess; and the friendship with Mr. Inness, who was many years my senior, was viewed with the reverent faith that the younger man should ever give to the elder, when that elder possesses the white wand of genius.

In the beginning, Mr. Inness paid absolutely no attention to me at all. He came and went through Mr. Hartley's studio because it was convenient to do so, and as the days went on and my friendship with Hartley increased, we began to have our luncheons together—and to this modest table in the studio, surrounded by all the paraphernalia of Hartley's craft, and often by the great figures in marble or clay upon which he was at work, Mr. Inness came and talked as only George Inness could talk; for to sit with him, if he chanced to be in the mood for conversation, was to sit as listeners, with only the occasional word of response which served to kindle a new flame.

Why he persisted in calling me "Lippincott" at first, I have never been quite able to understand, and how long it would have continued I have no means of knowing; but I took the matter in hand one day and spelled the name for him, emphasizing it in such a way that the mistake was cleared from his mind.

Throughout the long years which extended up to the time of his death, I saw him and knew him, and truthfully may say that I worked with him constantly. Though I have no claim to be a pupil of George Inness (and I think that no man may justly claim that he was really a pupil of Inness), all those men who sat in his presence for any length of time had of necessity to become pupils, for always was he master.

The man's personality was most interesting. He lived in Montclair, New Jersey, and came to New York on an early morning train. I have stood across the street and watched him as he walked from the elevated railroad station to his studio, and in every movement he showed haste and eagerness to get to the easel where some picture was baffling his best effort, or where some new theme that surged within his mind might find expression. In those days—the late '80's—his figure was already bent; his hair, worn long, might be called "shaggy," though when brushed it was a rich, curling mass; his eyes flashed behind spectacles; his beard was slender and thin, hiding a mouth that was very mobile, but with the beard removed would not, probably, have been handsome. Square of jaw, the whole poise of head on shoulders was suggestive of pugnacious energy and great eagerness—these points all convey in a slight measure a glimpse of the man. His hands—what strange instruments they were!—angular and bony; nails strong, and after a day's work not overclean, because of his habit of using them in his work—constant in their motion and gesticulation; a much chewed and half-burned cigar in his mouth; clothes of which he was quite oblivious, for of one thing positive assertion may be made: George Inness, mind, heart, and soul, was buried and engulfed in his work.

I have known painters who talked art *ad nauseam;* I have known painters who talked about themselves, their hopes, aims, plans, and particular works; but none was like George Inness, who, if he pointed a conversation with references to his own work, had always the mountain heights of beauty, of science, and of religion well in view.

Inness at Work

To watch him run up those dim, dirty stairs of the old Holbein Studios, which for long years many of us trod, push through the sculptor's room and into his own, and attack those canvases, was enough to make the blood leap along any man's veins, whether he were painter or onlooker. If the problem were a great one, the man wanted to be alone; if he knew that it was to be a battle, he purposed making the struggle by himself; but once that struggle was turned into conquest, then his need for an audience was great and urgent; and so the youngster across the hallway, the tyro, was called into the master's studio, and it was there I heard and learned precious things.

He possessed a trying habit into which his emotions had led him. If he came into your studio with some enthusiastic certainty seething in his imagination, if your palette and brushes and your picture were exposed, ready to hand, it would have been amusing, if it were not so serious, to see how utterly he would lose sight of your work in the expressing of the idea that bore upon him. Long ago I told the story of one of these visits to me, and the canvas he painted on is precious, because, though he destroyed six months' work in an hour, he gave me the most wonderful lesson in the management of pigment, the application of color, the juxtaposition of planes, masses, and values of color in constructive arrangement that I had ever had before or have ever had since.

An Overpowering Personality

And the little story about the great painter Wyant is significant of this insistent dominance—entirely genuine, almost childlike in its simplicity, yet tremendous in its force. Mr. Wyant had taken a studio in the Holbein, much to the gratification and pleasure of the rest of us, and Mr. Inness began to visit him—a companion more worthy. It was not long before Wyant began to show signs of uneasiness, and presently he said to me: "I've got to go. If I am going to paint Wyants I must go somewhere else, or else I shall be painting Innesses here." One who knows the wide difference in the potential principles underlying the art of the two men—in the one, a dynamic power; in the other, an exquisite, lyric beauty—can understand how the impress of the former force must destroy the harmony and sweetness of the latter; yet in his very actions Inness was showing the most extreme and genuine interest and faith in the work of Wyant, whom he thought a great artist. After a month's stay in the building, Wyant sublet his studio and moved away.

Mr. Inness was very easily imposed upon. I was very much amused one day, when in Mr. Hartley's studio, Mr. Inness came in and said, "Scott, let me have two dollars, please!" "Why, certainly, father," said his son-in-law, handing out the money, "but what are you going to do with it?" "Oh," he said, "there is a man in there who seems pretty hard up; I was going to let him have it." "Is his name

Inness?" said Mr. Hartley. "Why, yes," said Mr. Inness; "how did you know?" The answer was amusing. Hartley slipped into Mr. Inness's studio, and before he was quite aware of what was happening, caught a man there by the collar and improved his progress down the stairs by the use of his toe, to Mr. Inness' extreme astonishment and my amusement—and then said by way of explanation, "The rascal's name was 'Hartley' ten minutes ago when he was in here wanting two dollars from me."

There were times when the stress of work became very burdensome; when the pictures became recalcitrant, difficult; when he would almost break down from sheer effort to conquer difficulties; when nothing would "finish." Then he would say: "I must go out to nature. I must get an opportunity to study a little." And he would retreat for two or three days to his Montclair home, and in a coupé which he had arranged with easel and canvases, he would go out into the fields, even in the wintertime, and from the window of the coupé he would make direct sketches from nature—direct in the sense that tones and values, the underlying principles which the master could see in the effects of nature, would all be put down and registered directly upon his canvases. The composition might be only suggested by the place, but a freshened, invigorated palette—and better still, the freshened mind of the painter—would be the reward which came from this return to nature. For we are to remember that Inness' greatest pictures were the products of stored-up knowledge in his brain, and were executed in his studio. Those sketches done out of doors, or from his coupé window, were sources of great inspiration to him, and very beautiful they were to us who saw them later.

The Painter's Wife

At other times he found himself growing much fatigued and would ask his wife to come into the studio. I recall a very beautiful picture, as it seemed to me, of this great painter eagerly at work upon his canvases, talking almost incessantly, and the quiet figure of his sweet-faced, sympathetic wife, sitting in a corner sewing, or reading, bearing him company, giving him that solace which is of the spirit and which seemed to have for Inness the most soothing and the most strengthening of influences. There was no one, perhaps, who had so real an influence upon him as his wife, and in the great quantity of material which has been written about George Inness, the painter, all too little has been said of the wife—the companion whose presence and whose influence were as a guiding star to him.

In every effort to tell anything of Mr. Inness, the word "eagerness" forces itself on the pen, and perhaps no one word so completely describes the characteristic thing about him. Many, many times when pictures were going smoothly and beautifully to another's observation, when perhaps they alone needed time for drying, the master would set his canvases near the stove, and then forgetting them in his eagerness of conversation at the lunch-table or elsewhere, would return to find them blistered, burned, and much injured. But this never seemed to disturb him. The surface would be scraped, and with a new impetus he would repaint the injured surface.

A much more serious instance of his eagerness is the incident concerning the breaking of his right wrist. On alighting from the train at Montclair, he fell upon his right wrist and broke it. He appeared at the studio next day, with arm and hand in splints, and made light of a thing which ordinarily would be considered very serious by a painter. But ere many days had passed, to my great astonishment and anxiety, I saw Inness painting industriously, using his right hand, and holding the broken wrist with his left as he spread the paint over the canvas. Many times during that period, he would come for me and say: "Daingerfield, come in and spread this paint over the canvas for me, will you? My hand is not strong enough quite." And going into his studio I would spread certain colors under his direction; then, taking the brush himself, with the utmost *finesse* he would manipulate, with great delicacy and conviction, the crudely spread tones. The result of this injudiciousness in the use of his injured hand was that it was never afterward straight upon the wrist—the head of the bone being thrust to one side. Perhaps there is no incident concerning him which more completely illustrates the intense impulse to paint. There was no happiness for him if he was robbed of the privilege of painting.

Outdoor Life

He was extremely fond of walking in the country—not the long walks that the pedestrian would enjoy, but rambling, desultory excursions across the fields, gathering materials, studying the variations of light, and always seeking to arrive at some new principle which he could apply in his work.

I asked him one day how he estimated the size of the sun's orb in his sunset pictures. He said, "Generally I make it about one-twentieth of the space used." That is, on a canvas forty-five inches long, the orb of the sun would be two and one-quarter inches in diameter.

I asked him, again, how far from the eye he placed his nearest line of foreground. He said, "About eighteen feet." This he came to reconsider with a great deal of interest, after seeing some of the small circular kodak pictures which were just at that time becoming popular. Inness always held that visualization was vortexical, and that the nearest ring of the spiral fell about eighteen feet from the painter's eye. In the kodak pictures one readily could see that a very near-by thing, not properly within the range of artistic vision, would become important, often very beautiful in composition, and it interested him greatly.

I remember once when I went out to pay him a call at his Montclair studio—a visit which proved, alas, to be the final one I was to have with the great master—that we walked across the fields at the rear of his house, and he said, "I am trying to adjust the principle of construction in my work so that the nearest spiral of the vortex shall strike at my feet—so that I shall be able to paint all that is within the scene, including the objects which are at my very feet." How far he carried this principle I am not sure. I have never seen any canvas, even a beginning, which showed me that he accomplished the task he had set himself. I doubt very much if he did so, because in a few weeks after that visit he sailed for Europe, never to return.

Mr. Inness' home in Montclair was a large, rather rambling, and comfortable house, set in wide grounds, with stately trees surrounding it. There were many of his own pictures hanging in the house, and there was one room which contained only water-colors. Mr. Inness is never thought of as being a painter in water-color, but I used to study these sketches and pictures with intense interest. Some of them were merely tinted drawings done long ago; others were careful, elaborate studies, delicately colored, many of them of Italian themes and executed with exquisite understanding of perspective and distance. The precision of his touch, even in the extreme distance, was remarkable, and when compared with the broad suavity of his later work, of great significance. Then, too, there were the remarkable studies of Niagara. As I remember, they were done under the extreme stress which overtook him upon seeing the great waterfall, and being without his own materials, he borrowed a few watercolors and made some extraordinary studies. The breadth and dignity of design, the color, and the abandon with which they were executed, make them of rare interest in the master's work, because they were not approached in the usual water-colorist's spirit, but splashed and dashed with impulsive haste, and with no effort at what is usually understood to mean "finish." There were no pictures in any other medium in this room, and its charm was very great.

The painter's studio was not connected with his house, but stood at quite a distance off, approached by a vine-covered pathway. It was a large, frame structure with an ante-room, and one ascended two or three steps to the main studio. This was but sparsely furnished, a large, shadowy room with a balcony—used more for the storage of old canvases than anything else—and contained several great easels upon which stood pictures in various stages of completion.

Inness was fond of painting upon a canvas in its frame, so that he could get the effect of the gold as he worked. These easels were drawn up in a sort of half circle, sufficiently near the great north window which gave him light.

During this last visit which I paid him there, I was not very well, and we stayed only a very short while in the studio, and then, at the painter's invitation, we walked through the rear fields of his property, looked down over the gentle slope across the apple orchard which had served him so frequently in his pictures, and talked together on the theme which was ever uppermost in the painter's mind—the laws and principles of beauty as expressed in art.

Of a most versatile and imaginative nature, little things quickened his mind, and the slightest suggestion would kindle his vision into beautiful assemblages of compositional forms, expressed with full understanding of air or light or sun or shade.

I saw him once with a great chip in his hand, just an ordinary chip, newly cut from a tree. He held it nearer for me to see, and I discovered some crude charcoal marks upon it. He then told me, "I was out walking yesterday and saw an effect I wanted and had neither paper nor pencil with me, but I found this chip and a piece of charcoal, and got down the line and mass I want." The picture which grew from so crude a sketch was very powerful, and doubtless quite like the place and the moment which had impressed him.

This great master of landscape art was a dynamic, potential energy, seldom erring against good taste in his work. Always constructive in his drawing, he was true to the great law of beauty, and bitter always against whatever was affected, or untrue, or a trick.

The day will come when we shall find him, if not the founder of a great school of landscape painting, certainly the leader who pointed the way and revealed the opulence, the richness, and the beauty of American landscape.

Frederick Stymetz Lamb, "Reminiscences of George Inness" (January 1917)

[Like Elliott Daingerfield and Reginald Cleveland Coxe, the artist Frederick Stymetz Lamb rented studio space in the Holbein Building in New York, where he frequently came into contact with Inness. A native New Yorker, Lamb had studied in Paris with the French Academic painters Jules-Joseph Lefebvre and Gustave Boulanger. He and his brothers later founded the J. and R. Lamb Studios in Greenwich Village, where they constructed stained glass windows for Plymouth Church in Brooklyn, New York.]

It was my rare good fortune to have known George Inness at a time when I was able to realize that he was probably the most striking personality in the world of art during modern years—at least in America. When I made his acquaintance he occupied a studio at 139 West 55th Street—the Holbein Building—and my own studio was next to his. Thus it happened that we passed each other frequently, gradually becoming friends, and I was fortunate enough to see much of him at close range, thus coming to appreciate him both as an artist and as a man.

George Inness was born near Newburgh, New York, in a family of Scottish descent. He inherited that charming color-sense which made the Scottish School famous. He came at a fortunate time for American Art; for, while contemporaneous with the Hudson River School, he soon abandoned their standards, became an earnest follower of the Italian School, and painted, under its influence, many pictures of marked merit. But it was in the later years of his life when he abandoned the imitative for the expressive method that his work attained its greatest distinction.

In a peculiar way George Inness was a modern realistic painter, without knowing it—a memory student, without ever using the word. He developed a technique that was distinctly his own, yet never allowed it to dominate him; he controlled and varied this technique to suit the theme to be expressed.

While constantly referring in conversation to other schools of painting, he followed none, developing instead a style of his own. He was a master of his material in every sense of the word, working at times with a rapidity that astonished even those who knew him; and he never hesitated in one day's painting to obliterate the labor of weeks—if thereby he could improve, even in the slightest degree, upon his first work.

As others were realists in fixed states of nature, so Inness was a realist in the moods of nature. The fleeting effects, the passing shadows, the coming storm, the twilight, the setting sun—all were themes for his brush. No phase in nature was too delicate, no phase too fleeting for him to attempt: the early spring, the misty morning, the rainbow, the changing colors of the fall; the greens of summer, the frosty morning were a joy to him, and he revelled in their difficulties.

There have been poets, there have been painters, but few painter-poets that achieved his success.

In personal appearance Inness was slim, wiry, giving the impression of height, dark in color with strong features, piercing black eyes and hair worn slightly long. Although of Scotch blood he resembled the Norman English type. At times he reminded me of Dickens, then again of Tennyson, and again of Louis F. Day the remarkable English designer. If we look for a parallel in the American type, we would be forced to say "Yankee," although, perhaps, we would prefer to say Lincoln.

That Inness should have fallen under the influence of the Hudson River School was only natural. He followed their vogue, he studied their methods; but, interesting as was their work, it did not satisfy him. He painted realistically until, in his own words, he had painted every leaf on every tree, without result. The influence of Italy was strongly felt in America in those days. Story, Powers, Ball and a group of others were at work in Florence and Rome, and their work was constantly reminding us of Italy, that great storehouse of art. No wonder, then, that Inness should turn to Italy for his inspiration.

But, strange as it may seem, Italy, while it has endless material for figure composition, has little for the landscape painter. Still, he studied faithfully in this school and labored earnestly, producing many paintings of marked distinction. Yet he was not satisfied. The Barbizon School also and its products made a marked impression upon Inness. He knew them all, and his conversation was replete with statement, criticism and analysis of their work. An enthusiast, he was not sparing of praise. But in spite of this profound admiration one searches in vain in his paintings for any trace of their methods.

Inness the man was a fascination: simple and direct, clear of thought, quick of action, he was yet intensely human, and human with the simplicity which is the simplicity of a great mind.

The financial problem of his work he solved for himself in this manner: all the pictures of a certain size, on one side of the room, he valued at $3,000; others, slightly larger and on the other side of his studio, he valued at $5,000. The thought came to me that certainly some were better than others and therefore more valuable; but his point of view was explained a few days later when he came to my studio in a towering rage, claiming he had been insulted. It took several minutes to pacify him, after which he explained that a gentleman had visited his studio and after lengthy conversation, had left him a check for $2,000, with the request that, if at any time he had a picture less valuable than the others, to retain the cheque and forward the picture. Then, in a staccato way Inness exclaimed: "Doesn't the —— fool know that my bad pictures cause me a great deal more effort than my good ones?"

Again, late one afternoon, I was called to his studio to find him in great pain, for in those days he was a martyr to dyspepsia. He could hardly speak above a whisper, and, while his attendant and myself ministered to him to the best of our ability, there came a knock. I opened the door to find a butler waiting with the statement that he had come for *the* picture. Inness, drawing me to the side of the couch whispered: "There is the picture, but do not give him the frame."

Emerson says: "Say what you think to-day in strong language, and to-morrow in equally strong language, even if it be the direct opposite." This was the way of Inness. He came to my studio one day radiant, with the statement that, at last, after all these years, he had discovered the right method of painting. Being interested, naturally, I asked what it was. "Paint the undertones" he responded "in warm, rich color; then go over them with cool tones."

The next day he reappeared, with a face equally radiant, to state that he had again found the right method of painting. Upon being asked what this was, he said: "Lay in your canvas in soft, cool tones, and finish with warm, rich color." When I intimated, very diffidently, that this was the reverse of the statement of yesterday, he said most emphatically: "Yesterday I was a —— fool."

This intensity and abstractness of thought was one of his most interesting and charming characteristics. One day at lunch he spoke at great length of the action of the mind, and suddenly catching sight of a passer-by, said: "See that man? He is moving along the street with apparently no connected line of thought, and in a moment something may happen to change . . ."

Then, suddenly, Inness rose, took his hat from the rack, walked out and left us to pay for the lunch.

This singleness of purpose explains why, when once he had set his heart on some accomplishment, nothing could divert him.

He was good enough to admire some of the studies I had made while in Paris, and finally, through his brother-in-law, made me an offer to lay in certain figures for him in his landscapes. Realizing the impossibility of such a combination, I finally declined—only to receive the astonishing information that the dear old gentleman was very much offended. I saw that there was nothing left but an interview. Late one afternoon when the day's work was over I timidly approached the master. He was very gruff and demanded brusquely: "Why did you refuse my offer?"

"Well, Mr. Inness" I answered "it would probably be like this: the first day you would not say anything; the second day you would say 'umph' and the third day you would throw me out of the studio."

He sat for a long time in deep thought; then leaning forward he touched me on the knee and said: "You are right—you are right."

Many and varied are the stories told of Inness; but the fact that they remain fixed in the minds of his fellow-artists shows that each incident had its value as throwing some sidelight on his character.

A painting by a young man was once shown him for criticism. It represented a flock of sheep coming over a hillside with a few trees silhouetted against the sky. After gazing intently upon the canvas he asked for a palette, and in a few vigorous strokes had transformed the sky. A moment more of careful study and he said: "There is something wrong with those trees." Again a few moments work and the trees had taken their proper place against the sky. Then, nervously pacing the floor for a space he explained: "There is something wrong with that hill." Once more the brush flew to the canvas and the hillside was changed. A pause; the palette was set aside; with his eyes still fixed intently on the canvas, his hands clasped in his nervous way, he remarked: "Now, if you will paint out those sheep you will have a picture."

A friend, a young painter—for at that period his associates were mostly young—desired him most earnestly to come to his summer studio, look over his work and give him a criticism. All the young men were anxious to understand Inness' method of painting. The eventful day arrived, a Sunday, when Inness could spare the time. The young painter, knowing his guest's fondness for smoking, secured some of the best perfectos and awaited the visit. When Inness arrived he rushed at once to the studies and started to give his theories of painting. He was offered a cigar, took it nervously, biting off the end; then he lighted it, took two or three puffs, looked again at the canvas, threw the cigar in the fireplace and began his interesting analytical discussion and criticism. He spoke of color combination, showed methods of brush work and finally set aside both brush and palette. Taking his thumb he drew the color together with a few marvelous sweeps—as was often his habit—then excitedly seizing his friend by the lapel of his coat, he explained the reason at the same time leaving beautiful color combinations on the Sunday coat! At intervals this was repeated and when Inness left the studio his theories of painting had been explained, but the young painter's raiment was like Joseph's coat of old—one of many colors.

As to the merit of his different kinds of pictures there is much dispute and difference of opinion. Many admire his sunsets and claim them as his best;

others his fall tones; still others the frosty morning, the passing storm, or pictures that were accidental as to theme—being the means of recording strong impressions received under unusual circumstances.

My impression is that the pictures painted toward the end of each cycle will live and obtain the greatest distinction. For he worked in cycles, and each cycle had some important problem to solve. Few speak of his green tonalities—yet I have seen some of his summer greens that to my mind far excell [*sic*] many of the more popular, better known, sunsets.

In the later eighties Inness was in his prime. Picture after picture left his virile brush—each apparently more successful than its predecessor. No subject seemed impossible, no color combination too difficult; he worked with untiring energy and the work accomplished was of a volume difficult to realize. Yet he had times when for weeks he would struggle with some abstruse problem without result; afterwards, in a flash, the whole thing would be solved, and the canvas completed in all its glowing color. He worked with an energy and rapidity of touch seldom equalled, and day after day the fading twilight would find him stretched on his couch exhausted. Then, as he raised himself for an instant on his elbow to gaze on his canvas, he would say: "If I had had two hours more that would have been my masterpiece."

His technique was distinctly his own. Although scientific to the least detail in reference to his craft, yet, while working, he completely forgot all theories and forced his hand to obey implicitly his mind. At times, however, he tried strange experiments. One day I found him at work with little spots of pure color at different points of the canvas. Inquiry developed the fact that these were his gauges and were to remain as a key until practically the last stroke of the brush.

Is it to be wondered at that, with such intensity of purpose and mastery of technique, he won admiration as the greatest of American landscape painters, or that, in recent auction sales, his pictures have brought the highest prices ever paid for modern American work? And the end is not yet reached, for the future will undoubtedly record still higher values.

And yet, he was a man of moods. Many of his canvases are far below the standard of the average painter. He had great courage and dared to paint many things that even his friends would rank as inferior; but those were stepping stones to greater things—the experiments that led to those marvelous results that have since made his name famous.

Toward the end of his life he was seized with an unconquerable desire to see the sunset again from the Bridge of Allan, and his relatives, reluctantly giving way to his wish, took him to Scotland. The journey was long and tedious. They arrived in the late afternoon, with hardly time to prepare for the evening meal. Inness would not wait, but must needs go at once to his favorite spot. Time passed, the meal was over, and still he had not returned. Anxiety took the place of inquiry, and his companions began a search, and finally found him on the bridge—dead! His face was toward the setting sun, his last wish gratified.

His intrepid energy had kept him alive until he had accomplished his wish; then, like the Norse kings of old, his spirit floated out on the sea of golden light, and he was at home and at rest!

◆•◆•◆

C. S. Pietro, "The Art of John Austin Sands Monks" (April 1917 / excerpt)

[As noted above, John Austin Sands Monks was both a painter and printmaker who studied with Inness in Boston during the late 1870s. See above, pages 156–158, for George Inness, Jr.'s recollection of the relationship between his father and Monks.]

Mr. Monks is truly an exception in his work and in his ways. No one could look more the artist; there is a glint of alertness in his keen gray eyes that are touched with blues and gold, and the delicate contour of his face and the sensitiveness of his hands at once suggest the artist. His face has a spiritual look. He is kind, obliging and gracious, and never ceases to be the pupil of his master, George Inness. "Yes, he was like a father to me," he said with a trembling voice as he told of the early seventies when George Inness came to Boston to visit his friends. "One day when Mr. George N. Cass (with whom I was studying at the time) was showing Inness some of his recent work he passed over quickly a small canvas, 'hold on there, let me see that one,' exclaimed the master. 'That is not mine, it's the work of a pupil I have been teaching for a year' was the answer. 'Send him to me,' was the request of Mr. Inness.

"You can imagine my happiness at hearing such wonderful news. I ran practically all the way to Mr. Inness' studio. I was so convulsed with joy that I could hardly speak, and in response to my rapping, two sharp eyes peeked out at me through a small opening of the door, and a firm voice demanded what was wanted. I timidly said that I was the young man who had painted the little canvas which had made him send for me; thereupon the door swung wide open and a true welcome was extended. That was the greatest day of my life. He soon learned that I was left handed and placed me so that he was back of me and watched my work without interruption. He accepted me as his own son, brought me to the shores of Maine, to Connecticut and Vermont, to the fields, thick woods and plains, everywhere with him to paint and learn. His criticisms were always an effort to explain the best side of everything, and ever with the intense interest of tenderness of a father to a son." This is the simple story Monks has to tell of his eternal indebtedness to the great man who through all his life remained his teacher and best friend.

[David] Maitland Armstrong, *Day Before Yesterday: Reminiscences of a Varied Life*
(1920 / excerpt)

[Like Inness, David Maitland Armstrong was born near Newburgh, New York. He studied law at Trinity College in Hartford, Connecticut. He began to paint while serving in Rome as American consul-general (Chargé d'Affaires) to the Papal States and later to the Kingdom of Italy from about 1869 to 1873. He writes in his autobiography about an occasion in which he met Inness while sketching near the Pincio Hill. As Inness was in Italy from the summer of 1870 to the summer of 1874, the meeting probably took place between 1870 and 1873. Another meeting, in the White Mountains, probably occurred in the late 1870s.]

I was one day sketching one of these ruins, a small temple or tomb, the stucco a delicious yellowish tint, with a bright spot of white in the centre of the apse-like top. An almond-tree in bloom hung over it, and beyond was a jumble of delicate flowers and a touch of tender blue sky. I was busily absorbed when I looked up and saw George Inness and T. Buchanan Read. They had just finished lunching together and were in good spirits. Inness remarked, "Your high light in the arch is not bright enough." So, handing him my palette and brush, I said, "Do it yourself then," and without taking off his kid gloves he took the brush, mixed up some Naples-yellow and white, steadied himself and gave one dab just in the right spot. I sold that sketch later for a hundred dollars, but whether it was because of Inness's master touch I never knew. He was a small, nervous man, with ragged hair and beard, and a vivacious, intense manner, and excellent talker and much occupied with theories and methods of painting, and also of religion. I once met him in the White Mountains and we spent several hours talking together, or rather he talked and I listened, about a theory he had of color intertwined in the most ingenious way with Swedenborgianism, in which he was a devout believer. Toward the latter part of the evening I became quite dizzy, and which was color and which religion I could hardly tell! But, on the whole, he was an interesting man and undoubtedly one of the first of American painters. Unlike many great artists he was amenable to criticism, and when some friend suggested that he might change a sky he would promptly scrape out a gray one and try a blue. Crowninshield said that when Inness painted according to his theories the result was sometimes queer, but when he trusted altogether to his feeling his work was wonderfully fine.

Arthur Turnbull Hill, "Early Recollections of George Inness and George Waldo Hill" (1922)

[The Inness family spent the spring and summer of 1875 at the renowned Kearsarge House, formerly in North Conway Village, New Hampshire (the hotel was lost to a fire in 1917). There, Inness could paint the White Mountains, one of his favorite subjects. They socialized with the family of George Waldo Hill, a dentist by profession and an amateur painter and actor who lived next to Inness's brother Joseph in Brooklyn. Hill's son Arthur, a teenager at the time, later became a capable painter in his own right. The two families reunited when they moved to Montclair, New Jersey, the location, in all likelihood, of the repainting of George Waldo Hill's "finished" composition, described below.]

Born in the same year, much alike in character and temperament, both artists, of similar spiritual leanings and political beliefs, self-made and practically self-taught men, George Inness and my father, George Waldo Hill, formed an attachment early in life that lasted for many years and only closed with the unfortunate and premature death of the latter.

Although George Innes[s], Jr., often used to talk of my father very entertainingly when artists were gathered together and some of our members will no doubt recall such anecdotes in the old clubhouse in Twelfth Street, they may not have known just who Dr. Hill was. My father was a dentist by profession and a painter, actor and musician by taste and inclination. George Inness said: "Had your father adopted art as a profession—as I wanted him to—he would have made a great painter."

At an early date my father recognized the genius of Inness and proclaimed him as the coming American Master—as one of the greatest landscape painters of all times. This was long before the Civil War.

Father never tired of talking [about] George Inness. He bought Innesses and induced others to buy them. When I was born we had a fine collection of Innesses. Some of these canvases Mr. Inness had inscribed over his signature: "Painted for my friend, George W. Hill."

After the War my father had his dental offices at No. 5 Brevoot Place—10th Street—and in 1867 married my mother, Elizabeth Turnbull, daughter of John Turnbull of New York.

Speaking of this period, the late James McCormick, connoisseur and well-known art collector, said: "Your father had a salon where one could meet the celebrities and nabobs of the day. Such a thing is unknown in New York now." Among the celebrities Mr. McCormick had reference to were Junius Brutus and Edwin Booth, Lester Wallack and Charlotte Cushman. Whether my father took important parts with the Booths or with Wallack, we are not certain; but we know that he played CLAUDE MELNOTTE to Charlotte Cushman's PAULINE in "The Lady of Lyons," with great success.

My mother also was an ardent admirer of Inness, so that my own love for him was well inherited and cultivated from infancy through daily association with his works. I have no earlier recollection than of seeing Mr. Inness and his son, "Young George" at our house in DeKalb Avenue, Brooklyn. Our place had large grounds and was next to that of Mr. Inness' brother, Joseph Inness.

George Inness was a most remarkable man—his manner of working was entirely different from that of any painter I have ever seen. The energy of his attack upon a canvas (in his case it was literally an attack), the rapidity and accuracy of his drawing and brushwork and the amount of space he would cover in a few moments, was simply marvelous to watch. At such times his eyes fairly glowed and snapped and he would often talk while he worked, in this rapid way, expressing his thoughts and giving his reasons, scientific and artistic, for what he was doing at the moment.

I will never forget my first impression of seeing Inness work in my father's studio. I stood in great awe of my father and by keeping quiet was allowed to stay in the studio and watch him paint. One day as he was touching over quite a large canvas—finished and signed—Mr. Inness came in. He looked at the picture on the easel and there was some discussion. Inness evidently had a different idea from my father of the way that particular subject should be treated. At any rate he finally jumped up, grabbed the big palette from the painting table, seized a large tube of white and starting at the small end of the palette had squeezed out the whole tube by the time he reached the thumb-hole. Taking up a big brush, with one swift backward scoop he lifted that entire lot of white and "plunked" it squarely in the middle of the sky.

Then began that rapid brushwork—that scrubbing, rubbing, spreading of the paint across the canvas without seeming to lift the brush from its surface which I have never seen anyone else do in anything like the same way. The whole thing was done without, so to speak, stopping to take breath; other colors, black, blue, orange, had followed in quick succession after the white, and in a few moments the color scheme of the picture was completely changed. It was very wonderful to me—whether father agreed with what Inness had done or not. I remember that he took the picture down and turned it to the wall. They were both strong-willed men, and while they usually agreed at times had some very warm controversies, it made no difference in their friendship and they evidently enjoyed it.

Inness appeared severe in his criticisms at times to those who did not know him, not even sparing his own family on occasion. But his comments were always very original and often more apt to induce a laugh than to excite resentment.

Although only a boy at the time I well remember an incident where he criticized and complimented his wife in the same breath. Mrs. Inness was a beautiful woman and a lovely character and received, I am sure, the full measure of her husband's affections; but her grasp of the histrionic art evidently did not always meet his expectations.

It was at North Conway, White Mountains. Mr. Inness and my father had gone on one of their sketching trips in May, 1875, and we all followed later. We stayed at the Kersarge [*sic*] House, a famous resort in those days, especially for Bostonians.

During the summer father had a series of private theatricals, one of the plays being "Richard the Third," which was staged in an old school house on the Kersarge Hotel grounds. Mother attended to the costumes for the first performance, which was so successful that the play was repeated later, this time the costumes being ordered from Boston.

Mr. Inness and my mother did not take part and I sat with them near the stage. I remember how handsome Young George looked as PRINCE

EDWARD, all in black velvet with a long black cloak, and Mrs. Inness made a beautiful LADY ANNE, but the appearance of my father as the misshapen and deformed GLOSTER was so awful to me that when it [c]ame to the part of the meeting between GLOSTER and EDWARD and father drew his sword—a very real sword with a long glittering blade—and killed Young George I sprang up and screamed with fright.

This was my first "tragedy"—and I was very fond of Young George. They must have calmed me, however, for I can still see, in the scene of GLOSTER'S wooing of LADY ANNE, my father on one knee baring his breast and Mrs. Inness brandishing his sword over him.

The criticism and compliment Mr. Inness paid his wife came later, as we were walking back to the hotel. My mother said, "Well, George, what did you think of Lizzie?" "Tame—tame, weak—weak" and then, more quietly—"but beautiful—beautiful."

For many years I have read and heard the opinions *pro* and *con* of artists, color makers and others on the advisability of placing pictures out in the sun to dry. It may be of interest to painters to know that this was the practice of Inness—at least at the time of which I write. The long back piazza of the Kersarge was filled with canvases of Inness and my father during that summer. Most of Inness' work has stood wonderfully and many of my father's pictures are as fresh as if painted yesterday.

We have a glowing "Winter Sunset" by Inness, dated 1857, in which the vermilions, cadmiums and blues are as fresh as the day they were painted. This picture in breadth and freedom of treatment, in color and style, could as well be dated 1887—thirty years later. It is so characteristic that no one but Inness could have painted it—which only goes to show how great and prevalent is the misunderstanding to-day regarding Inness and his work.

My father began teaching me to draw at a very early age. He was a "stickler" on drawing and is said to have confined himself to the use of black and white in various mediums until he was almost thirty years old. Inness held the same opinions as to the need for hard grinding with the pencil before taking up color. I can imagine what he would say to some of the artists who today start their pupils painting "still-life," or even from the living model, with canvas, brushes, pigments and oils, the origin, properties or use of which is absolute Greek to them and before the hand has been trained to make a straight, respectable looking line on paper.

My father died in 1878 and it was several years before I again saw Mr. Inness. His suggestions, advice, illustrations, on construction, composition, the use of color and of mediums, were harder to follow than to remember; for his terse, epi-grammatic expressions and directions made a deep impression—in fact, anything Inness ever said is hard to forget. "Do little bits," said the Master; "put away your palette, take a sketch-book and pencil—don't try to make a picture—do little bits, do lots of them, come inside and *if you've got a soul you'll paint a picture—if you haven't, you won't!*" Strong meat for a youngster to digest. For sketching in oils Inness advised using only linseed with a little turps added, as a vehicle. As to colors, he said: "You can use almost any pigment made if you know how."

His method of work when beginning a new canvas (however much has been said to the contrary) was very scientific and thoroughly understood from the ground up. He used warm, transparent reds, browns or citrons, as the undertones to cover his drawing. Over these undertones were superimposed the final colors painted with the desired solidity. Inness was such a master of color that he knew to a nicety what the results would be. Of the final effect and how to obtain it he said to me: "Paint your picture in the natural colors—true to nature—just as you see it. Let it dry—good. Take a warm color and thin it out—such as gamboge, yellow ochre, raw sienna—whichever seems best—use your judgment. Spread it thinly—rub it in—over your picture, then while it's wet go over and touch up your high lights and your shadows. You'll have sunlight—all sunlight—warmth—and you'll have pulled your picture together." This may sound easy—but do it! For a lesson Mr. Inness gave me in construction and composition he used a large and superb "Indian Summer" that he was working on. I was so enthralled with the color and atmosphere of the picture that I must have appeared stupid as he talked on structural forms, dimensions, distances, spaces, masses and lines. "Seventy-five feet across the base line"—sweeping the stick end of his brush along the bottom of the forty-five inches of canvas. "Twenty-five feet back to that tree," indicating the largest one at the left. Then the girth of that tree—the distance to the next one and its size. The character of the objects and the reasons for their selection—the point of sight, the horizon line, the vanishing points—and so on through the entire scene with an exactness and certainty that was amazing. One might have thought he was an architect laying out a large structure and yet this picture was a veritable poem—an unsurpassed creative work.

George Inness had little use for what he termed "the frumpery of art." He never gave teas or entertained socially in his studio. One day having received an invitation from Mrs. Joseph Inness, I went with herself and youngest daughter, Kitty, to an affair in West Fifty-fifth Street, where the artists in the Holbein Studios were holding an afternoon reception. Mr. Inness' name appeared first on the card, his studio then being in No. 139, where were also Dearth, Deming, Ochtman, Marie Guise and DeCost Smith.

There were a number of visitors in the studio, but no Inness and people were much disappointed. Somebody said Hartley might know where Inness was and on inquiry he was located in a nearby restaurant. When told there were visitors that wanted to meet him he answered: "Nothing but idle curiosity—let them look at the pictures—they're on exhibition—I'm not." And nothing would induce him to leave.

It was the same way with the titles of his pictures. He rarely named them— Mrs. Inness did that. After dinner one evening at Grove Street, Montclair, I was admiring one of the masterpieces that hung in the living room. Mrs. Inness noticing my admiration said, "Do you like that, Artie?" and then turning to her husband—who was walking up and down the room clicking his heels together, a way he had—"That's a picture of Medfield, isn't it, George?" Mr. Inness came over and squinting through his glasses replied, "Medfield, Medfield—never saw the spot in my life!" repeating the last sentence as he turned away. Dear Mrs. Inness probably thought an attribution to some particular place or spot would enhance the picture in my eyes—but the "Old Man" failed her that time.

◆·◆·◆

Sadakichi Hartmann, "Eremites of the Brush"
(June 1927 / excerpt)

[Son of a well-to-do German trader and Japanese mother, Sadakichi Hartmann became one of the most important art critics of his generation. He befriended many of the leading Gilded Age American artists, including John Singer Sargent, Abbott Thayer, Ryder, and Inness. In this reminiscence, he recounts his visits to the homes and studios of several American artists. The text in brackets is Hartmann's. Immediately preceding his recollection of Inness, cited here in full, he describes how Winslow Homer lived "in hermit fashion on a little island on the New England coast," discouraged visitors, and disliked reading about art.]

George Inness was more accessible. After forty years of bad luck, recognition at last came to him. He had made the laborious climb from the thin, detail-loving technique of the Hudson River school, from panorama-like composition, Lorraine sunbursts, and Düsseldorf sentimentalism, to the dignity and breadth of the Barbizon artists, and finally to a dramatic colorful style of his own. He had kept up his enthusiasm and was a spirited and interesting talker. At one occasion, during a visit I made to his new home in Montclair, we were discussing the various arts. "It always needs the same something," he exclaimed, "in all the arts, whether you work as a painter, sculptor, architect [he accompanied each word with an expressive gesture] or as actor or dancer." And the old gentleman actually got up and pirouetted about the room. "You need rhythm," he said, "and that must come from within. It cannot be taught. It must be there," and he patted his chest. When I departed and we stood on the porch, we involuntarily grew silent, gazing at the landscape before us, a regular Inness of the later years. It was a sunlit afternoon in early Spring. Everything looked so fresh and moist—the ploughed fields, the young foliage, the green and yellow grass, the distant woods.

"Ah," he called out, making a sweeping gesture with his arm, "if I could only have seen things thirty years ago in the same breadth as I see them now!"

"Think of the fun you would have missed!" I retorted.

"Yes," he laughed, "the ability to see things broadly is a matter of conquest."

"Or of eyesight," I ventured. "No, you can't make me believe that!" and he waved his hand as I walked away.

S. C. G. Watkins, "Reminiscences of George Inness, the Great Painter, as I Knew Him"
(14 April 1928)

[A graduate of the University of Pennsylvania School of Dental Medicine, S. C. G. Watkins lived in Montclair, New Jersey, from 1876 until his death; he befriended Inness and became his dentist. This account was first published in the *Montclair Times*.]

My first acquaintance with Mr. Inness was on a day in the summer of 1889, when he appeared at my office, No. 13 North Fullerton Avenue, Montclair, in the need of some dental work. It was a very hot, dry, dusty day when the streets of Montclair were not provided with the good sidewalks which we now have; consequently there was a good deal of walking in the paths or in the streets, either of old country roads or the old-fashioned macadam, and in either case there was a great deal of dust which would naturally be kicked up all over one's shoes and clothes in walking through such roads.

Well, that day Mr. Inness arrived at my office, it might perhaps be said, looking worse for wear, as he was thoroughly covered with dust, and by the uninitiated would not be suspected of being Inness, the great painter. When he was let into the office, being so thoroughly covered with dust, perspiring freely and hair all mussed, with a scraggly beard, it is no wonder that my assistant sized him up and looked him up and down before seating him in the reception room, but she sized him up as being something out of the ordinary and not a common working man or tramp, so she allowed him to remain in the reception room. She came to me and said: "There is a very peculiar looking man in the reception room. I don't know what to make of him. I feel that he is a high type of something but I can't tell what. He doesn't seem at all ordinary." Well, of course my interest was aroused when I went in and met him. I certainly agreed with what she said—that he was unusual and yet of a high type, beyond the ordinary.

He soon told me who he was, and of course that explained everything. I got very well acquainted with Mr. Inness and from that moment to the time of his death I saw a great deal of him. He appeared very frequently at my office and invited me to come to his studio, which I did, and the more I was at his studio, the more I wanted to be there, as it was a perfect fascination. I would sit [for] hours and watch him paint.

Enthusiastic About Work

I will never forget one day when he came to my office. It was earlier than usual—about 2 o'clock instead of 4 or 4:30 in the afternoon, as it had always been before. The instant I met him he began talking enthusiastically about his work which he had been doing that day and the wonderful picture he had painted. He jumped to his feet from the sofa and described his picture as having a quality in it which he had been trying for years to get, and now he had accomplished it in a very short time and now he could carry it to any extent.

"That quality is something I have been after all my life and have just reached," he said. "I painted on that picture one forenoon last week and a couple of hours today and finished it, and I have the best picture I have ever painted in my life. I can now go on to any extent." He was so enthusiastic that every nerve was tense, and if he had had a canvas and paint there, he would, no doubt, have rushed at it with the vigor of youth. His enthusiasm knew no bounds. That was wherein he excelled. When he worked, his mind was concentrated on what he was doing. The outside world was nothing to him. His whole being was in that painting. He was placing his soul on that canvas. His whole being, body and soul, was so wrapped up in the intensity of his work that it could be truly said it was his soul's work, and his canvases were different from others from that fact.

A true artist is not easily satisfied with his work. He will paint his picture and have the feeling, perhaps, that it is grand; that it is the best he ever did, yet tomorrow, or next week, or next month, when he comes across that same picture, it may seem to him to be, as Inness would express it, "perfect rot." Instantly the work was destroyed—out of sight forever. The great Inness was that kind of man. I have known him to paint fifteen pictures on one canvas. I have seen him paint eight on one canvas myself, and when each one was finished, he had the feeling that it was as good as he ever did, but yet, after a few days, or a few weeks, when he would look at it in a different mood, his feeling would be that it was trash. Instantly the brush would pass over it and destroy it.

Painted at Terrific Pace

Inness was a terrific worker. He worked whenever it was daylight; he work[ed] so hard and so incessantly that he would not take time to eat; his family would have to take his lunch to the studio, or go to the studio and compel him to come to the house and eat; he was an intensely enthusiastic man; enthusiastic over his own work. In fact, I have seen him stand in front of a picture and paint, with every nerve under tension, every muscle up under strain; he would be in a half squatting position in front of the picture, painting like a boy at play, and quickly jump back about five or six or eight feet, bend down in a crouching position and again rush forward, brush in hand, and strain his eyes at the picture with such intensity that they would bulge from his head and his hair fairly stand on end. And that is just where he excelled, where he was ahead of others: that intense enthusiasm which made his pictures what they are, for he put his soul right into them. I once said to his wife that I had seen his eyes fairly bulge from his head when he was working. She spoke up quickly and said, "I have seen his hair stand on end." I could almost believe that was the case. Yet he was a simple man, in a way. He would receive suggestions from anyone. I once said to him in looking at a picture, a sunset, "Isn't that sun a little peculiar in color? Would it not be better if it had a little more orange in it?" Instantly he grabbed the tube of orange, put a little on his thumb and rubbed it into the sun—jumped back a couple of feet, looked at it and said, "That does help it; that does help it; that is an improvement." Who is there among the artists of a similar type who could have received a suggestion like that and applied it instantly, from one who knew so little about it?

"Big Man in Many Ways"

This showed his greatness, for only a great man could have done it, and he was a big man in many ways. He wanted to work all the time. He didn't want to take any recreation, as his soul was in his work and his work was his life. But he had a noble wife who studied the man and knew what was best for him—better than he did. She would plan vacations and carry them out, and he was so in love with her and so under her mind in a way that he couldn't work if she was not near by. On one occasion she went to the studio in the forenoon at about 11 o'clock and said to him, "George, come in now and take a bath." He instantly said, "What the devil is up now?" She, in her calm way said, "We are going to Florida this afternoon on the 3 o'clock train, and I want you to come in and take a bath and change your clothes." "No, I won't," repeating it several times, with some damns thrown in. "I have certain work to do and it has to be done and I must do it." "Well, all right, George, if you can't, I will go to Washington and stay over night and you will come down tomorrow," knowing full well that he could not work when she was gone and that he would follow her. She went to Washington and stayed over night and went to the train the next day, knowing that he would be there. Sure enough, he was there. She boarded the train and they went on to Florida. He might just as well have gone, for she had gone and after that he couldn't do anything.

Inness cared but little about his personal appearance. His wife always bought all his clothes. She would go to the city and buy two or three suits at a time. When he was in bed, she would take out a new suit, take the things from the pockets of the old clothes, put them in the new ones and put the new suit beside the bed. In the morning, when he got up, he would put on his new clothes, not knowing this, and go on to work with them. When they were too soiled, the wife would repeat the same operation with another suit—and so on.

Trip with Harry Fenn

I spent Sundays with him for several years, perhaps two or three Sundays a month, so that at the time of his death I knew him, perhaps, better than any man. We went on vacation trips together for a few days at a time. I will never forget one trip when he and Harry Fenn (another famous Montclair artist) and I went to Oakridge, N. J., in 1891. They enjoyed themselves very much the first evening.

The hosts pretty nearly lost their patience as they had to wait dinner for us. There was a beautiful field of rye just outside the house and the sun nearly setting, with fleeting clouds in the sky which frequently cast its peculiarly beautiful lights and shadows on that field of rye, with a brisk breeze blowing, keeping it in constant action. Mr. Inness and Mr. Fenn forgot all about dinner while viewing the different pictures in that field of rye from different points of view, and admiring the beauty as none but an artist could. After several urgent invitations to come in to dinner, I succeeded in getting them into the dining-room. The next morning we went to Clinton Falls and the Old Forge, walking a distance of a mile and half each way. Inness loved to walk, but he didn't like long walks, evidently, for he insisted that it was five miles. The Old Forge was the last of the old forges in New Jersey which were used in Washington's time for making pig iron and is now owned by the city of Newark. They would mine the iron in that vicinity and then make it into pig iron. They sent it in saddle bags on mules back to Elizabethtown, now Elizabeth, N. J., to be worked into different kinds of iron. Mr. Inness was intensely interested in the Old Forge and in Clinton Falls and expressed a great desire to paint it, but never got at it, as he was always so busy in his studio he never could find time unless someone would make all preparations and just take him right away. In the afternoon we drove part way to Green Pond; then I took them up through the woods and over the mountain.

In this instance the face of the mountain had actually fallen off and the rocks were leveled off, many of them six, eight or ten feet across, perfectly flat, lying on the ground on a slant on the side of the mountain. Mr. Fenn and I worked our way down through the crevices between the rocks, but Mr. Inness would sit on a rock and allow himself to slide until he would come to the end of that and slide again, and so work his way down the mountain. He had on a new pair of trousers. It is needless to say it was not very good for the trousers. Mr. Inness got very tired on that trip. I cut a cane at Green Pond, which he carried in walking back, but it was not sufficient support to him and he insisted that I had walked him over ten miles that afternoon. That cane I now own and prize highly. When Mr. Inness returned to the boarding house, he discovered that the cork had gotten out of his flask and the contents were in the bottom of the satchel. He immediately became very much disheartened and disconsolate and Mr. Fenn and I could not console him sufficiently to keep him from insisting upon returning home on the first train, which he did.

Interested in Sparta Scene

On another trip we went to Sparta and there his enthusiasm knew no bounds. He was interested in the beautiful hills and valleys, coves and little clusters of trees and great spread-out pasture fields and the herds of cattle and sheep, stone fences and orchards. His enthusiasm was something grand to witness. Again he expressed a very strong desire to get up there and paint some time, but he never did.

We were out walking one hot dusty day when we were both very thirsty. We started to enter a dooryard to get a drink of water. The woman saw us coming and immediately slammed the door and we could hear her bolt it. I presume she thought we were a couple of tramps.

Mr. Inness was so loath to leave his work that it was very difficult to get him to remain away from his studio very long and he nearly always went home sooner than he expected. He could rarely stand it more than a couple of days on those short trips. He would have a picture in his mind and would be anxious to get to his studio to put it on canvas, and once he felt that way there was no use in talking to him. Home he went.

In June, 1894, the Sunday before he went to Europe, I called on him in his home and found him not feeling well; consequently he had remained in the house, but after talking for a few minutes he said, "You do not want to stay here. We will go to the studio," and we did so. He was very talkative that morning and took pictures out which had been stored away in corners back against the wall and which I had never seen, although I had been going to his studio for years. Up to that day I had never seen his figure pictures, but he showed all of them to me and told me about his figure work. He said that he was tired of painting landscapes and that from that time on he was going to turn his attention to figures and be known as a figure painter. Suiting his action to the word, he grabbed a brush and began painting on one of his figure pictures. He acted peculiarly on that day and when I left the studio, instead of sticking to his work as he had formerly done, he left the studio with me and walked to the street. We stood and talked there and I again urged him, as I had been doing during the morning, to take a trip to Europe. He consented, which was something he would never do before. He went into the house when he left me and said to his wife, "We will go to Europe this week." On Monday they went to New York, secured passage and sailed on the following Thursday.

That day I was with him in the studio was the last day he ever painted. I saw him use the brush for the last time. Afterwards his wife told me that while in

Europe he acted differently from what he ever acted before; that in traveling around from city to city he had visited the museums and galleries and had walked so much that she was a complete wreck. When he had been in Europe before he had always been working, working, working, but this time he never took a brush in his hand. He was always looking, studying, talking about and discussing different men's work.

His Death in Scotland

Finally they reached Scotland, Bridge-of-Allen, the place where he died. He thought it the most beautiful place he had ever seen. They reached there in the morning and, in talking with a gentleman in the hotel, he told him that he was so pleased with the place that hereafter, every summer, he would close his studio and come over to Scotland to Bridge-of-Allen and spend the summer. After luncheon he asked his wife to take a drive around the country. She said, "No, George, I am so tired from tramping around through these museums that I must lie down and take a rest." "All right," said he, "I will go out for a walk and about 4 o'clock I am coming back with a carriage for you and we will take a drive." He left the hotel for a walk and had been gone about half an hour when a messenger arrived at the hotel, stating that Mr. Inness was dead. He had been walking through a beautiful valley, admiring the scenery such as he loved to paint, and while in that frame of mind, studying nature and enjoying it to its fullest extent, he threw up his hands and dropped unconscious. He was brought back to the hotel unconscious and died in a very short time.

While in Scotland during the summer of 1927 I took occasion to visit Bridge-of-Allen, as I had been for many years anxious to see and locate the place where Mr. Inness fell unconscious, and the hotel where he died. From the minute description of the place given to me by Mrs. Inness after her return home and through the courtesy of Alexander Morrison, who was solicitor and town clerk at the time, I was able to locate the place, which was about 800 feet up the river above the old bridge which crosses the River Allen from which the town receives its name. He was carried from there down the river to the Royal Hotel on the main street about a quarter of a mile, where he died Aug. 3, 1894.

It had always seemed to me his work was finished on that Sunday that I saw him last. He acted differently that day from what I had ever seen and from that day to the day of his death he appeared differently: in being persuaded to give up his work and take the trip and in giving it up without any resistance, in spending his time in Europe without working, but, rather, in visiting the galleries and studying and resting. He was brought back to New York and lay in state for a couple of days at the National Academy and was then interred in Rosedale Cemetery, Montclair.

J. Henry Harper, *I Remember* (1934 / excerpt)

[Joseph Henry Harper joined Harper & Brothers publishing house after it had been started by his elder brothers in 1831. Some of their most important publications include Herman Melville's *Moby Dick* in 1851, Charles Dickens's *Bleak House* in 1853, and Henry James's *The Ambassadors* in 1901. Harper & Brothers merged with Row, Peterson & Company in 1962 to become Harper & Row, which continues to publish in the United States and England. Harper befriended many American painters during the late nineteenth century and often visited their studios. Here, he recalls Inness's habit of spoiling his work through excessive repainting.]

I called one day on George Inness, the artist. He was just coming out of his studio and I told him I wouldn't detain him, but would return some other day. "Not at all," he said, "come right in." He then told me that he had been working on a canvas, which he showed me, until he had carried it beyond the finishing-point, and that now he was distressed at not being able again to restore it to its completed state. He remarked that in his opinion many pictures were spoiled by over-finishing. If an artist could only realize when a picture was really completed there would be a great many more successful paintings.

Eliot Clark, "Notes from Memory"
(Summer 1957 / excerpt)

[Eliot Clark recalls the experiences of his father, the painter Walter Clark, N. A., when the elder Clark rented studio space, during the 1880s, next to Inness in the Holbein Studio Building in New York.]

In the untold depth of experience certain flashes endure in memory illumined by the spoken word.

My father, Walter Clark, was a landscape painter, a member both of the National Academy and the Society of American Artists. As a child I grew up unconsciously in the association of artists, of studio talk and the smell of paint and turpentine. In his younger days my father's studio was next to that of George Inness in the Holbein Studios. The two-storied buildings were erected by tax-payers on either side of 55th Street between Sixth and Seventh Avenues in New York City. Before the coming of the motor car the street-floor level was used as stables, while painters and sculptors occupied the sky-lighted studios above. The studio was a workshop. Few artists lived in their studios. There was no central heating. On school holidays it was great fun to join my father and work in the studio. Inness had left the Holbein to live in Montclair, New Jersey, before my memory begins, but I well recall my father's comments on his methods and criticisms.

The "old master" was intensely emotional and temperamental, but always kindly and constructive in demonstrations and helpful advice. My father had started a landscape in warm transparent monotone. Inness was interested in the composition and by way of suggestion impulsively took a dab of cobalt blue from the palette and rubbing it in at a decisive point in the sky, exclaimed, "Now take that as your keynote." He had envisioned the canvas at once in its completion and naïvely thought the young painter could do likewise.

Inness was a symphonic colorist. He had started a large canvas, sunset with barn in the middle plane. As my father was watching, he took some light cadmium and with the brush placed a spot effectively in the foreground. Then he said, "My problem now is to make that chicken look white."

The art of Inness is too unthoughtfully associated with the Barbizon School. In his European travels he had studied the early masters of landscape painting, particularly Constable, Turner, and the Dutch painters. His life work covers a vast evolution from the scenic beauty of pastoral landscape to the ultimate synthesis of tonal form. His versatility and dramatic use of color has [*sic*] no counterpart in European painting. In his mature period he was intensely individual. Continuously experimenting, every picture was a particular problem. As a follower of Swedenborg, he was deeply imbued with metaphysical introspection. In its organization a picture should have cosmic significance, the key to which was the relation of the part to the whole; the universe the manifestation of its Divine Source; the all a part of the One.

Impetuous by nature and emotionally stimulated, Inness would frequently repaint a picture as if it were a fresh canvas. At other times he would complete a picture at one painting. I recall my father speaking of a large canvas on which Inness had worked during several years. Unsatisfied with the result he scumbled a light neutral half-tone over the entire surface, allowing the underpainting to come through. When dry he then completely repainted it with semitransparent color glazes. Always the light underneath should qualify the overpainting.

On one occasion Inness was showing some pictures to visitors. They had all admired a particular part of a certain picture. Inness made no remark, but when the visitors left he abruptly went for his palette and began to paint out the admired part. My father said, "Why, I thought that was what they all liked." Inness replied, "Damn it, they shouldn't have seen it."

George Inness, Jr., began his career as a cattle painter wishing to depart from his father's influence. My father had acquired one of Junior's pictures[:] two cows standing before a woodland pool. When Senior saw it he was delighted. "Why that's not bad for the boy; but the landscape needs simplifying." Always acting on impulse, he began to illustrate; becoming absorbed he painted freely over the canvas until coming to the cows he said, "I guess I had better stop, I don't know enough about cows." My father said later to Junior, "George, the Old Man liked your picture, but I'll have to ask you to sign it again. He even painted out your signature." Junior replied, "Well, I don't mind signing the Old Man's picture."

The enthusiasm and intensity of Inness was contagious. Wyant at once time had a studio in the same building, but left when he realized that the proximity of Inness was overpowering.

BUSINESS LETTERS

Letters to the American Art-Union (1847–1850)

[Established in America in 1842, the American Art-Union (see Fig. 34) operated on the principle of joint association. Revenue from modest annual membership fees would be spent, after operating expenses were paid, on contemporary art; these works would, in turn, be redistributed among the membership by lot. Although, according to Joy Sperling, the institution had become so suc-

FIG. 34. Samuel Wallin, *Gallery of the Art-Union*, frontispiece, *Bulletin of the American Art-Union* 2 (May 1849).

cessful that there were five other art unions in America by 1850, the one in New York was the largest. The letters written by a young George Inness and reprinted below reveal the careful balance he sought to strike between selling his work at its proper value and avoiding offense to the selection committee.]

To the Committee of the American Art Union
New York // Oct 4th 1847
Gentlemen   accompanying this I send for your inspection, a picture entitled recolections [*sic*] of a chase on the Lakes, at sunrise[,] which if you feel inclined to purchase I shall be happy to sell   The price of the picture & frame $112 Picture alone $100

               Respectfully your obdt servant // Geo. Inness

Gent.
    Respecting my small Landscape sent you for sale—I have named $50 as its value—But—being unproved—will value it at $25—provided you give me $175 for my larger picture
               Your obt Servt // Geo. Inness
               N. Y. 7th Dec / 47
To Committee of the Art-Union

Gent.

I am obliged by your offer for my large Landscape – & do not doubt but that you intend to be liberal.—circumstances prevent my accepting it—I may be too partial in my estimate, but consider, that if I threw off $25.00 from my price— say $175.00   The frame having cost over $25.00   You will find my picture with the money

Your obt Servt // Geo. Inness
N. Y. 7th Decb / 47
To Committee of the Art Union

[Written in another hand: Recd Feby 24]
New York   Feb 23 1849
Gentlemen

I have recd your notice, and although you may think $400 a large sum for a picture by a young artist, yet as on this picture, I have spent every effort, and sustained considerable loss by not painting small pictures I cannot help feeling as if I should have a little more than you offer. The present price will not pay me at the same rate as you paid for my "Peace and War" of which I could easily, while painting this, have painted four and sold two at private sale for $200 each. I do not wish to ~~you~~ upbraid you as desiring to get the picture at under value for none but Mr. Geo Austin have seen the picture ~~for~~ either finished or framed a just estimation of it, therefore, cannot ~~not~~ be made. If now the committee will be so kind as to call and see the picture as it stands I think they may be willing to give me my full price or at least what I named to Mr. Austin as my lowest one.

Yours Very Respectfully, // Geo. Inness
Corner of Broadway & Franklin St.
(Thinking it may give you too much trouble to call upon me I send the picture with this and submit it to your consideration. G. I.)

[Written in another hand: Rec May 24]
Thursday Morning May 24 / 49
Gentlemen

I have several pictures of which I am most anxious to dispose even at a price much below what I had considered their real value   wishing to leave the City on account of the most wretched health induces me to lay the present offer before you in hope that you may consider it worthy of acceptance   I would not offer so many pictures were it not that in my present situation I cannot well leave the City without a smaller sum than $500.

I have our picture at your rooms   Our old mill prise [*sic*] $226 with the frame at the Academy[,] one Early recollections &c. $330   A large Moonlight and one picture of scene Near our village   The former $279 with frame   the latter $226 &c

I offer the whole, the frames having been paid for, at any price you may feel willing to give me not less than $500

Very Respectfully yours // Geo. Inness

———◦•◦•◦———

[Written in another hand: Rec Oct 17]
Oct. 14th / 49
Gentlemen

The picture I send you is entitled the Watering Place   Its price is $175 Price of frame $15

Yours respectfully // Geo. Inness
506 Hudson st.

———◦•◦•◦———

[Written in another hand: Rec Nov 30]
Nov 30th 1849
Gentlemen—

I offer to your notice a picture entitled Religion giving peace to the world price $100   price of frame $13.00

Yours very respectfully // Geo. Inness
506 Hudson st.

———◦•◦•◦———

[Written in another hand: Recd Aug 15]
To the Art Union—
Gentlemen—

I find that during my recent illness that my father has placed in your hands 4 pictures—on which he has received from you $100.00   You now offer me $155 for two   The Mill ⎫
                 a Study ⎭ including the frames.

My father had no authority to act for me, but I am glad to acquiesce in what you consider to be for my interest.

As circumstances require me to sell my pictures, I must accept your terms, but hope that you will reconsider your ~~former~~ decision & give me in addition the cost of the frames, viz,

for the Mill	$ 28.00
" " Study	3.50
	$ 31.50

which I consider ~~reasonably~~ sufficiently low.

~~Your obed Servant~~

I also call your attention to the two Pictures,

The Gloomy days of '76	$ 300
frame	40
	340
A Composition	100
frame	13
	$ 113

I consider these prices also sufficiently low——but am disposed to meet your price for reason already stated——

Your obt Servt // Geo. Inness
New York   15th Aug / 50

———◆·:·◆———

[Written in another hand: Recd Oct 30]
Tuesday Oct. 29th 1850
Gentlemen

As I am led to supose [*sic*] that you will not purchase the pictures I have offered you at least at the prices named, I send you three others in hope that you may either purchase these alone or make me an offer for the five. I think that the small picture which I have before offered you may be fiting [*sic*] for distribution. I there[fore] offer you the four small ones for $375.00 the frame to be paid for, or if it suits you I will sell the whole for $500.00 ~~you pa~~ including the frames or not as you see fit

Yours very respectfully // Geo. Inness
506 Hudson

———◆·:·◆———

[in another hand: Recd Decb 14th 50]
Mr Monk

Please deliver to the American Artists Association the two pictures belonging to me which are in your gallery on exhibition   The one entitled The Gloomy days of Seventy-six[,] the other an upright landscape about 20 [x] 24
Yours &c Geo. Inness

Letters to Samuel Gray Ward

(7 January, 21 November, and 30 November 1852)

[Samuel Gray Ward (FIG. 35), an art collector and the American agent for the British banking company Baring Brothers, corresponded with Inness and began collecting his paintings in 1852. See above, pages 132 and 150–51, for information on and a photograph of Ogden Haggerty, Inness's first patron. Ward and his wife, Anna Hazard Barker Ward, were longtime friends of the Haggertys.]

New York   7 Jan. 1852
Sir

I understand from Mr. Haggerty that you have an order from Mr. Sturges of Liverpool, for a picture the price of which is to be $100.00   I have just painted an American subject of the required price. If however you have not yet disposed of the commission and are willing to wait until I have returned from my summer sketching I will paint something from nature expressly for the purpose. As $100 is at any time very desirable I take the liberty to write you this and hope that you will not purchase until you have seen what I have to show.

Yours Respectfully // Geo. Inness
806 Broadway [New York]

FIG. 35. Samuel Gray Ward, photograph, c. 1860, Emerson Papers, Harvard University, bMS Am 1280.235.706.29, photo album picture #27.

New York   Nov 21st 1852
Mr. Ward
    Dr Sir   Tomorrow I shall have Mr Sturgis' picture finished   As you expressed yourself pleased when you last saw it I take the liberty of asking you for money   I should not do so but that three shillings is all I possess in the world and I know not where to get more   I dread asking Mr. Haggert[y] as I [have] been almost entirely sup[p]orted by him since I have been back from Europe
                    Yours Respectfully // Geo. Inness
                    806 Broadway [New York]

New York   Nov. 30th '52
Sam G. Ward Esq
Dear Sir
    Tomorrow I send you, by Adams' Express, a box containing the picture which you saw at my studio. You will find it (the picture) considerably lower in tone than when you saw it last but, I hope, with increased colour & transparency as well, and also the dreamy obscurity of a lowering day better represented. I pray you sir excuse an inadvertency, perhaps, I should say an indelicacy in the letter I wrote you last sunday week. Do not impute the <u>feeling</u> to me. I wrote in haste that I might be in time for the mail and did not think of what I had omited [sic] until the letter had gone. I am perfectly aware that I have never recd an unqualified commission to paint the picture I send you and therefore look upon the matter as altogether a speculation on my part. The frame that surrounds the picture is not suited to it, and I merely send it, having none better, that the picture may have all the advantages I can afford to give to it
                    Very truly yours // Geo. Inness
                    806 Broadway // N.Y.

Letters to Roswell Dwight Hitchcock

(19 November and 2 December 1860)

[Roswell Dwight Hitchcock (FIG. 36) was a minister of the First Congregational Church in Exeter, New Hampshire, from 1842 to 1852. In 1852, he became

FIG. 36. Roswell Dwight Hitchcock, photograph, n. d., Amherst College Biographical Record: Class of 1836, c/o Richard J. Yanco.

FIG. 37. George Inness, *Sunrise*, 1860, oil on canvas, 15 x 26 ³/₈", Collection of the Farnsworth Art Museum, Rockland, Maine, Gift of Mrs. Mary A. Boudreau, Ocean Point, Maine, in memory of Roswell Dwight Hitchcock, 1957, #57.1062.

professor of natural and revealed religion at Bowdoin College, Brunswick, Maine, and, three years later, professor of church history at Union Theological Seminary in New York. One of his many books, *Hitchcock's New and Complete Analysis of the Holy Bible*, was published in 1870. He served as president of the Union Theological Seminary from 1880 to 1887. The second letter accompanied Inness's *Sunrise*, 1860 (FIG. 37).]

Medfield(?)   Nov. 19th 1860
Prof Hitchcock Dear Sir
    From what you said when I saw you last and from further conversation with your wife I supose [*sic*] that you have a desire to posess [*sic*] one of my pictures at some future period. Should you at any time act upon such a desire I should be pleased if you would commission me directly insted [*sic*] of purchasing through another, as I could promise to give you a much better picture than any you have seen of mine at such a price as you might consider yourself justified in paying. Nothing would please me better than to have one of my best efforts in your possession for I know noone [*sic*] in whose hands a good picture painted by myself would led [*sic*] to greater profit
                    Yours Respectfully // Geo Inness

Medfield   Dec 2nd 1860

Dear Sir

When I recd your note of the 21st Nov I was endeavouring to finish a picture which I had commenced in the month of June. Although I had intended to ask considerably more than the amount of your commission $100 I determined that if it finished to my satisfaction I would send to you. Of course I cannot say that my desires are perfectly realized but the picture in all its subjective qualities pleases me better than anything that I have as yet painted. I consider this subjective the strong side of all morning and evening effects. And to see in most of my moods the charming side of everything. I must confess though that however willing the spirit, the flesh has a wonderful preference for Turkey & mince pies over mush & milk. I haven't quite got to <u>Food</u> yet. The effect of my picture is to represent the sunrise.

You will find it at Nichols [*sic*] rooms where I thought best to send it so that you might see it in a frame. Mr. Sandicor (?) [Snedecor] 768 Broadway has a frame of the right size and character which I should like you to put upon the picture if you do not think it to [*sic*] expensive

Yours truly // Geo Inness.

Letter to Horace H. Moses (14 January 1866)

Eagleswood   Jan 14th 1866

My Dear Moses

I have sent to the care of Childs & Jenks a picture framed and boxed addressed to you   Will you please see that it gets into the right hands. I should like to have sent you something better if I could have done so

My price for such a picture is $300

Yours Truly // Geo. Inness

Letters to Thomas B. Carrol[1] (11 May–10 August 1868)

[undated]

Mr. T. B. Carrol   212 Fifth Avenue

Dear Sir

Will you be kind enough to let me know if you have sent your son to Quebec and if you have what you know of the constitution there. I lost the circular which I brought from there[.] ~~last year~~ Can you send me yours if you have it.

The main thing that I wish to know is of the expense of puting [*sic*] my boy there. I wish to send him from home if I can afford it.

Yours Truly // Geo. Inness

21st

New York   May 11th 1868

Thos. B Carrol Esq

Dear Sir

I beg that you will be so good as to excuse my neglect in not answering your letter sooner   I sat down a few days after having recd. it to do so but something interrupting I did not do as I intended and from forgetfulness it has been neglected until the present time.

I do not care about working upon the picture which you bought at Snedicors [*sic*] but shall be very happy to paint something for you, if we can agree as to terms   Please call and see me when you are in town   I thank you for your invitation to visit you in the country and do not know but that I may like to avail myself of your kindness for a few days in the summer

Yours Truly // Geo. Inness

July 1st 1868

Mr Thos. B Carol

Dear Sir

I have finished painting upon your picture and I believe the universal opinion is that it is very much improved. One hundred and fifty $150.00 is the least that I can charge you and as I am just about starting for the country and need all the money that I can raise I shall be glad to hear from you   My family start[s] for Leeds Green co. on Monday next but I shall probably remain in town for a week longer. I am painting in Mr Chapmans [*sic*] room no. 377 Fulton st. Brooklyn at present it being to[o] hot to paint in my studio in Fifth Avenue ~~it being~~ which is next [to] the roof   Please let me hear from you and address me at the place I have last mentioned

Yours Truly // Geo. Inness

Tuesday July 7th 1868
Mr. Carrol
Dear Sir

I find that it will be impossible for me to go to Troy with you tomorrow as it is necessary that I should attend to some matter in regard to my family. Please send me a note at Leeds and let me know just where to find you and I will ~~and I shall~~ do myself the pleasure of calling upon you ~~at the first~~ within a week or two

Yours Truly // Geo. Inness

Leeds Green Co. // July 1868
Thos. B. Carrol Esq.
Dear Sir

I should like very much to join you on your trip north, but I do not think it wise for me to have the course of study that I am at present pursuing interrupted. Should I get my brain excited with the grand scenery of the St Lawrence it would be likely to disturb the determination which I have found to use this summer for close study. I think my best plan will be to stay here with my family until Sept when the children will have to return to school   I shall then make my visit to you and after that return to my studio. I shall on my visit to you be able to show at last one study painted with a closeness and fidelity that I think will a little surprise you

Yours Truly // Geo. Inness

Brooklyn   Aug 8th 1868
My Dear Mr Carrol

I recd. your last note, in which you make me the offer of $300 for the picture at Snedecors [*sic*], just as I was leaving Leeds. I determined not to answer until I had well reflected on the matter. And now I will make you a proposition in return. If you will give me $500 you may have the picture at S. [Snedecor's] framed and I will finish the large one which I have in my room <u>perfectly</u> to your satisfaction.

This proposition may look to you as being extravagant when compared to the one you made me but let us look it carefully over. In the first place the picture in Snedecors is one of my most perfect productions and easily worth more than the $600 which I ask for it in proof of which let me state to you that two picture[s] of the same size and no whit better or more attractive which I was obliged to sell last fall ~~at~~ under prise [*sic*] were sold within two months by the first purchaser for $850 each   This picture is fresh never having been exhibited in New York. The picture which I worked on for you is a fine composition and can be made perfect in all respects should I spend sufficient time upon it   What I have already done $250 would not have paid me for even at the poorest prise I have recd. for my work   Now supose [*sic*] you keep the one I left with you at $200

First payment on large picture	350
Paid for retouching	150
For perfecting large one and one at Snedecors	500
	1200
Very small one I present	

Here you have two large pictures   one medium size and one very small all handsomly [*sic*] framed for $1200   Now I know that $600 and over can be realized for one of the large pictures during the winter leaving you three pictures handsomly framed for $600 which is certainly a very small prise. I know that I shall paint no more such pictures until I am certain of what I feel to be a proper prise but stick to my small elabourate pictures for which I can always get a prise. Cant [*sic*] you come into town soon and see me about this and see the small picture which I have finished. I shall be in my studio in New York
Yours // Geo. Inness

August 10, 1868
My Dear Mr. Carrol
You did not misunderstand me in regard to what I said to you in New York It was not my intention to charge you any thing for what I may do further to your picture   I consider your kindness in loaning me the money upon the small pictures deserves some return and therefore I am determined to have the picture give thorough satisfaction
I hope to be able to finish my visit to you about first Sept   if you can let

me have the $200 a day or two before that it will oblige
> Yours Truly // Geo. Inness
> 212 Fifth Avenue

Letter to Barry Alden, Esq. (30 December 1868)

New York   Dec. 30th 1868
Dear Sir
   I have no autograph of either of the mounts [?]
> Yours // Geo. Inness // Barry Alden Esq

Letter to S. A. Coale, Jr. (14 October 1869)

[Samuel A. Coale, Jr., was involved with organizing some of the many exposi-
tions and art fairs held in St. Louis during the late nineteenth century.]

New York   Oct 14/69
Mr. S. A. Coale, Jr.
Dear Sir
   I have to express to you my thanks for your favour as well as for the attention
on your part by which an honour has been bestowed upon me
   I am very sorry that I cannot remember what picture it is that you have but
I am as well pleased at the pleasure you express in having it recognized as of
superlative merit as if it were one direct from my present hand
   I have recd. one of the catalogues only and none of the papers which I regret
   Should you at any time find yourself in our city I trust that I may have the
pleasure of making your acquaintance
> Yours Truly // Geo. Inness
> 212 Fifth Avenue

Letter to A. D. Williams (13 August 1872)

[The painting to which Inness refers in this letter, which was written to its first
owner, is *Lake Nemi*, 1872, Museum of Fine Arts, Boston.]

Albano, [Italy]   Aug 13th 1872
Mr A. D. Williams
Dear Sir
   Your picture was shipped on the 21st of June with several others to W. & E. [Williams & Everett, Inness's dealers] with directions to them to deliver it to you. I thought this the better way, so it would save some expense to both you & them. I trust that you will find the picture of Lake Nemi one of my very best, as I intended it should be, and I am happy to say was so looked upon by all who saw it at my studio.
   You can assure Mrs. W. that among the many ladies who saw my pictures before I sent them away there was not one, who did not like hers better than any I had. I hope she may be as well pleased with it, the knowledge of which would be very grateful to
                    Yours truly // Geo. Inness

Letter to Mr. Williams (8 January 1874)

Rome   Jan 8th 1874
Mr. Williams
   My Dear Sir
   I have to-day made arraingment [*sic*] with Mr. Hooker for a loan and have given him an acceptance for 6000 francs payable with interest on the 28 Feb This with the returned draft will make me indebted to him about $2100 Gold if I can take up my acceptances when due I can borrow until things are in a better condition   I am rather lothe [*sic*] to send the pictures which I am preparing for the Salon to London for sale ~~for sale~~ and hope of sales among Americans this season is so small that I trust but little to it   Please let me know if I can expect anything from you in time
                    Yours Truly // Geo. Inness

Letter to J. C. Dodge (9 June 1874)

[The painting to which Inness refers is *Lake Albano, Sunset*, c. 1872, National

Gallery of Art, Washington, D.C. Nicolai Cikovsky, Jr., discussed the letter in his catalogue entry for Inness's *Castel Gandolfo* (1876, Portland Art Museum) in Cikovsky, Jr., and Quick, *George Inness* (1985), p. 134.]

Paris   June 9th 1874
Mr. J. C. Dodge
Dear Sir
    The picture, which you have bought of me, is a view of Lake Albano taken from near the Franciscan Convent which is situated on the east side of the lake and the garden wall of which you see on the right. On the opposite Shore is Castel Gandolpho [*sic*] or as it is generally called by Italians, Castello.
                Yours Truly // Geo. Inness

[Inness attached a note to the letter: "Paris June 9th 1874 // Recd. of Mr. J. C. Dodge Seven // thousand five hundred francs ƒ7500.00 // for the painting above described // Geo Inness"]

FIG. 38. Charles Frederick Ulrich, *Thomas B. Clarke*, 1884, oil on panel, 8⅜ x 6", National Portrait Gallery, Smithsonian Institution, Washington, D.C., NPG.89.202.

Letters to Thomas B. Clarke
(1878–93)

[By the turn of the century, Thomas B. Clarke (FIG. 38), a lace and linen manufacturer in New York, had become one of the most famous collectors of American art. He served as Inness's agent during the late 1880s and early 1890s and amassed a large collection of his paintings. For additional references to Clarke in this volume, see pages 27, 30–31, 134–35, 138, 167–69, and 276.]

[undated # 1]
    I am very much pleased that the sale has been effected and can easily believe that the general knowledge of it and its exhibition in Washington will give us a good start   I am

just now painting a Yosemity Valy [*sic*] 25 x 35 and will probably finish it this week   You spoke of some Lady who wanted a picture   If it can be made available at once and you can find out what she wants I will paint it right away

Yours T[ruly] // Geo Inness

------◆◆◆◆◆------

If this Valy picture is a success I will paint some others of that reagion [*sic*]

------◆◆◆◆◆------

[undated #2]

My Dear Mr Clark

I will have a 30 x 45, perhaps two, for you on Friday   I did not feel well yesterday and made a look on the Rainbow and wiped off what I did so that it is just where it stood   I think I had better leave it for the present.

Yours Truly // Geo Inness

------◆◆◆◆◆------

[undated #3] // The Pines // Montclair, N. J.

My Dear Mr Clarke

In thinking over our matter I am inclined to the opinion that the simplest way will be for you to pay me $1000.00 for 30 x 45s as they are delivered, for the present at least, you selling for not less than $2000.00 except by special agreement. I will hold at the same price and credit you with $500.00 on each sale   20 x 30s 750.00 to be sold for not less than 1250.

You not to sell pictures by other artists

Or if you prefer it have a percentage of say 50 per ct net over frame of $75.00

My intention was, as soon as our arrangement was made, to let my studio as I should not need it

Yours Truly // Geo. Inness

------◆◆◆◆◆------

Mont Clair   Sept 26 1878

Mr T B Clarke

Dear Sir

I send you a picture of a gray day—Winaukee River [in New Hampshire]. If you care about keeping it send me a check for $75.00 which will makes [*sic*] us right $150.00 for picture   I have one or two of the small uprights commenced but not finished. Have done but very little lately   What is the matter I don't know but cannot work

                    In haste // Yours Truly
                    Geo. Inness
over
[on following page:] Should you not wish to keep the picture I will send for it in a day or two

———◆•◆•◆———

Montclair Oct. 4th 1878
My Dear Mr. Clarke
    I did not send the upright as a specimen of autumn but merely as something new which I thought might be desirable to you   The changes are now beginning to be strikeing [*sic*] and very vivid   [A]s soon as I can get out I shall I trust find strength to make a few small studies   Can you afford to let me have a $100.00   I have felt obliged to ask for an offer from St. Louis and hope to hear today   I presume one that I can take will be made from aletter which I rec'd from them a few days after the opening [?]   in such case I can return you the money and have enough left to enable me to try and get myself in order again
                    Yours truly // Geo. Inness
Excuse the pencil as I write with great difficulty and am greatly exhausted

———◆•◆•◆———

Studio   March 7th 1884
My Dear Mr Clarke
    I did not think of your wanting the 16 x 24 at your house before the exhibition and let it go down with the other pictures   If you desire it however Sutton can send it to your house[,] though we should like it for the exhibit
                    Yours Truly // Geo. Inness
American Art Association
Please deliver to Thos B Clarke on order the 16 x 24 ~~Sunset~~ Mountain Lake Sunset and oblige
                    Geo Inness

———◆•◆•◆———

[letterhead: Atlantic House. Ocean Ave., facing the Sea.
G. C. Austin, Proprietor. Ocean Beach, N.Y.]

Aug 12th 1888

My Dear Mr. Clarke

I have found it necessary to leave Montclair for a while and came here to rest. Precisely when I should return I cannot say but I shall let you know when I do. I have a number of pictures which I could soon finish but I find that to work now is labour thrown away.

At present I am in a good deal of pain from indigestion which with too close application has brought on what the doctor says is neuralgia of the spleen. I ~~suppose it~~ am better of it than I was when I left for this place but I feel rather more like groaning than writing so that I shall bid you good by [*sic*] with the expectation of seeing you at Montclair upon my return.

Yours Truly // Geo. Inness

Studio   Dec. 23rd 1888

Dear Sir

Since through Mrs. Hartley you gave me carte blanche to do as I thought best with with [*sic*] your picture, I have finished it according to my idea of what the subject demanded. As you declined to allow me to restore you the original surface intact which could have been done perfectly I feel that I have a perfect right to say that the canvas was never in a state which any artist whose opinion I respect would not have perceived to be more worthy of me than it was as you bought it

If you still feel that I have robbed you of a good picture and gain you an inferior one ~~the~~ it is now your own fault   All that I can say further is that the picture will become very much richer in tone in a few months when it can be varnished which will reveal a great deal[,] which will by that time become comparatively lost, <u>perhaps</u>—for I am not certain   I do not fear however that as it is competent judges will pronounce it quite equal to my best work in all that goes to make a good work of art and a truthful representation of nature

Yours Truly // Geo Inness

To Thos. B. Clarke Esq

[undated; 1889?]

My Dear Mr. Clarke

The picture Evening is off at last and I presume you will have rec'd it by the time you get this.

I do not want the picture offered for sale just at present as I have not quite decided as to the price I shall fix upon it   Besides it is painted for Chicago and if to [*sic*] late to go with the others it can be sent at my expense   It has been painted in my bedroom in a very small and low light so that I do not know how it will look under other circumstances but as it appeared here I think it to be my most complete [*sic*] and beautiful work   in haste

Yours Truly // Geo Inness

Monday Jan 7th 1889
My Dear Mr. Clarke

I expected to go down today but my cold is bad again and with this weather it is unsafe for me to go out.

I am in first rate spirits and have worked all the time although my cold has troubled me a good deal at times. There is but very little to do to a number of the pictures in the studio   I shall probably bring something in tomorrow if I can get into town

Yours Truly // Geo Inness

The Pines   Montclair N.J.
Oct. 17 89
My Dear Mr. Clarke

I have recd the draft from Mr Palmer all right and have sent acknowledgment

I enclose Mr. Potters [*sic*] letter to you   I have red. [received] from Mr. P_____ a letter stating the [*sic*; that] he like[d] the picture very much and desires me to notify him when I "have a picture which I would like him to have"   I want you to see what I have and you can tell him ~~about~~ how they compare with my other work   I have a smashing Sunset[;] the whole canvas is a mass of splendor away up in key and I only want to hold [onto it] until I make up my mind whether I shall lower it in tone   I shall not to do so at present   You will find in a number of my last works a certainty much greater than in any others

Yours Truly // Geo. Inness

Palmer House, Chicago, October 31, 1889
My dear Mr. Clarke:

Just as I was stepping into the carriage on Tuesday for the train I remembered that I had not paid my dues at the Century for the November term, and as I knew Hartley had no more ready money than he needed, I asked him to write to you. I find that I have neglected my own account until there is only about fourteen dollars to my credit, so I inclose my wife's check for the amount.

On our arrival here we took a moderate board at seven dollars, which my wife thought would answer our purpose for the two or three days of our intended stay here. Thinking that Mr. Palmer had an office here, I called upon him as the first best thing to do. As soon as registrations were made, I found myself received with the greatest cordiality, and in a few moments we were occupying D. E. on the first floor front, with every convenience, and a pile of extra dinner-tickets for friends, and a couple of large vases of elegant fruit, enough to last us a week. Of course I had to accept what Mr. Palmer insisted was only a great pleasure to him.

I then called upon Mr. Ellsworth, and then there was another instance that we should at once make his house our home. Mr. Palmer insists that we shall stay here until Monday at least, so that I shall probably get no nearer the point of our destination before the middle of next week, probably Thursday. My necessary visit to the studio on Monday last upset me somewhat, but I am feeling a great deal better this morning, and I have no doubt but that I shall be all right in a day or two.

I intended to write to you further about picture matters, but I will leave that for a few days when the ground will be further opened and I shall be in better condition.

Yours truly, // George Inness.

[In the hand of Elizabeth Inness]
Delivered to Mr. Thomas B. Clark // Jan 3d 1891, two pictures. // The Pasaic [*sic*] River from Kearney Station. size 30 x 45.   The Storm 30 x 45 // Geo. Inness // The pictures are fearfully dried in will be ready to varnish by Monday

---

The Pines // Montclair, N.J. // August 2nd 1891
My Dear Mr Clarke
   I have recd. your check for $4000 for the Sunset in the Woods bought by the

Corcoran Art Committee—all right
                    Yours Truly // Geo. Inness
over [reverse blank]

[Siccatif (or "siccative") is a drier made with lead and manganese. A small amount added to oil paints accelerates the drying process to as little as eight to twelve hours.]

[Letterhead: Ocean View House // Siasconset, Mass.]
Aug 20th 1891
My Dear Mr Clarke
    I presume by the time you receive this you will have recd. the three pictures for which please send a receipt   I think the Autumn should be held at $2500.00 as it is an exceptional picture and a very unique piece of art. I took the cow out of the Moon picture as I found it too small to allow of the foreground takeing [*sic*] its proper relation and to have made it larger would not have done   The pictures will need Siccatif & turpine [turpentine] half & half in a few days probably which Decker can do. Look across them against the light for they may be full of dry spots already. I have kept the Moon picture a little fresher than when you saw it which is what I wanted as this time is so short a time to what it would be difficult to give otherwise as clearly.
    I shall return on the first of Sept. when I hope to finish the two large pictures in a few days so as to have them ready for you to show. I calculate that after this rest a month or two will bring a large amount of work to a finish
                    Yours Truly // Geo. Inness

Jan 18th [1892?]
My dear Mr Clarke.
Please make all checks for money due me payable to my daughter Mrs. Helen Hartley and oblige
                    Yours Truly // Geo. Inness

[ca. June 1892]
My Dear Mr. Clarke

I send you a study painted out of doors. I do not know if it is finished enough for the market but it has qualities that are very easily lost so I send it and leave the matter to your judgment   I intend to paint this thing for a while not being in a mercantile humor for the present. The other picture is I am afraid [?] a little worried   I need a change and shall take it by painting out of doors. I have chosen a subject for this afternoon if the Sun is out. If I can go a little further at the first go I think these will be wanted

                    Inness
[Written on the reverse of part of a letter that had been sent by Clarke to Inness and dated June 1892]

⸻⋅•⋅⸻

[Letterhead: The Pines // Montclair, N. J.] // [1892?]
My Dear Mr Clarke
    I have been very much disturbed with my stomach since I saw you last. In fact then I was far from being in proper order. This comes from nervous exhaustion on account of over work. The work I did on those large pictures wore me more than I was willing to acknowledge to myself. And then there is another thing. Those large pictures worry me. I must see to having them out of the way. The two pictures I promised you will be finished soon and then after a day or two of change, which I must take, I shall drop everything untill [sic] the large ones are out of the way. They will not take long if I determinedly ~~drop everything else~~ do this. As fast as they are finished I shall remove them from th̄home Studio and then I will have a clear seeing for the smaller works.
    The Marine has bothered me for about a week   The Storm I could easily have got out of the way but that is not my stile [sic]   I must get what I want when I am in ernest [sic]   And now the Marine has it. I was determined that it should be at last equal to any landscape that I was capable of and now I have it. Splendor, dramatic interest and the refinement of truth seem to be there now. The compleation [sic] is a mere matter of a little patience
    I hope to finish the Storm approach tomorrow, and if it is what I want I will wire in the afternoon. I will send neither picture however until they are surpassing, nor[,] if they are what I want, will I sell to [sic] them to any any [sic] one but Ellsworth or Halsted for less than $2500.00. I tell you my boy unless I am very much mistaken and have lost my cud, you are going to see something that will make people believe there is a 'God in Israel' yet. French

painting and bombast to the contrary notwithstanding.

Yours Truly // Geo. Inness

———— ❖ ————

Montclair, N.J. // Dec. 30th 1892

My dear Mr Clarke

I should like to see you before we leave for the south which we do tomorrow, but I am not well and I want if possible to finish the Moonlight before [it is] time to leave   I am inclined to think that my days of impetuous painting are ended and that I shall be obliged to consider longer and do less. Still have a large number of pictures which only want carefull [*sic*] consideration and little work comparatively, at well separated intervals to bring to a greater degree of perfection than any I have got compleated but I must take my time

At present I am not well being nervous and rather depressed [—] from the fast I presume [—] that I am not constantly at work.

If I can only restrain myself in this aspect and stick to a diet of rice or food of a like kind I presume that I will come out all right   My not haveing [*sic*] observed some rule in regard to work is the cause of a return of my troubles and I am satisfied has retarded me   I did not carry either of the two last pictures I sent you as far as the one you sold to Halsted as I needed more time.

This Moonlight will I think quite equal it I hope tomorrow, if my stomach will allow. If not I shall take it with me with enough others to keep me employed while at Tarpon Springs   I shall do the best I can for you but as purchasers seem to come along very slowly I cannot see that there is any particular use in showing anything more unless it be so extraordinary as to command buyers if possible, when I shall tell them that if they want pictures of by myself an unequaled excellence, I must have an extraordinary price if in case of success and that I shall choose to judge of for myself

I do not care to exhibit at Chicago. I have no pictures which I care to put out of my own control for a great length of time and I presume that those who want pictures painted by me feel the same   besides I consider the big exhibits the cause of art degradation

Yours Truly // Geo. Inness

[continuation of previous letter]

31st // Find I can't get the Moonlight done and yet if I could feel right for about three hours I could send you both. Kost wants to get his Boston friend

to take the Autumn at $2500.00. Something will come of it but what he can-
not tell   I shall hear from him by the time I get to the Springs when I will
let you know   Kost thinks the picture extraordinary and wants me to let it
go as it is but I know what an hour's work will do as soon as I am in condition
and will not.

[on margin:]
Will have the pictures soon enough probably to ~~let you~~ start them off in about
a week and there are two others [that] will come in a few days after   If I should
begin in feel right well from the change[,] which I probably will[,] pictures will
come fairly fast if wanted

———◦•◦◦•◦———

Tarpon Springs Florida // Jan 6th 1893
My Dear Mr Clarke
    I should be obliged to leave to your judgment the Chicago exhibit affair as I
am in no condition to push myself at present   You will be wise, I think, to let
it be understood quietly, that I have been been [*sic*] preparing for that exhibit
finding it impossible to obtain the pictures I wanted from those who had purchased of me, but that under an overpressure of work I have found myself so
frustrated that I am unable to perfect what has been commenced
    The large 10 foot picture could go in a pinch as a center to such smaller ones
as you may be able to collect and these should be of my very best finish if possible. There is then the oblong and the upright of both 6 x four feet, about,
which if I could work upon about a week in good spirit would be all that is
wanted. Again, there is the square one exhibited at the review exhibit of S. A. A.
[Society of American Artists] though I should want to see it again and maybe
work a day upon it Then the others, same size, Rainbow, which would need a
frame and a little work to make it telling
    The question now is when would these four pictures be needed
    I am preparing a studio better than my former one and expect to be at work
on Monday or as soon as my pictures arrive   I am not at all strong yet but I
begin to feel sound
                    Yours Truly // Geo. Inness

How about the Corcoran picture   would they let that go [?]

———◦•◦◦•◦———

Tarpon Springs // Jan. 23rd, 1893
My Dear Mr Clarke

I have today sent you by express two pictures 22 x 27 one Afterglow—Southern Florida, the other A Breezy day vicinity of Montclair.

I want these pictures to net me $800.00 cash, which framed at $1250.00 leaves you 450.00 or one third and fifty dollars over   I think that three of this size, of good quality, can be sold more easily than one 30 x 45 since Elsworth and Halsted are about filled up.

Perhaps by the way they may take another run on these.

I have two other sizes with me, besides several 30 x 45s, one 22 x 27 and the other 24 [x] 34 and hope to send you one of each next week. As you have about seventeen or eighteen of the 30 [x] 45s and sales getting to be limited, I have thought it best to send no more at present particularly as I have determined to finish no more at the old prices.

I have no longer the strength to work as I have done and the smaller sizes require less exertion even though they may take as much time, beside with the smaller sizes our clients will be more extended and receipts greater for both of us in the end. I have recd. no answer from you in regard to the Chicago exhibit which is to be made well if at all.

I have recd. a letter from Mr. Chas. Karty whom I referred to you, after making some explanations as to the cause for my not being ready. I would much rather not bother with the thing but if I exhibit it must be of my most important and best works and this I cannot do without having spase [sic] reserved until first of April as I explained to you. I will not exhibit at all however if obliged to compete
                    Yours Truly // Geo Inness
[Postscript:] You have sold only one small picture out of several which I have unwillingly sent you at your suggestion

These I send at my own and as I get my hand in I presume something better still may be done although I think these should sell if anything will just now

***

Tarpon Springs, Flo. // Jan. 31st 93
My Dear Mr Clarke
I expect to send you two pictures on Thursday the 2nd Feb—one 24 x 36 and one 25 x 30. You have a frame 24 [x] 36 I believe. If you have none 25 x 30 there is a very fair one with Shadow Box and Glass, I believe, at Montclair. I shall write further on sending.

Your have not written as to whether I can eschew competition at the Chicago. Please let me know certainly, as if not I shall on no account send anything   In regard to the fine art loan exhibit I will have nothing to do with it as long as Mr. Butler is its president.—This is final

I do not feel satisfied with the schedule you propose for Chicago. I do not intend to compete yet if I do exhibit it will be an injury if it is not a telling one. As for the large Storm I shall probably never do anything more to it as there is no object and I cannot afford to throw away more time. It is however so grand in its treatment that it will make a fine center, one row up, for smaller pictures. However let me know just what you expect to show at Orleans of mine, in what connection and how you will be for space if you have art objects &. My opinion still is that the principle benefit will be in the notoriety that a loan exhibit of my pictures will give and the increase of sales in consequence privately or heretofore

Williams and Everett of Boston took special pains to show my pictures privately and sold

Doll and Richards made a general exhibit and sold nothing.

Sutton did the same with like success. People seeing a number of pictures for sale will not buy   They must rather be made to believe that but few came into the market, if possible I think. In case you make simply a show from what you have take[n] [from] me   Halsted would let us have his collection for my special benefit and perhaps some others. If it is to be a general exhibit of American art art [*sic*] objects &, I do not care about being in it. Chicago will be of much more benefit to me. And now in regard to the schedule. I think that the first six might do well enough but insted [*sic*] of the Mill Pond and September Afternoon[,] the Tarpon Springs upright belonging to you[,] send the Rainbow with Cow [—] would be better. 'Threatening' is a fine picture but I think the glass kills it, and so with the Spirit of the Night.

Mr Nickerson has a fair picture—wont [*sic*] he let that go? Also, Palmer, wont he let one or two of his go? Now I propose to finish at once the fine 30 x 45 and 32 x 42 which I have with me and send them. These will take me but a short time as they are all in fine order and I am feeling pretty well. They will all be very rich in colour, finished sufficiently and strikingly. How about frames? I want no glassed and have one frame [at] home good enough.

I wish I could look over the sky of your Sunny Autumn as that picture should make a mark. I could trust George's judgment and could tell him just what to do if necessary, the probability is that five minutes would do everything wanted. I expect all that is wanted is a little Dvoes no. 2 Naples yellow rubbed over the

blue with drying oil. ~~would do all that is necessary~~
Yours Truly // Geo Inness

———— ◆·⋅✦⋅·◆ ————

Tarpon Springs // Feb 12th 1893
My dear Mr Clarke

I have just recd. yours of 8th inst   The receipt for the $2000.00 was sent you and I presume has been recd by this time   I intended to write to you before this in regard to the two pictures promised but have been puting [*sic*] it off from day to day in hope that I shall be able to say that they had been expressed [sent by express mail].

but I have found myself failed every time I touched them until yesterday If I am all right on Monday morning, tomorrow, which I presume I will be[,] the 24 x 36 will be finished   I shall not send it at once however as I have a box ready to contain it with the other picture which another day as successful as yesterday will probably complete. I think you are probably right about the Florida picture which I sent you with the other 22 x 27 though I think it probable that it may, when dry and varnished, become clear in the shadows and the picture become more brilliant   The same trouble I found was attaining in the picture I expected to send and so determined to retain them   There appears to be a constitutional change going on in my system & I find that I must wait until my energies are restored before I can make much head way   I find myself very well and make a start to pitch in my old fashion but I soon tire and then my good work of the short time is injured with the bad work of the forced endeavour   This is apparent in the two 22 x 27s   I might have painted three or four like the Breezy Day while I was straining myself by over work to ~~finish the other to a greater degree of~~ make the other all I wanted

I determined to let the first one go although it was not all I wanted but I believe the 24 x 36 is within two hours of being pretty near the mark[:] rich, clear, firmly painted and interesting. So that what I have to do as a new lesson in life is to regulate my working hours and try to do only what can be done in these.

Until lately when I became disgusted with the slow progress I could take a clear canvass and under the impulse paint a satisfactory picture, but I find that this way will answer no longer as it is when the first sense of dissatisfaction comes that I should stop. I know I have consequently of this habit assembled a great number of unfinished work[,] most of the smaller ones of which can be finished in a morning as soon as I can habituate myself to the new working habit which I feel satisfied is to be a success. However you will see shortly from what I send

You have not informed me yet whether I shall be obliged to enter into competition   Please see about it as all rests upon that whether I send or not. Also let me know when the pictures will have to be on hand   How will it be about the jury of selection? Finding myself under the necessity of limiting my working hours I shall wait until I have sent off the two pictures before I think any further of the Chicag[o] affair and let go what can go for if I get in any haste toda[y] for that[,] I shall get all upset again

I think you will hear from me again in two or three days

Yours Truly // Geo. Inness

Tarpon Springs, Fla. // Feb 1893

My Dear Mr Clarke

I have at length sent off the two pictures after constant delays caused by this miserable indigestion   On these pictures I make the same arrangement as with the two smaller ones sent previously, viz, one third for yourself and two thirds for myself I paying cost of frame. The larger picture is more ~~finished~~ unique than any of the 30 [x] 40 that you have been selling and I want for it the same price[:] $2000.00. If I were buying I would prefer it at the same price   The upright is not so finished and I leave it to your judgment to ask 16 or 1800.00 though I intend to establish that latter figure as the price of that size and depend on the 20 [x] 30 and 22 [x] 27s   I have not quite got into the habit of work again for the smaller pictures but as fast as the nervous prostration and indigestion from my previous describing has past I feel certain that I shall be able to give you things in these sizes that will be in constant demand   I have come very near the mark in the 24 x 36 but will soon send something a great deal beyond it as I am convinced by work that I am doing both small and large   I shall send two 32 x 42 by the first of next week if my health admits of my working partly for two or three days. These I shall want to go with what you have selected for Chicago or if there is no time, to be put in place of two of them   With these I think there will be no doubt of success ~~although~~ notwithstanding that I am not able to obtain what I should select of my work

I am much pleased at the deffinate [*sic*] condition of the Seney affair and also that you have been able to arrest [?] the Chase [?] attempt

Yours Truly // Geo. Inness

[The following are notes on a letter written by Inness to Clarke. The location of the letter, which was sold in 1992, is at this time unknown.]

[Tarpon Springs, Florida // 4 March 1893]

   Inness explains that he has been ill, "so weak that I could hardly crawl about. Of course painting has necessarily amounted to very little." He turns to the matter of his painting sales. "You have yet on hand about fifteen [paintings], [if] out of those none are worthy of a purchaser, I do not see what is the use of painting more in the same way. Most of them are as good as the average of those that have been sold. I have no intention of sending any more until I am completely satisfied, and then I shall ask such a price as I think they deserve. Your interest will not be less, but mine will be more, as it should be. . . . [At] present I feel that we must depend more upon small pictures though I do not think I shall paint anything for less than \$1250.00. The little work I have been able to do seems to be very successful and I think that sometime through the next week the two 32 x 42 will be off and then shortly two smaller ones."

[In the following letter, Inness refers to the painter and fellow Swedenborgian William Keith, with whom he shared a studio during a trip to Monterey, California, in 1891.]

May [1893]

My Dear Mr Clarke

   I shall be very much obliged if you will give my friend Mr Keith an opportunity to see the exhibit if possible before he leave[s] on Saturday for Europe.

   I shall ship the Niagara (American Lower Fall[s]) Tomorrow

           Yours Truly // Geo. Inness

Letters to Isaac Bates (9 October–12 November 1878)

[Isaac C. Bates was Trustee, President, and Corporation President of the Rhode Island School of Design. An avid collector of American art, he bequeathed his vast collection of paintings, including works by Frank W. Benson, Winslow Homer, William Merritt Chase, Charles W. Hawthorne, and Inness, to its museum.]

Mont Clair N.J. // Oct 9th 1878
Mr Isaac C. Bates
Dear Sir

I was so ill when your letter reached me that I was unable to answer   I have been up and about for a few days and have been working a little upon a small picture commenced before I was taken ill   The painting of which I speak is an upright 12 x 14 price $150.00   I am very much pleased with it, so much so, that, if you like, I will send it [to] you for inspection   I have a frame which suits this picture and as I never like to have a picture seen without a frame I propose to send [it] framed. I am disposed to treat persons commissioning pictures with the utmost fairness   And you may depend I will not send you a work that will not be Coveted   Should my proposition meet your approbation I will send with this understanding that should you not desire to keep the picture you are to return [it] to T. A. Wilmurt 54 E 13th St free of expense   Should you keep the picture you to [*sic*] take the frame at $20.0[0]. The original cost of this frame was $22.00   it has been a little abraided and I deduct the cost of retouching   I hardly think you would be able to get the frame for less than $25.00. I shall return to the City on the first of Nov. and shall then be found at N. Y. University.

Yours Truly // Geo. Inness

Mont Clair N.J. // Oct. 18th 1878
Mr I. C. Bates
Dear Sir

I have thought it best to send you the 12 x 14 but without frame   Should you not desire to keep it return it to me at the N. Y. University, Washington Square

Yours Truly // Geo. Inness

New York // Oct 25 1878
Dear sir

I have just recd. your note sent to Mt Clair   As I have another upright of same size nearly finished which I presume Mr. Clarke will like as well as yours I had better perhaps accept your offer particularly as "Cash is cash" just now   I have two 10 x 14 Naragansat [Narragansett], which I am now working at, either of which would I think suit you   One is a Morning Sun   Sun seen in upper part of the picture   Colors cool and fresh   Friends think it a perfect idyll The other is fully up to it——a mellow evening effect. Certainly as fine in sentiment as anything I ever did and I think more masterly. They are both pictures which have been laying about me for a long time which I have just taken a notion to finish

> Yours Truly // Geo Inness

--·•·--

New York // Oct 28th 1878
Dear sir

I sent to you on Monday last a small picture   Will you please inform me if you have recd. the same   And give me your decision in regard to it. Should you not intend to keep the picture will you oblige me by sending it to me at once   I have a person waiting for it in case you do not take it

> Yours truly // Geo Inness

To Mr. I. C. Bates   N. Y. University // Washington Square

--·•·--

New York // Oct 31st 1878
Mr I. C. Bates
Dear Sir

I have recd. the check for $125.00. I had forgotten that I had mentioned to you that I did not expect to be in New York until the first of Nov   Still I had half expected that you would address me at Mt Clair   The letter was unaccountably delayed there   I shall probably have finished the two pictures next week   And will send them on as soon as I am thoroughly satisfied

> Yours Truly // Geo. Inness

--·•·--

[Undated; c. 31 October–12 November 1878]
Mr. I. C. Bates
Dear sir

I painted over the sky of the small picture the other day but have been so busy with larger work that I have not been able to finish what I began to do. If you can wait until next Tuesday or Wednesday I can send you the picture very much improved on what you saw it

> Yours Truly // Geo. Inness

--·•·--

New York // Nov 12th 1878
Mr I. C. Bates
Dear Sir

I find that I can send you only one of the pictures of which I wrote to you as I am so much occupied with some larger work which I feel it necessary to finish that I cannot pay proper attention to the completion of the other just at present Should you like the one I send you can have it for the same price as the other This with the companion a cool silvery picture will be the last pictures of a size similar than 16 x 24 that I shall paint, they cost nearly as much time as much larger pictures and the remuneration is to [*sic*] little to make it an object, so that any small thing that I may do hereafter will be but a slight sketch   I have lately painted several of these small sizes and then find it would have been wiser to have let them alone

Should the picture or the price not suit you please return the two at New York University

Yours Truly // Geo. Inness

—◆•╪•◆—

Fragments of Letters to Genevieve M. Walton
(1878–79)

25 November 1878 // Autograph receipt of $25.00 in partial payment for "one month's tuition in painting."

—◆•╪•◆—

Durham, Connecticut, 26 July 1879 // "I have not yet had the article I spoke of published and as I find it hardly the thing for the lighter magazines, I do not know when I shall make use of it. Should I do so before long, I will send it to you."

—◆•╪•◆—

Letter to Moses S. Beach (September 1879)

[Moses Sperry Beach was the son of Moses Yale Beach, publisher of the *New York Sun*. Moses Sperry, who invented a cutting device that allowed printing on a continuous roll of paper and a process for printing both sides of a newspaper sheet at one time, was a close friend of the Reverend Henry Ward Beecher, who is mentioned in this letter. Writer, editor, abolitionist, women's rights activist, and renowned Brooklyn minister, Beecher was also a well-regarded art collector and, at one time, owned at least eight paintings by Inness. The date of September 12, 1879, appears on a previous page of this manuscript.]

Milton   Sept 1879

My Dear Mr. Beach

I fear from a letter which my wife has recd. that you was [*sic*] put to a great deal of unnecessary trouble on account of the box which I have recd. by Boston Express.

Please accept my thanks for your kindness in this instance as well as for many favours.

I have just recd. an invitation from Mr. Beecher offering me his cottage but I am obliged to decline his generous offer as I <u>must</u> be in the city during the Autumn. I am the more sorry as I should probably have the pleasure of seeing him on his own 'dunghill' and be in the possibility of further continuing our relations of the Summer.

Please remember me to all.

Yours Truly // Geo Inness

———•·•·•———

Letters to Sylvester Rosa Koehler (September 1879)

[Inness corresponded with the Leipzig–born Sylvester Rosa Koehler on etchings he was making after his painting *Scene on Hudson*. At the time, Koehler was the first curator of the print room at the Museum of Fine Arts, Boston; he would subsequently publish widely on the subjects of art education, printmaking, and painting. The first letter accompanied an impression of the etching (FIG. 39).]

My Dear Mr. Koehler

Mr Wellstood is to send you to day, a proof of an unfinished plate by myself I intended to make a free open etching, but as this is the first I have done except a little tinkering in an engravers office when a boy   It was natural that there should have been a little unevenness in the work so that it has become necessary to work it up with graver & ~   I will send you a proof of it finished in a few days

G Inness

[Inscription at bottom of letter in another hand: "Recd. Sept. 24/79. K."]

———◆◆◆◆———

[letterhead:] Steel Plate Engravers and Printers, 46 Beekman Street, New York; dated Sept 27 1879

My Dear Mr Koehler

I send you another proof of the etching[.] I do not know that I shall attempt to carry it further as this picking with the graver is such long indeed tiresome work and don't pay

I shall prefer to do the work with pure etching and if I commence another shall make that my aim as I have nearly got the hang of the thing

Yours Truly // Geo Inness

FIG. 39. George Inness, *On the Hudson*, 1879, etching, 7¼ x 5½" (plate), Montclair Art Museum, Montclair, New Jersey, Museum purchase; Acquisition Fund, 1991.8.

———◆◆◆◆———

[Inscription in Inness's hand on a card attached near the print]: "On comparing with my first proof I feel quite satisfied that I can very much improve the plate by a careful use of the burnisher   will send another proof on Monday // Inness"

———◆◆◆◆———

Letter to J. Carroll Beckwith (13 January 1881)

[Inness writes to the artist J. Carroll Beckwith to resign from the Society of American Artists. The SAA was officially formed in 1877 by artists who felt that the National Academy of Design had become too conservative an institution; they held their own annual exhibitions. Some other artists in the group included the sculptor Augustus Saint-Gaudens, Ryder, La Farge, Wyant, and Louis Comfort Tiffany. See Inness's interview "Strong Talk on Art," pages 82–86, above, for his ideas on this subject. The SAA merged with the National Academy in 1906.]

Jan 13 1881

My Dear Mr Beckwith

In regard to your notice from S. A. A. I do not feel called upon to pay anything for which I have not made myself personally responsible

I allowed my name to be used with those of other N.A.s for the furtherance of that Society at the solicitation of its first president with the understanding that active membership could not be expected on my part

As the S. A. A. is now fully fledged I think it better that it be left wholly to the younger artists   I shall be very much obliged to you therefore if you will be so kind as to present this my resignation to the proper office and oblige

Yours Truly // Geo. Inness

———◆•✦•◆———

To Julian Alden Weir (25 April 1881)

[Inness writes to the American Impressionist painter Julian Alden Weir. After studying at the Ecole des Beaux-Arts in Paris and traveling throughout Europe in the 1870s, Weir settled in America and became a member of both the National Academy of Design and the Society of American Artists. He was elected president of the Academy in 1915. Although it is not clear to which article in "the Post" (the New York *Evening Post*) Inness refers, the art critic George Sheldon wrote a chapter on Inness in his 1879 book *American Painters*.]

April 25 1881 // Julian Weir Esq

Dear Sir

I did not understand what you meant when you spoke to me in the street to day until after a word with Mr. Sheldon   As I very rarely see the Post, Mr. Sheldon has been a friend of mine for several years but on what he publishes you must not hold me responsible as on art matters we in many parts very severely disagree. In regard to this particular matter I may or may not have illustrated an idea by some high sentence as he uses. I do not remember   The thing is older however than my acquaintance with you for precisely the same remarks and and [*sic*] answers were made and quoted years ago   Should it however have been my misfortune to have offended you I have done you no imposition for he who fires a gun is alone responsible

I never interview[ed] again although sometimes people interview me and whatever I consider as done for reason and justice I consider as right   So that although I would not willingly offend you you are at liberty to consider me as offender or not as seems good to you

Yours truly // Geo. Inness

━━━━━━•┅•┅•┅•━━━━━━

Letter to Thomas Wigglesworth (13 March 1884)

[The letter is not in Inness's handwriting and bears the letterhead of the American Art Association in New York. It appears to have been written by the Association on his behalf.]

March 13th 1884 // Mr Thomas Wigglesworth
Dear Sir

Your favor of the 12th Ins't received and would state in reply that we would prefer the picture "Olive Grove" near Rome. If perfectly convenient to yourself would like to have it shipped the later part of next week. Messrs. Doll and Richards are perhaps the best ones to pack &c. of course at our expense. With many thanks for your kindness I remain

Very respectfully // Geo Inness.

per American Art Association
I would mention that the title of the picture you have of a New England landscape is "<u>The</u> <u>Old</u> <u>Homestead</u>."

━━━━━━•┅•┅•┅•━━━━━━

Letter to Edward Gay (16 November 1885)

[Fleeing the Irish potato famine, Edward Gay and his parents emigrated to America in 1848. Gay revealed a talent for art and, in 1862, went to Karlsruhe, Germany, to study painting. He returned to the United States in 1864 where, in the coming decades, he produced numerous placid renditions of the landscape in and around New York. He died in Mount Vernon, New York, in 1928.]

Nov 16 1885
My Dear Mr Gay

I had intended to write to you some days since about your splendid success in the large picture at the Academy but I have been very busy and with my general disinclination to write letters I did not fulfill that intention.

But I will now express to you my belief that your picture of "Washed by the Sea" is the finest piece of nature in tone and colour that has ever been on our walls. To my knowledge nothing of local force is sherked and the tone is natures [*sic*]   The gradation leaves nothing to be asked for and the greater part of the picture is magnificently rendered   The lower sky is perfect but the upper clouds might be improved and the blue although fine in quality needs to be reduced with darker tone[,] leaving the darkest spots as they are   The water line does not appear quite level owing to the droping [*sic*] of its tone at the left   There are few thing[s] on the right hand of the picture which can easily be benefited with a few touches

There was at first some opposition to my oppinion [*sic*] but after I had got it hung in the present place[,] there was a general agreement that I was about right.

In haste   Yours truly // Geo. Inness

Letter to Edward D. Adams (11 January 1888)

[Edward D. Adams was the original owner of Inness's *Sunset* (1888).]

The Pines // Montclair, N. J. // Jan. 11, 1888
Dear Sir:

I have recd your check for $2000.00 in payment of painting 30 x 45 inches entitled '<u>Sunset,</u>' purchased for you by Mr. Clarke.

The money is convenient but your very kind and appreciative letter enhances the value of your signature in my eyes very greatly I assure you.

The picture is not particularly a view of any special place. My endeavor having been, without any very marked attempt at extrordinary character, to give the luminosity of the Sunset. In this I hope that I shall have succeeded to the satisfaction of all your friends as well as I have to that of yourself and wife.

With many thanks for your favor, I remain
Yours truly, // Geo. Inness
Edward D. Adams. Esq. // New York City

Letter to [J. Francis] Murphy (29 January 1889)

[Inness is widely viewed as the source of inspiration for the Tonalist movement at the turn of the century; J. Francis Murphy was one of the movement's most active leaders. See the Selected Bibliography for Murphy's account of Inness painting in the Catskills, published in George Chambers Calvert, "George Inness, Painter and Personality."]

Montclair // Jan. 29, 1889
My Dear Mr. Murphy,

I trust you will excuse my not answering your very kind note sooner but—. I will do so now however, in such measures as I can, to acknowledge to you the pleasure I feel in the knowledge that the general feeling among our artists is that I fully deserve the measure of success that has come to me. I think that the time is rapidly approaching when numbers among us will be acknowledged to stand at least fairly alongside of much of the European art that has absorbed in great part large amounts of money which could have been deservedly spent among us.

The wind has blown from the east for so long a time that it has seemed almost hopeless to expect that it would ever begin to blow from the west. I have reason to hope however that I shall be able before long to give the other side a puff of our quality.

Yours truly // Geo. Inness

Letter to Jervis McEntee

(n.d.; after February 1885 but before 1891)

[Jervis McEntee, an artist of the Hudson River School, studied painting with Frederic Church in New York in 1850. He opened his own studio there in 1858. Like Inness and Ryder, he would occasionally accompany his paintings on exhibition with brief passages of poetry.]

The Pines // Montclair N.J.
My dear Mr. McEntee

I should have answered your very kind letter immediately upon its receipt but for an atack [*sic*] of rheumatism which had disabled my right hand the using of which is still difficult

You may be assured that I fully appreciate the kind spirit of your generous congratulations which of the many being recd is—with me—the first and foremost

Of course the only way in which I feel at liberty to look at this turn in affairs is that of a piece of bussiness [*sic*] transaction. I realy [*sic*] believe it to be however the beginning of a general acknowledgement of American art ability as one of the necessary features of our national developement [*sic*] and the cause, in general terms[,] lies in the fact that which was in one form becomes what is in another form as the earth turns its face to the Sun

Yours truly // Geo. Inness

Letter to William T. Evans (undated)

[Born in Ireland in 1843, William T. Evans made his fortune in railroad construction and became an important patron and collector of American art. He gave American paintings to the National Gallery of Art, Washington, D.C., and American Impressionist and Barbizon landscapes to the Smithsonian American Art Museum. In the late nineteenth century, he purchased George Inness, Jr.'s home in Montclair, New Jersey, and later donated thirty-six paintings, including works by Frederic Church, Inness, and Ralph Blakelock, to the Montclair Art Museum.]

139 W. 55th Street // New York City
Dear Mr. Evans

Your check for $800.00 has been duly received

I am sorry to hear of your lameness but hope you will be able to come with your friend on Sunday next

I think with you that the picture cannot be touched again to advantage except about a half hours work at the top corners which appears to me not quite equal in finish to the rest of the picture   this however is a mere bagatelle

Yours Truly // Geo. Inness

Historical Figures and Colleagues

Reverend Dr. John Curtis Ager (1835–1913)
Washington Allston (1779–1843)
Benjamin (B.) Altman (1840–1913)
David Maitland Armstrong (1836–1918)
Moses Sperry Beach (1822–1892)
J. Carroll Beckwith (1852–1917)
Henry Ward Beecher (1813–1887)
Clark Bell (1832–1918)
Albert Bierstadt (1830–1902)
Ralph Blakelock (1847–1919)
Marco Boschini (1605–1681)
Adolphe William Bouguereau (1825–1905)
Gustave Boulanger (1824–1888)
Frederick Bridgeman (1847–1928)
Edgar Spier Cameron (1862–1944)
William Merritt Chase (1849–1916)
Frederic Edwin Church (1830–1900)
Eliot Clark (1883–1980)
Walter Clark (1848–1917)
Thomas B. Clarke (1848–1931)
Darius Cobb (1834–1919)
Stanwood Cobb (1881–1982)
Thomas Cole (1801–1848)
John Constable (1776–1837)
Clarence Cook (1826–1900)
Jean-Baptiste-Camille Corot (1796–1875)
Correggio (1490–1534)
Pierre-Auguste Cot (1837–1883)
Gustave Courbet (1819–1877)
Thomas Couture (1815–1879)
Reginald Cleveland Coxe (1855–1927)
Jacob Coxey (1854–1951)
Bruce Crane (1857–1937)
Elliott Daingerfield (1859–1932)
Alexandre-Gabriel Decamps (1803–1860)
Eugène Delacroix (1798–1863)
Chauncey Depew (1834–1928)
Thomas Wilmer Dewing (1851–1938)
Narcisse-Virgile Diaz de la Peña (1807–1876)
Asher B. Durand (1796–1886)

William T. Evans (1843–1918)
Marie François Firmin-Gerard (1838–1921)
Mark Fisher (1841–1923)
John Flamsteed (1646–1719)
Henry George (1839–1897)
Jean-Leon Gérôme (1824–1904)
Régis-François Gignoux (1816–1882)
Palma il Giovane (Jacopo Negreti, 1544–1628)
Johann Wolfgang Goethe (1749–1832)
Philip Guston (1913–1980)
Ogden Haggerty (1810–1875)
Edmond Halley (1656–1742)
Joseph Henry Harper (1850–1938)
Jonathan Scott Hartley (1845–1912)
Sadakichi Hartmann (1867–1944)
Charles W. Hawthorne (1872–1930)
Arthur Turnbull Hill (1868–1929)
James Ripley Wellman Hitchcock (1857–1918)
Roswell Dwight Hitchcock (1817–1887)
Arthur Hoeber (1854–1915)
Winslow Homer (1836–1913)
George Inness (1825–1894)
George Inness, Jr. (1854–1926)
Elizabeth Hart Inness (1833–1903)
Helen ("Nell," "Nellie") Hart Inness
    (1861–1931)
Julia Goodrich Roswell Smith Inness
    (1853–1941)
William Keith (1838–1911)
Sylvester Rosa Koehler (1837–1900)
John La Farge (1835–1910)
Frederick Stymetz Lamb (1863–1928)
Jules-Joseph Lefebvre (1836–1911)
Claude Lorrain (1600–1682)
James Steele MacKaye (1842–1894)
Valentin Magnan (1835–1916)
Homer Dodge Martin (1836–1897)
Jervis McEntee (1828–1891)
Jean-Louis-Ernest Meissonier (1815–1891)
John Stuart Mill (1806–1873)

Jean-François Millet (1814–1875)

John ("Jack") Austin Sands Monks
    (1850–1917)

J. Francis Murphy (1853–1921)

William Page (1811–1885)

Pierre Puvis de Chavannes (1824–1898)

George Gardner Rockwood (1832–1911)

Théodore Rousseau (1812–1867)

Albert Pinkham Ryder (1847–1917)

Augustus Saint-Gaudens (1848–1907)

John Singer Sargent (1856–1925)

Napoleon Sarony (1821–1896)

George I. Seney (1826–1893)

George Sheldon (1843–1914)

Roswell Smith (1829–1892)

Marcus Spring (1810–1874)

Rebecca Buffum Spring (1811–1911)

Emanuel Swedenborg (1688–1772)

Louis Comfort Tiffany (1848–1933)

Titian (Tiziano Vecellio, c. 1488–1576)

Constant Troyon (1810–1865)

J. M. W. Turner (1775–1851)

Sir William Cornelius Van Horne
    (1843–1915)

A. T. Van Laer (1859–1920)

Samuel Gray Ward (1817–1907)

Julian Alden Weir (1852–1919)

Archbishop Richard Whately (1787–1863)

James Abbott McNeill Whistler (1834–1903)

Alexander Helwig Wyant (1836–1892)

Elihu Vedder (1836–1923)

Felix Ziem (1821–1911)

References

(The texts are listed in the order in which they appear in this publication. Microfilm texts are cited as reel/frame numbers.)

INTERVIEWS

"A Painter on Painting," *Harper's New Monthly Magazine* 56 (February 1878): 458–61.

E., "Mr. Inness on Art-Matters," *Art Journal* 5 (1879): 374–77.

"Strong Talk on Art," *[New York] Evening Post* (3 June 1879): [3].

"His Art His Religion. An Interesting Talk with the Late George Inness on His Theory of Painting," *New York Herald* (12 August 1894): 4:9.

WRITINGS *(Letters to Family Members, Letters on Art, Essays, Speeches, and Poems)*

Inness, George. Letters to Elizabeth Hart Inness (1855–84), in George Inness, Jr., *Life, Art, and Letters of George Inness* (New York: The Century Co., 1917), pp. 82, 108, 111, 148–52, 155–58, 162–64, 167–68.

———— [probable author]. "The Sign of Promise," exhibition pamphlet (New York: Snedicor's [*sic*] Gallery, 1863).

———— [probable author]. "Inness's Allegorical Pictures," *[New York] Evening Post* (11 May 1867): [4].

————. "Colors and Their Correspondences," *New Jerusalem Messenger* 13:20 (13 November 1867): 78–79.

"The Logic of the Real Æsthetically Considered," *Boston Daily Advertiser* (12 April 1875): 4.

Inness, George. Letter to Nellie [Helen Hart Inness] (13 February 1877), in Inness, Jr., *Life, Art, and Letters of George Inness*, op. cit., pp. 199–202.

————. "A Plea for the Painters. Letter from the Artist Inness," *[New York] Evening Post* (21 March 1878): 2.

————. "A Poem and a Statue. Mr. Inness Explains his Poem," *New-York Daily Tribune* (11 April 1878): 6.

————. "Artists and Critics. George Inness Replies Again to 'C. C.'—Distinction Between Deserved Correction and Illogical Abuse," *New-York Daily Tribune* (13 April 1878): 5.

————. Letter to the Editors of the *[New York] Evening Post* (16 March 1881); reprinted with commentary under the heading "Extraordinary Incivility," *Art Interchange* 6:7 (31 March 1881): 75.

————. *A Letter from George Inness to Ripley Hitchcock* [23 March 1884] (New York: privately printed, 1928). Reprinted with the permission of the Montclair Art Museum, New Jersey.

————. Letter to Editor Ledger [Letter on Impressionism] (Tarpon Springs, FL, late 1880s–early 1890s), in Inness, Jr., *Life, Art, and Letters of George Inness*, op. cit., pp. 168–74.

————. Letter to the Editor of the *New York Herald* (9 March 1889). Rare Books and Special Collections, Princeton University Library, Call # C0140, General Mss. Misc, Box I [Inness], folder AM12814. First published in the *New York Herald* (10 March 1889): 16; reprinted in Inness, Jr., *Life, Art, and Letters of George Inness*, op. cit., pp. 198–99 [version transcribed].

————. Speech on Henry George, published in "The George Dinner. The Great Banquet at the Metropolitan Hotel," *Standard* 7:4 (22 January 1890): 10.

————. Statement on *Sunset in the Woods* in letter to Thomas B. Clarke, 23 July 1891. Special Collections. Grenville H. Norcross Autograph Collection. Massachusetts Historical Society, Boston. Abbreviated transcription by Clarke in Rare Books and Special Collections, Princeton University Library, Call #C0140, Box I [Inness], folder AM12814.

————. "Unite and Succeed," *The American Federationist* 1:6 (August 1894): 119.

————. Poems, undated. Transcriptions from the following sources: "The Leaves and the Brook" from "Poems by the Late George Inness, The American Corot," *Illustrated American* 17:257 (19 January 1895): 69; "Exaltation," "Destiny," and "[Untitled]" from Inness, Jr., *Life, Art, and Letters of George Inness*, op. cit., pp. 97–98, 101–6; *The Illustrated American* also published "Exaltation," "Address of the Clouds to the Earth," "Whirlwind," and the first third of "The Pilgrim." Typescript copies of the first half of "The Leaves and the Brook," "Love," "Despair," "Address of the Clouds to the Earth," "The Pilgrim," and "Exaltation": LeRoy Ireland papers, Archives of American Art, Smithsonian Institution, Washington, DC [hereafter: AAA], 995/1029–36. Ireland papers lent for microfilming to the AAA by Chapellier Galleries, New York.

REFLECTIONS ON INNESS'S LIFE AND WORK

George Inness, Jr. *Life, Art, and Letters of George Inness*, op. cit., pps. 8–9, 14, 17–19, 42, 45–46, 61–64, 67–68, 91–95, 117–19, 123–32, 135–37, 140–47, 190–92, 195–97, 251–53, 283–84 (excerpts).

Sheldon, G. W. [George William]. "George Inness," *Harper's Weekly Magazine* 26:1322 (22 April 1882): 244–46.

Cameron, Edgar Spier. "The Cusp of Gemini" (c. 9 October 1882), unpublished autobiography, Edgar Spier Cameron papers, AAA, 4291/1294 (excerpt).

"Homage to George Inness: Memorial Services in the National Academy of Design," *New-York Times* (24 August 1894): 8. Reprinted in part in Inness, Jr., *Life, Art, and Letters of George Inness*, op. cit., pp. 210–19.

Cobb, Stanwood. "Reminiscences of George Inness by Darius Cobb" (c. 1894), *Art Quarterly* 26 (summer 1983): 234–42.

Daingerfield, Elliott. "A Reminiscence of George Inness," *Monthly Illustrator* 3:2 (March 1895): 260–68.

Coxe, Reginald Cleveland. "George Inness," *Scribner's Magazine* 44:4 (October 1908): 509–12.

Daingerfield, Elliott. "Inness: Genius of American Art," *Cosmopolitan* 55:4 (September 1913): 518–25.

Lamb, Frederick Stymetz. "Reminiscences of George Inness," *Art World* 1:4 (January 1917): 250–52.

Pietro, C. S. "The Art of John Austin Sands Monks," *Fine Arts Journal* 35 (April 1917): 258–60 (excerpt).

Armstrong, [David] Maitland. *Day Before Yesterday: Reminiscences of a Varied Life*, edited by his daughter Margaret Armstrong (New York: Charles Scribner's Sons, 1920), pp. 198–99 (excerpt).

Hill, Arthur Turnbull. "Early Recollections of George Inness and George Waldo Hill," *New Salmagundi Papers, Series of 1922* (New York: The Library of the Salmagundi Club, 1922), pp. 109–15.

Hartmann, Sadakichi. "Eremites of the Brush," *American Mercury* 11:42 (June 1927): 194.

Watkins, S. C. G. "Reminiscences of George Inness, the Great Painter, as I Knew Him," *Montclair Times* (14 April 1928): 28; reprinted in the author's *Reminiscences of Montclair* (New York: A.S. Barnes and Company, 1929), pp. 107–18 [version transcribed].

Harper, J. Henry. *I Remember* (New York and London: Harper & Brothers, 1934), pp. 224–25.

Clark, Eliot. "Notes from Memory," *American Artist* 21: 6 (Summer 1957): 72, 87.

BUSINESS LETTERS

Letters to the American Art-Union. BV American Art-Union, Letters Received, The New-York Historical Society, microfilmed. 4 October 1847: 13/164; 7 December 1847 (2 letters): 14/140–141; 23 February 1849: 4/170; 24 May 1849: 4/171; 14 October 1849: 5/36; 30 November 1849: 5/157; 15 August 1850: 6/superimposed on 132; also available in LeRoy Ireland papers, AAA, 995/998–99, typed transcription: 995/1001; 29 October 1850: 6/243, also available in LeRoy Ireland papers, AAA, 995/988.

Letter to Mr. Monk (14 December 1850). American Art-Union papers, Letters Received, The New-York Historical Society, microfilmed, 6/339.

Letters to Samuel Gray Ward (7 January, 21 November, and 30 November 1852). Samuel Gray Ward and Anna Hazard Baker Ward papers, Houghton Library, Harvard University, Cambridge, MA, bMS Am 1465 (707, 708, 709).

Letters to Roswell Dwight Hitchcock (19 November and 2 December 1860). From transcribed copies. The Farnsworth Art Museum and Wyeth Center, Rockland, ME.

Letter to Horace H. Moses (14 January 1866). Artists' Correspondences, AAA, D-10/1358.

Letters to Thomas B. Carrol[l] (11 May–10 August 1868). Misc. Mss. I, George Inness letters, 1868, n.d., Folder 10F1, The New-York Historical Society.

Letter to Barry Alden, Esq. (30 December 1868). Rare Books and Special Collections, Princeton University Library, Call # C0140, General Mss. Misc., Box I [Inness], subf. 2.

Letter to S. A. Coale, Jr. (14 October 1869). Princeton University Library, Rare Books and Special Collections, Call # C0140, Box I [Inness], folder AM13365.

Letter to A. D. Williams (13 August 1872). From transcribed copy. Object file for *Lake Nemi*, Department of the Art of the Americas, Museum of Fine Arts, Boston.

Letter to Mr. Williams (8 January 1874). The Historical Society of Pennsylvania, Philadelphia.

Letter to J. C. Dodge (9 June 1874). Object file for *Lake Albano, Sunset*, Department of American and British Paintings, National Gallery of Art, Washington, DC.

Letters to Thomas B. Clarke (1878-93). Rare Books and Special Collections, Princeton University Library, Call # C0140, General Mss. Misc, Box I [Inness], folder AM12814: undated #1 and #2; 26 September 1878; 4 October 1878; 7 March 1884; 12 August 1888; 23 December 1888; [undated; 1889?]; 7 January 1889; 17 October 1889; 3 January 1891; 2 August 1891; 20 August 1891; 18 January [1892?]; [ca. June 1892]; 30 December 1892; 6 January 1893; 23 January 1893, 31 January 1893. Undated #3: LeRoy Ireland papers, AAA, 995/983.

Letter to Thomas B. Clarke (31 October 1889). In Inness, Jr., *Life, Art, and Letters of George Inness*, op. cit., pp. 189–90.

Letter to Thomas B. Clarke (12 February 1893). Charles Henry Hart Autograph Collection (entitled "History of art in America as told in a remarkable collection of autograph letters and documents of 18th, 19th, and 20th centuries"), AAA, D5/144; also available in LeRoy Ireland papers, AAA, 995/1024–25. Inness's page numbers have been omitted from the transcription in the present volume.

Letter to Thomas B. Clarke (February 1893). LeRoy Ireland papers, AAA, 995/1019–20.

Letter to Thomas B. Clarke (4 March 1893). Described and quoted in *Kindred Spirits: The E. Maurice Bloch Collection of Manuscripts, Letters and Sketchbooks of American Artists, Mostly of the Nineteenth Century, and of Books, Pamphlets, and Other Contemporary Publications Relating to Them* (Boston: Ars Libri, 1992), Part II, p. 48, #283; reprinted in LeRoy Ireland, *The Works of George Inness: An Illustrated Catalogue Raisonné* (Austin: University of Texas Press, 1965), p. 445.

Letter to Thomas B. Clarke (May [1893]). Keith-McHenry-Pond Family papers, 1841–1961, Bancroft Library, University of California, Berkeley, Banc Mss C-B 595, carton 5.

Letters to Isaac Bates (9 October 1878; 18 October 1878; 25 October 1878; 28 October 1878; 31 October 1878; [Undated c. 31 October–12 November 1878]; 12 November 1878). Rhode Island School of Design Archives, Isaac Comstock Bates Scrapbook of Artist Correspondence, 1877–1889.

Fragments of letters to Genevieve M. Walton (25 November 1878; 26 July 1879). Listed in *Kindred Spirits*, op. cit., Part II, p. 48, #282.

Letter to Moses S. Beach (September 1879). LeRoy Ireland papers, AAA, 995/976.

Letters to Sylvester Rosa Koehler (1879). Department of Prints, Drawings, and Photographs, Museum of Fine Arts, Boston. Gift of Sylvester Rosa Koehler.

Letter to J. Carroll Beckwith (13 January 1881). George Inness manuscript file, National Academy Museum Archive, New York.

Letter to Julian Alden Weir (25 April 1881). Julian Alden Weir papers, 1869–1966, AAA, 70/46–47. Lent by Mrs. Caroline Weir Ely; microfilmed by the AAA; owned by Brigham Young University.

Letter to Thomas Wigglesworth (13 March 1884). Curatorial department, Albany Institute of History and Art Library.

Letter to Edward Gay (16 November 1885). Edward Gay and Gay family papers, 1852–1975, AAA, D30/719–20; typed transcription, D30/721.

Letter to Edward D. Adams (11 January 1888). From transcribed copy. LeRoy Ireland papers, AAA, 995/1016–17. See 995/1015 for a slightly different transcription of the letter.

Letter to [J. Francis] Murphy (29 January 1889). From transcribed copy. LeRoy Ireland papers, AAA, 995/1018.

Letter to Jervis McEntee (n.d., after February 1885 but before 1891). Jervis McEntee papers, AAA, D30/452–53.

Letter to William T. Evans (undated). William T. Evans letters, AAA, 4055/25. Originals in the possession of Robert Price.